Praise for *Tales of the*
Pumpkin King's Cameraman

"At the time of *Nightmare Before Christmas* there weren't many stop-motion movies being made. Many of us, like Pete, were hugely influenced by *King Kong, Clash of the Titans,* and all of Ray Harryhausen's films. Stop-motion felt like a dying art, so having the opportunity to do *Nightmare* in this medium was very important to me.

It takes an unusual person to work in stop-motion; imagination, patience, technical ability, and a strong artistic vision. Pete has all of these qualities, and I had the pleasure of working with him on many films. Watching him work was like seeing a giant hovering over a quiet village or a mad scientist in his laboratory, bringing inanimate objects to life; finding ways, both high-tech and low-tech, to solve problems; and delicately, tactically bringing the beautiful miniature sets to life. Pete's unique style gives you an insight into this special world and the weirdness, excitement, depression, humor, anger, loneliness, and creativity of it all."

—**Tim Burton**, filmmaker

"Pete Kozachik—the most important and innovative stop-motion cinematographer in history (as well as the best-looking)—has written a fascinating book about his adventures in filmmaking, filled with wry humor and tons of practical tips on how to actually make the magic happen."

—**Henry Selick**, a long-time collaborator of Mr. Kozachik's, is the Academy Award Nominated director of *Coraline, The Nightmare Before Christmas, James and the Giant Peach,* and *Wendell & Wild*

TALES FROM THE
Pumpkin King's

PETE KOZACHIK ASC

with Katy Moore-Kozachik

RIVER GROVE
BOOKS

Published by River Grove Books
Austin, TX
www.rivergrovebooks.com

Distributed by River Grove Books

Design and composition by Greenleaf Book Group
Cover design by Greenleaf Book Group
Cover images used under license from
©Shutterstock.com/Dn Br; ©Shutterstock.com/anthonycz

Publisher's Cataloging-in-Publication data is available.

Print ISBN: 978-1-63299-379-3

eBook ISBN: 978-1-63299-380-9

First Edition

For Katy Moore-Kozachik, in love and gratitude.
And for anyone who wanted to work on films in
the stop-motion "Renaissance," welcome, to my life's work.
I've done my best to write what it felt like, working on a show.

—Pete Kozachik, ASC

Tales

FOREWORD

Many years ago, I was crewing up Industrial Light & Magic to start the visual effects work for a comedy film, *Innerspace*. A military test pilot is shrunk to the size of a tiny dot and injected accidentally into someone who imagines he is being possessed.

Our shots needed to show the soldier's journey from fat cells into arteries, stomach, lungs—whatever disgusting, gooey, throbbing body parts we could think of. The goal, remember, was to be funny.

The solution was to make the body's insides out of large rubber carvings that were kind of recognizable, painted pinkish, and covered with lots of slimy gel. Keeping it dark added a sense of wonder to the journey.

Quickly, our staff cameramen came onboard, the ones who I knew could handle a job that would be different from our usual blue-screen motion control photography. This would be more of an improvised live-action shoot—small, cramped, and messy. Each camera jockey would need to create film noir movie lighting: low key, mysterious, with shadows and strange glows coming from just around the next slimy blob. Small motors would be needed to push, pull, and pump plastic, rubber, wood, and metal parts. Even the set construction would be largely directed by the cameraman in order to jam so much stuff into very small spaces, including the camera.

I had seen Pete around a few times at ILM and knew he had worked with my old boss, Phil Kellison, from my early days making effects commercials for TV. Now, with *Innerspace* starting up, we got together and quickly realized we had many of the same friends and interests. As kids, we both shot stop-motion home movies and were entranced by Ray Harryhausen's fantastic creatures, especially the Cyclops from the *7th Voyage of Sinbad*. His experiments with camera tricks were something I also practiced, and in the process, we had both made discoveries that carried over into our professional careers.

Both of us are curious about how things work. Taking a camera apart might lead to rebuilding it as part of a specialized optical printer that solves a specific problem. Deconstructing and reconstructing is an important learning process. It's not that difficult if you take the time to learn how and why a device was originally made. Having a holistic interest helps too, as does a can-do attitude.

Over the next many months, Pete and the other crew members did a fantastic job on *Innerspace* by exciting the viewer's imagination while also telling an amazing and funny story. And when it came time for the Academy Awards, our screwball comedy actually won the Visual Effects Award that year.

Pete's credits and skills grew with every visual-effects film he worked on. We ran into each other a few times and discussed the films we'd seen and worked on, both old and new, good or bad, and why we liked them or not.

As I was getting deeply involved with ILM's Computer Graphics Department, Pete was offered the director of photography job for an all stop-motion film, *The Nightmare Before Christmas*. Every bit of his knowledge would need to be reconfigured into a new, unknown paradigm for making stop-motion feature films. I encourage the reader to pay close attention to Pete's recollections of this film and his subsequent stop-motion films. The results are astonishing.

It wasn't long before Pete's masterful lighting and camerawork got the attention of the members of the prestigious American Society of Cinematographers, and he was invited to join the organization in 2006.

Pete writes in a relaxed and sometimes ironical tone that mirrors the real Pete Kozachik that I know. His deceptively casual writing style will pull you into his world of wonderment, curiosity, persistence, imagination, enjoyment, and satisfaction. You will read and feel how he became a skillful technician, the master of his craft, and an artist: a maker of cinematic emotions.

—**DENNIS MUREN**
ASC, visual-effects artist

Shock and Awe

Throughout the studio, each department was busily prepping away, separated for the most part like isolated islands. We hadn't yet coalesced into a company. That wouldn't happen until we had a tangible point of focus to rally us out of the abstract. It was a tall order since we didn't even have a script.

What Henry did have was a song, Danny Elfman's "What's This?" where Jack Skellington discovers Christmas Town. From that, work flowed for all of us, starting with Henry and his story team. Joe Ranft and his guys churned out storyboards to illustrate the song. Suddenly, everyone had work to do, work that would end up on the screen!

Henry picked one shot out of the thirty-six shots boarded, shot number "WHAT-32." That would be the shot we'd begin the movie with. WHAT-32 was a good choice in my opinion; no pussyfooting around with a simple shot. It was a big one, a big exterior set, where we'd define the look of Christmas Town.

There would be lots of animation, major camera move, false perspective, and animation effects in-camera. The shot was our shakedown cruise, testing all systems.

There was another reason that it was a good pick; the shot called for just one puppet—the only puppet we had.

You probably know the shot: Jack riding on a train that's puffing out cotton balls. Jack jumps off, lands on a toboggan, skis down a hill, past houses, runs into candy cane arch, falls back into the snow. A busy shot!

Several departments worked on-set, shoulder to shoulder, politely stepping on each other's feet. It helped us bond as a company.

Chris Peterson and I were searching for a look that would work for the whole sequence. Chris came up with adding color gels to the specials, red on red houses, green on green, spilling onto the nearby snow.

The elaborate camera move really needed my motion-control rig, but hiring it for the first shot felt a little awkward. It got more so, when I had to replace a burned-out driver.

All in, our first shot took six weeks! When the shot was finished, when animator Trey Thomas shot his last frame, we projected it as a loop. The shot ran continuously, over and over.

On the first couple runs, the room was silent. I didn't know why, maybe some kind of shock, or not knowing if it was good or bad.

Then, came clapping, laughing, and cheering, like a sports event. As the celebration subsided murmurs, rolling eyeballs, and silence came. Reality was sinking in; we'd spent a month and a half, and had one shot in the can. Anybody know how many shots in a movie?

This was going to be a big project. Really big!

CHAPTER 1

It's Alive!

It was the summer of 1958, the year of the Cyclops. I had been glued to the screen all through *The 7th Voyage of Sinbad*, mesmerized, until a fire-breathing dragon wrung a giant Cyclops's neck. This was my Monster Totem. At that point, Mom decided to reel me back to reality.

She leaned down and whispered, "Look at how they move. Do you think they're robots?"

Cowabunga! At seven years old, I had the scoop! President Eisenhower had a fleet of giant robots! They could be deployed to some Cold War hotspot, covered with rubber monster suits. So watch it, Commies!

Months later, I applied my flawed theory to an even more exciting film, *King Kong*. Apart from the fantastic creatures and that preposterous story, *King Kong* was also the first movie I noticed having a "look." There was a dreamy atmosphere I liked. The jungle scenes especially looked more elegant, as in an old fairy tale. No matter that it was an old, black-and-white, fuzzy TV image. I was captivated.

As a third grader, I spent hours after school at a newsstand. I remember dark, creaky floorboards and the scent of newsprint and tobacco. The reading material was more interesting than what we had in school. *Mad Magazine* was a favorite, and so were comics—superheroes, sci-fi, and horror. Quaint nudie mags were nice, too, when the proprietor wasn't watching. But most intriguing was a diamond in the rough, the magazine *Famous Monsters of Filmland*. Forrest Ackerman's articles were illustrated with black-and-white publicity stills and behind-the-scenes peeks.

This was heady stuff; it was my first inkling that movies were made by (somewhat) regular people who had names and did particular jobs. I read about actors, writers, directors, and makeup artists. I saw step by step how Dick Smith made a foam-rubber monster mask perfectly formed to exactly fit one actor's face. I admired his skill.

Flipping to another page, I found the very Cyclops and dragon that had been inhabiting my psyche since I was seven—my Monster Totem. But they weren't giant robots. They were just standing on a table, like puppets. A smiling man was towering over them. Were they . . . small robots?

As I read, my whole theory was debunked and replaced with a better, simpler explanation. The smiling man, who was named Ray Harryhausen, had somehow made these creatures himself. And, somehow, he had made them perform as well. One guy had done the whole job, not a factory full of army men.

Mr. Harryhausen Was My Hero!

Once those creatures were pared down to toy scale, I became fired up to make such a film. It was within reach. There were many details missing from the article, including how to make the figurines and how to make them move, but I found clues in several sources, beginning with other issues of *Famous Monsters*. Subsequent issues described movable rubber figurines that could be posed and reposed sequentially in small increments. Each pose was shot on a single frame of motion-picture film, building up a performance that came to life only when the film was projected. The process had a name: stop-motion animation.

Later, in 1962, I read the short story *Tyrannosaurus Rex*, Ray Bradbury's salute to his friend Ray Harryhausen. Within the story was a tantalizing description of the protagonist making a stop-motion dinosaur. One step in particular, "glue plastic sponge over lubricated skeleton," had me baffled. What was that skeleton all about? Another photo in *Famous Monsters* solved the mystery: This type of skeleton—a complex jointed frame—had been used in *King Kong*, and there it was on the page. Most of the joints were cousins of the stiff ball joint in a car's rearview mirror. The contraption was called an *armature*, and it had been invented by Kong's creator, Willis O'Brien.

In parallel with the crafty techniques employed by my heroes, I was taken by the concept drawings and still frames, specifically from *Kong*. Something about the lush jungle scenes resonated with me; they had great depth, thanks to layers of misty backgrounds, separating rim light on trees and characters, and foreground vines that framed it all in silhouette.

Stop-motion was usually described as a tedious, boring process, one that taxed the patience of the animator, but to me, it sounded like a challenge and a lot of fun. I wanted to give it a try but was missing a lot of the basic skills, not to mention the equipment.

In 1963, Flip Ferington, a family friend, taught me to shoot, develop, and print photos. With that, shooting movie film seemed a doable thing. One of Flip's *Popular Photography* magazines had an article titled "Build a Movie." To make a complex animation puppet, you would simply "snip the characters out of foam pillows and skewer them on bendable wires."

Snipping foam with scissors turned out to be straightforward, and in a few hours, I had a crude 10-inch allosaurus that could actually stand up and be posed. Toothpicks filled out his dentition. Then came a brontosaurus and a caveman.

My studio started with an ancient 8 mm camera and a roll of black-and-white film. Flip provided her tripod, and I would shoot outdoors, where there was a sunny spot dressed with sticks to suggest a jungle scene.

It took a while to shoot the first frame. I guess it was something like writer's block. Finally, I moved the bronto in several increments, making it take a step toward a tasty-looking tree, and then shot some more frames without movement to give a brief pause that I thought should be between strides.

Having broken the ice, I slowly got into the zone, rhythmically moving in, repositioning the creatures, moving out and shooting a frame. It was a great feeling to be so focused, keeping the current movements going while planning the next movements. After three days, I had something—not sure what—in the can.

Black-and-white film had to go all the way to Chicago for processing. A week later, it came back, and I was still apprehensive. Lights out, and off we go. There's the Bronto. How come it's not moving? I wait a little more, and still no motion. Bronto should be moving by now. What's wrong?

It moved. Then it didn't. Then it moved and stayed moving, crudely taking steps toward the caveman. The allosaurus ripped off a chunk of bleeding Bronto blubber and then exited, leaving the caveman in safety. It was jerky and halting all the way. But it was alive!

Ecstatic, I pondered what to do next.

Nephew of Kong

My discovery of a dark, rabbit-fur purse in a trash can provided the answer. I would make a Kong puppet covered with that fur and pit Kong against my allosaurus.

This time, I set up in the bedroom and guessed at an exposure, which turned out a bit dark. The animation was too slow overall. Lesson learned: Estimate how many frames a movement should take. And get a light meter!

The crude results buoyed my confidence, inspiring me to tackle a more ambitious project: I could remake my favorite movie in glorious 8 mm black and white. This could get costly—maybe $50, I figured. I needed a job to finance the project. Luckily, the *Detroit Free Press* was looking for paperboys. I loved the job; I could walk through the sleeping neighborhood and think, undisturbed.

My English teacher was liberal enough to allow us to make a film as an assignment in communication. I seized on the opportunity to cast my classmates and to shoot on the auditorium stage. I figured I could get one sequence for the new Kong finished by Mrs. Brown's due date. I had been experimenting at home, making a foam stegosaurus with more realistic skin by coating him with liquid latex. The new dino fit right into a scene in *King Kong*.

When the scene was shot and edited, it was well received, especially by the guys who'd performed in it. Everyone had a laugh at their expense: seventh graders trying to look like rough-and-tough sailors. Of course, I had to step in as the hero, putting the stegosaurus down with a final shot. I created the muzzle flashes by scratching the film stock with a pin.

Lucy, my puppy love, was playing the heroine. After some uninteresting talking (in a silent film), we got to the kissing scene. As we were about to shoot the scene, I realized that I had never kissed a girl. It had looked easy on TV, but I got nervous about actually giving her a smooch. I skipped that moment, but I had no problem in directing my savage natives how to kidnap the leading lady! As planned, I took the project beyond what was assigned, moving toward covering the whole story.

At some point, I wanted to put my actors and creatures in the same shot. To begin, I borrowed a hacksaw and modified the camera to carry two films, sandwiched together. It seemed to be the way to go. One film was raw, and the other film was already developed, shot with live actors, and would act as the background. Shoot through it at a Kong puppet, and you end up with both images together. That required wet film—developing 8 mm movie film—using the bathroom as a darkroom. It all worked, but the process was very cumbersome and not precise enough. This may be the simplest and best way to get a humble double exposure.

Somewhat more than a year later, the model biplanes finished off Kong, shooting him down from the Empire State Building's gleaming tower. The tower, made of coffee cans and cardboard, was shot in the laundry room of our apartment complex. One tenant kept coming back, coaching me to "quit adjusting and shoot." I kept telling him, "I *am* shooting."

Half a dozen dinosaurs and tiny humans and two giant apes later, I had learned a lot. Besides the crafts involved, I learned to soldier through the tedious moments and live within a budget. I also learned for sure that I really did like doing this stuff!

Ray Harryhausen and Pete Kozachik having tea on *Corpse Bride*.

Pete's *King Kong*.

CHAPTER 2

The Age of Aquarius and Baking Dinos

om; my brother, Steve; and I left the Midwest just before the Summer of Love, bound for Tucson, Arizona. When we got off the train, I looked up a special section in the yellow pages: between motels and motorcycles was "motion picture producers and studios." Now that I was this close to Hollywood, I knew there must be something going on. Yes, there was one studio, Aztec Films, and it was within walking distance.

Chuck and Ron, brothers from Brooklyn, were making industrials and educational films, but they were also into Harryhausen and horror movies. Chuck was the cameraman, and Ron was interested in makeup. I showed them my *Kong*.

They approved: "Some of this, it's better'n that shit ya see on TV."

To my 15-year-old ears, that was a special compliment, but I knew my stuff wasn't anywhere close to that good.

Ron clued me into foam latex—where to get it and how to use it. I'd use that valuable inside info someday for sure. Chuck laid a hefty box of vintage *American Cinematographer* magazines on me. As I read through them, the real pro filmmaker's world opened up to my dazzled eyes. I've subscribed ever since.

If that was all that came of it, I would be very grateful. But not much later, Chuck called and asked if I could assist for him on an educational film. This was my first film job and a good reason to play hooky.

I happily moved lights and props at his direction, soaking up new knowledge in the process. He showed me how to load his Bolex camera, and I vowed to own a machine. It had every feature that I wished for on my Kong film.

Reentering my sophomore year, I was hoping for some Wild West vibes, and I got what I wanted the day I joined my new classmates in English class. Unlike prim Mrs. Brown back in Michigan, this lady could hock like a cowboy in a dust devil and drop a loogie in a steel trash can. *Bwang*! And in the lunchroom, students were engaged in a "yee-haw" contest.

My favorite subjects—science of any branch, English, and art—were still here. The electives were amazing. In graphic arts, a real, live photographer taught you how to light studio photographs, shoot on 4×5 negatives, and massage them in the darkroom. On the school newspaper, a real journalist critiqued my photos for composition and storytelling.

I made a couple of short films as class projects. One was regular cel animation, showing the life cycle of a star. It didn't play well, with me narrating live as cartoon deuterium atoms came together and flew apart, but the next film did.

For English class, I made a short film, a kind of "Age of Aquarius" version of Harryhausen's four-armed, snake-tailed dancing girl in *Sinbad*. Because it was the era of peace, love, and understanding, I made her topless.

This puppet was a new experiment in fabrication, closer to how the pros did it. I started by sculpting the character in oil-based modeling clay, and then I made a two-sided plaster mold around it. Then I mixed the base color with vinyl paints and mixed a little of that into some white liquid latex. Painting a couple of layers of that into the molds resulted in rubber skins, front and back. To keep the shape, I stuffed cotton into both skins, with a black iron wire armature in the middle. More colored liquid latex fused the seams, and I painted details with other colors in latex.

The main advantage of this method was the extreme detail—much more advanced than my crude, snipped-out shapes in urethane foam. The cotton within didn't do a great job of holding the shape, and the next level of sophistication, injecting liquid latex foam into the mold, was beyond my means at the time.

I asked a hippie girl I'd befriended at our apartment building to do some heady dance moves from the exotic and mysterious East while I filmed her for animation reference. A record of Ravi Shankar doing his sitar thang provided the mystic tunes. The animation was a slight improvement, but the result was not very interesting: no story.

Toward the end of high school, Mr. Marcek's physics class suddenly came to life on the big screen. *2001: A Space Odyssey* featured realistic spacecraft, gracefully demonstrating Newtonian kinematics. Nothing had come close to this realism or its beauty. The accompanying Strauss waltz was right on; it brought out the elegance of the austere dance. I wanted to put that kind of motion on the big screen someday. My date wasn't so much into the show. She snuggled and nuzzled, but the only body in motion I was fixated on was a space station.

A part-time job at a grocery store financed various other experiments, mostly to do with a film I had been dreaming of making for some time. It would be an instructional piece, set in the Age of Dinosaurs and depicting their rise and fall in all its savage grandeur.

To date, I had nothing to show that was even close to a low-budget professional film. But this one had to be sellable to an educational-film distributor because it was going to finance my college degree.

That was the ideal, and the grocery-store job was reality.

A year into college, I was dividing my time among school; homework; my girlfriend, Jeanne; the grocery store; and making rubber dinosaurs. The latter took the hindmost position.

I was stealing time at my dormitory desk, sculpting plasticine dinosaurs, while John, my wildlife-conservation roommate, was stuffing kangaroo-rat pelts; Gary, our Vietnam-vet roommate, was reacting to battles with plastic soldiers; and James, our ROTC roommate, was polishing his brass and popping his zits.

Off campus was Walt, a retired machinist, who lived next to Jeanne's house; he let me make armatures in his home machine shop. They were crude, more wire than ball joints, but at least those theropods could stand on their own two legs.

Next door, I was allowed to mix foam latex, pour it into plaster molds, and cook it in Jeanne's mom's oven (twice). After stinking up the house with sulfur fumes on two late-night casting sessions, I was politely asked to find another laboratory.

Dinosaur making was curtailed until the next year, when Jeanne and I married and moved into an apartment with a nice gas stove. At one point, I heard of liquid urethane foam, which makes its own foam bubbles! It was cheaper and less stinky than latex, but it was tougher to flex. I used it on a couple of critters, but Mother Nature's product (good old latex) prevailed.

I filmed nothing until 1974, after I had graduated and finished my first and only year as a middle-school science teacher. Let me tell you, that profession is harder than anyone who hasn't done it can imagine. I salute teachers, the good ones out there in the trenches who are enriching young minds and civilizing kids whose parents have dropped the ball. I loved the kids, but the job was not for me.

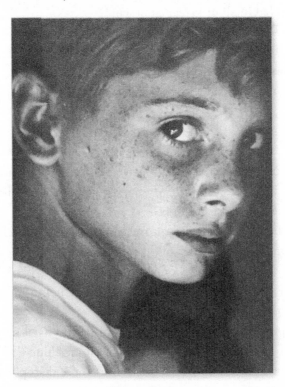

Young Pete.

CHAPTER 3

KZAZ!

The dinosaur film remained on my to-do list, but a new job took center stage. Harry West, program director at the local independent TV station, KZAZ, took a gamble on hiring me as a control-room tech. What I brought to the table was mostly eagerness, a little background messing with film, a diploma that showed I could start and finish things, and the tie I wore in my cold-call interview. Harry seemed to like me well enough, but it's a good bet that wearing that tie closed the deal.

When I was a teacher, my yearly salary had been $7,500. The TV job paid about half, $2 per hour. But I had no regrets; this felt like the right move.

I started in the control room as technical director, threading 2-inch-wide videotape reels on the two massive record-and-playback machines. Things could get frenetic when several 30-second commercials ran back-to-back.

A couple days later, I was also running the video switcher, where any of the video sources could be switched on air. In addition to the videotape machines, a pair of film projectors, a slide carousel, and two studio cameras out on the stage floor were tied in to the switcher. The director on duty would tell me to cut from one source to another. He made all the calls on picture and controlled the audio sources.

It was fun, especially when we were doing live on-air production. Mine was the sign-out shift, from 6 p.m. to 2 a.m., when we signed off for the night. That included the evening news, where the director communicated with the two cameramen by headset, calling for specific angles on the two newscasters and calling for me to cut to feeds from the cameras and the other video sources in the control room. The director followed a printed script, the same one the newscasters were reading, and he communicated with the newscasters via hand signals from the cameramen during the broadcast and via loudspeakers during breaks.

Unlike shooting a movie, there was no time to ponder; the director was riding the whole show, framing and cutting in real time for 30 or 60 minutes. I was in awe of the director's focus, his nimble mind processing so much at once. I sure was glad I wasn't doing that job!

Two weeks into my employment, Harry called me into his office. "Pete, tonight's your trial by fire. I had to fire the director, so you're directing the news." And then, after he saw my face, "You'll be fine. I'll be watching at home."

Do you know those nightmares where you're naked in a crowd or showing up for a test you haven't studied for? This was both, plus thousands of viewers' eyes glued to what I was doing.

The journalists, John Scott and George Borozan, were clued in, and they were cool as cucumbers. Some of that coolness wafted my way, but I didn't know all I needed to and was keenly aware of it.

We got through the broadcast with plenty of hiccups and a dead interval caused by the need to replace a microphone. John and George fed me clues while on air: "George, I'm going to pass the next story to you." The next show after the news was *The Twilight Zone*.

Over time, Harry put me on directing several live shows. On Saturday we broadcast professional wrestling, where fat bikers with face tats came into the control room to plan out who would jump on whose head. They were all cordial in the control room but snarling blood enemies in the ring. They even had little old ladies in tennis shoes cheering from the bleachers—the gladiators' moms.

Running the church shows on Sunday morning wasn't so exciting. It was about running videotapes, each featuring a smarmy televangelist. I sometimes wondered if anyone was watching. I decided to find out: Between shows, I slipped in a public-service bulletin about birth control. Wow! The phone lit up with a live one bellowing, "Get that sewage off the air!"

Sunday noon was time for *Telefiesta Mexicana*, three hours of nonstop, live, south-of-the-border music, banter, and advertising. My Spanish was weak, but the hosts, Oscar and his lovely wife, did a great job throwing cues to me for the next event. They signaled with a change in nuance and then froze in a smile. I liked Oscar. Sometimes after a show, he'd take all of us—crew and performers—to celebrate at his favorite Mexican restaurant. The show had essentially zero budget, but we had fun. One time, while a crooner was lip-syncing, I stepped out of the sound booth to prep a slide commercial and soon felt a tug at my pants. A little kid squeaked, "Can you fix the record? It's skipping."

We also taped local church shows on location: two cameras in the church and me in the van, directing and switching. The 2-inch video recorder took up most of the van's space. It was great fun; the cameramen and I worked as a sharp team. The operators knew exactly what I was calling for, and they framed up in a matter of seconds.

One show featured a red-faced Holy Roller laying on the fire and brimstone, and the other show starred a considerably slicker pastor who brought his professional acting skills to the pulpit. He knew how to play to the little red lights on the camera.

His banter tended to move along smoothly in volume and cadence, and he delivered the final word in an intimate downbeat. I enjoyed anticipating that shift and emphasized it with a cut to a closer frame just before. He gracefully flowed with my cuts, as if we'd rehearsed it.

Both shows included choir segments, which provided a creative challenge to make the subject interesting. The cameras were on wheels, so the guys could get different angles and make moving shots. I would call for specific frames in shorthand: "Camera A two-shot on Ma and Pa Kettle. Cam B slow pan the choir top row. Cam A close on bald guy. Cam B close on the cute girl." (They liked that last one.)

Harry was great to work with, and I learned a lot just watching him work. He would create dynamic sports-program openings by cutting in snippets of video to the beat of hard rock. He used the cumbersome pair of videotape machines we were also using on air. By today's technology, the gear was painfully user-unfriendly. (Harry said the video switcher came from an Otis elevator.) But he put out work that stood out among the productions in town.

When at home, I was shooting those rubber dinosaurs, now in 16 mm! I had found an old Bolex, still useful when shooting miniatures. I concentrated on a sequence that echoed a scene in Disney's *Fantasia*: A brontosaurus, a stegosaurus, and several trachodons are peacefully munching green tinfoil leaves by a lake. All's well until an allosaurus attacks—in color! The 9-minute scene came off as classroom material, maybe usable in a 1950s B movie, but nothing more.

The scene had some in-camera split-screen shots of animals wading in water that I'd photographed at a real pond nearby. That trick was a bit dangerous, because I was double exposing over the latent animation. A mistake would have required a reshoot.

To create a fearsome storm, I animated lightning effects right on the backdrop and augmented them with short, staccato frames blown out by a bright light. Rain would be added later—much later.

At work, I transferred it to 2-inch tape and added a temp music track. On that Saturday afternoon, with the bosses gone, *A Jurassic Pictorial* went on air unannounced. No schedule, no permission, no complaints, but a few people called in.

It felt good!

Opening Scene and Ghouls Paint the Town

The first set we see is a real show-off shot: the camera twisting straight down and landing in a circle of trees, each containing a portal to a different holiday town in its trunk. We lit for an October evening sun, low shadows and golden color, with a weak blue gelatin to feel the chill.

The shot becomes a roller-coaster ride through a graveyard. Singing ghost shadows darken the headstones as we fly by. Now we're in moonlight, which casts sharp shadows and looks almost neutral in color. In fact, the whole movie would be in black and white if Disney had let Tim have his way! This shot was one of the prickliest and most contrast-heavy in the movie, but we needed a tiny bit of ambient light and a few special lights to see the pumpkins.

You can see a lot of "lighting with paint" all over on the edges on the stones. The ghost shadows were cartoon-animated and projected on the

---

1 The "interlude" chapters are meant to give you the feel of a typical day on the studio floor with the camera crew and our coworkers. If you have a DVD copy of *The Nightmare Before Christmas* running, you can navigate to the subject you're reading about using the time code.

headstones. We used Luxo Senior—an articulated arm, like an adjustable office lamp, holding the camera—on this shot, and we used every inch of its floor track while extending its arm as far as it could go in both directions. That enabled us to span that long, skinny set, but just barely.

Everyone in the camera crew had a hand in the opening sequence. It was a big one, with 27 sets and 40 shots that included lots of big camera moves, crowd shots, and effects. Right at the start, we had used Luxo Senior to the hilt, which made it plain that we needed another big motion-capture rig. The quickest solution was to interest Phil Tippett in selling his half-ownership on the rig we'd built together. Phil agreed to a fair price. According to one production person, it was going to "save our butt." From then on, the rig was referred to as the Butt Saver.

"I am the one hiding under your bed" was a short shot featuring a one-purpose puppet consisting of a pair of toothy jaws and two disembodied glowing red eyes. No flesh, just an armature painted black. The eyes were on stalks so they could spread apart to help the effect of zooming in closer than we could.

The singing vampires had pools of light from overhead in their creepy haunt. We borrowed that from *The Godfather*. Vito Corleone wouldn't like our treatment; we made our pools of light a bit harder.

The vampires actually weren't intended to be in the film. Rick Heinrichs sculpted them as study maquettes, much smaller than full-size puppets would have been. But with all the oddball characters in *Nightmare*, we decided a few smaller vampires wouldn't be too hard to swallow and skipped making the big ones.

As the scene takes us outside and into the town, we had a motivation for using color lighting: fire orange fit in very well as torches. To tie in a little the look of Sally's kitchen, I went back to Dean's green sewer glow. It worked best at stinking up the darker shots.

We also had to soften the lighting just a little to make it easier to understand *Nightmare*'s baroque scenery and characters. The puppet-fabrication team was suddenly knee-deep in making a throng of extras for the show's biggest crowd shot. The specifications were simple: look appropriately weird, be able to stand, and be able to clap hands without breaking.

Three animators were going to work together on the wide shot of Jack triumphantly greeting the ghoulish crowd. The shot would include a grandiose camera move and several torch fires, each double exposed on the same piece of film.

The shot would take a long time to animate, and nobody wanted to shoot it again for any reason. Under a bulletproof lighting and camera setup, I got a promise from the animators that nobody would touch the camera. Any bumps would show up when we burned in the torch fires.

Two weeks later, the animation was finished, and the animators had gone rogue, racking over the camera regularly; they couldn't guarantee a bump-free shot. They had voted for us to shoot the fires on another strip of film. That might make it fixable if we needed a fix.

I had to smile; there was no choice. Indeed, the shot was full of bumps, and we were lucky to have Buena Vista Visual Effects available to fix it.

Shooting shadows.

CHAPTER 4

A Few New Tricks

Business was never great at KZAZ. Providing content every minute of every day, an independent in a small market had a hard time competing with national network affiliates. At one point, business dropped enough that I was cut down to part-time. I took it as an opportunity to take classes in mechanical engineering. Whatever the subject, our instructors instilled in us the credo "An engineer can do for a quarter what anybody else can do for a buck." The fun part was learning how to draw plans and then make them real with lathes and milling machines.

Another bonus: I was introduced to computing. The first computer I ever laid eyes on was a Control Data 6400. It took up an entire floor of the University of Arizona's budding computer-science building. The system included rows of tape drives, a furiously chugging line printer, and a hard drive the size of a washing machine that boasted *2 megabytes*. All of it was contained in a glass room.

We learned the programming language Fortran and modeled physics stuff we found interesting. You'd sit down at a keypunch machine, type a line of code, and keep punching cards until you were done. Then some guy with a scraggly beard would take your stack of cards and run them through the card reader. The next day, you'd pick up your printout. It was pretty much the same anticipation cycle as when you sent film off to the lab. Did the film come out?

I was fiddling around with Estes model rockets, so I tried modeling a rocket's trajectory and velocity second by second. There were no graphics back then, just reams of paper columns of numbers, but it was fascinating. Look how this column slowly gets bigger, then gets bigger faster, then gets smaller, zero, then negative. A velocity curve! Cool!

I had no idea that years in the future, I'd be looking at such columns of data on a glowing CRT monitor, describing the trajectory of a camera move.

Alex and Dino

Fun as it all was, there was a missing element. I started going AWOL from classes to visit Alex Hankocy, head of the film department at the University of Arizona. I had questions; he had answers. My focus was how to proceed after I'd shot everything on the dino film. The next step was called *postproduction*: editing work prints, cutting A–B rolls, mixing sound, and working with labs in Hollywood. Alex had done it all and was happy to share his experience, even though I wasn't a film student.

I continued shooting the dino film, including the requisite "educational" intro, a little history of reptiles starting with invertebrates (displayed as a praying mantis eating a moth's head). Modern-day versions were exemplified by my beloved pets: Bruce, the iguana, and Spot, the rosy boa constrictor.

Of greater interest, the early dinosaurs included fish with legs, an oversized salamander stalking a giant dragonfly, and a sailback lizard who was defending her nest from a plucked-chicken reptile. The final scenes included pteranodons scooping up fish to feed the babies and a battle between a T. rex and a triceratops.

I'd been splicing the film together as I finished a roll, so there was a rough cut right there. There were no prints; I had made the cut with the camera original. That's low budget!

The procedure was almost reasonable, as I only filmed the exact shot length I intended to have in the film. That's one of the advantages of animation: You can stop on a dime, reframe, and continue the action at another angle. Alex didn't approve, and today, I don't either. I was cocky, a mix of ignorance and unwarranted optimism. Alex asserted that he was going to make a black-and-white work print of the film. The decision was unilateral. I wasn't allowed to destroy my original film while editing sound—not on his watch! He would charge $40 all in. Is that a lot? No, a thousand-foot work print would be a gift.

My first task was to recut the entire film—the right way! I had been cutting and splicing in a way that looked extremely bush league, like TV news cutting film. From Alex, I learned to cut A–B film reels, "the movie way." The film looked just like a movie on each cut.

Another benefit in A–B reels is that you can use it to get a poor man's double exposure. That's how I burned in raindrops.

With a shiny new work print in hand, it was time to record sound. For an over-the-top narration, I used Rich Heatley, the chief engineer at KZAZ. His baritone voice was perfect for my melodramatic lines. He triumphed over tongue twisters like "*Struthiomimus*" and could work up to the desired level of hokum on lines such as, "When he walked, the ground trembled with a sound of *thunder!*"

The sound effects consisted of me in the announce booth with a boxful of things to crunch, snap, splash, and punch and a record of thunder and animal noises. The animal sounds were better slowed down, sometimes played backward. I did some heavy breathing, chewed an apple, and made slurping sounds to round out the effects.

With all my sound transferred to magnetic film, I could line up all those sounds with the pictures. Synchronizing sound with the work print was simple: use a sync block. The device had identical film sprockets on the same shaft, rigged to hold mag film in sync with picture. Turn the shaft and hear the sound as the mag film goes under a magnetic sound pickup. Cut and splice that roar next to the open jaws of T. rex. Splice thunder next to lightning.

Alex had a complete mixing theater right across from his office. The system consisted of three sound reels that were slaved to a projector with the work print. Roll the system and adjust the volume for each track as the film runs. All three tracks get recorded onto sound-reel number 4. If it went well, there's your soundtrack. What a blast!

The A–B reels and the single soundtrack shipped out to a big-time movie lab in Hollywood. With Alex's help, I phoned instructions in to a rep, Jack West. Back came a color sound print of *Dinosaurs: Giants of the Past*.

Wow, playing with the big boys!

I showed it here and there. Stop-motion dinosaur freaks were complimentary, but a class of eighth graders rated it as "cool but dumb." That was as far as it got, but not for that reason. The challenges of distribution turned out to be more than I expected.

I had been naive about music. Did I really think I could lift cuts from classical-music records without paying anyone? *I'll deal with it later*, I thought. Wrong! The music company wanted more money than I'd spent on the whole production. A local distributor, part of the university, agreed to take on the film if I would recut it and replace the music. I couldn't cough up the dough for that, and as time moved along, we both got tired of negotiating. For all I know, the original reels are still in some corner of a film vault at the lab. Lesson learned.

I Could Do That!

Working at KZAZ allowed me to observe local commercials in production. Once, I helped some agency guys set up a shoot in our studio. One asked the other, "How come everything we do turns to shit?" I wondered that, too.

Well, budgets in town were mostly about $1.98, so the local storekeeper was encouraged to narrate (mumble) the commercial himself, looking like a yokel in a home movie.

I started thinking about making local commercials myself. Friends working at the NBC affiliate had seen my dinosaur film and mentioned it to the new general manager, Jon Ruby. He was from Chicago and was looking to spiff up production at his station. Jon was interested in creating an animated station ID, the graphic logo you'd see before every show in those days.

Graphics wasn't my strong suit, but I pitched Jon the idea of NBC's channel number, 4, rotating obliquely to be revealed as a 3D shape, then rotating back to the 2D view, where it now appeared as the letter N of NBC. Jon was quick to get it and liked the idea. I quoted him the princely sum of $150. He looked at me funny for a moment, then said it would be fine with him.

Now I had to figure out how to do it. Initially, my experience with mechanical drawing was the path; there are ways to derive any view of a solid from two flat views. But complications arose, and I chased down a professor who had been experimenting with wireframe graphics drawn with a computer. Back in 1974, that stuff was in its infancy.

I gave him 3D mechanical drawings of the 4 and the N, dimensioned like a machine part, and he printed out both rotations on paper. I filled in the transformation by hand, deciding which lines making up the 4 would carry through to be what lines making up the N. All the drawings went under clear animation cels, where I traced the lines in red and blue cel paint. Once that was shot over a black card, the job was done. Jon Ruby was happy with his logo, and I was thrilled to see it come up on TV.

Another Chicagoan in Tucson broadcasting, Mark Schwartz, wanted a TV spot for his Top 40 radio station, KTKT. Mark was quite animated himself, very positive and full of energy, a great guy to work with. He went for my pitch: cartoon monolithic call letters erupting up from the desert as the ground heaves in an earthquake. I sneaked in a lizard riding a chunk of desert floor. The lizard alone made him chuckle.

I was much more interested in stop-motion, but the word *animation* meant "cartoons" to anyone in broadcasting or advertising. What if I made a demo piece—without dinosaurs—to prime the pump?

There was an intriguing sign over a local car wash that depicted a smiley green octopus. I whipped up a cartoony stop-mo puppet of the octopus and animated a 10-second shot of him washing a model car. I brought it to a sales rep and asked him to help me get Mr. Octo interested in a full-on TV ad.

It didn't excite the guy managing the car wash. He pointed out that they wouldn't want to show a car being so roughly handled. I really wanted to make a spot with that octopus. Like a rube, I came back with an ambitious storyboard and agreed to shoot it on spec.

A month later, I transferred the film to videotape with the sales rep. We thought the piece was nice. A live actor is washing his car on a hot day, wiping sweat off his brow. He steps in a washing pail, falls back, and lands in the cradling tentacles of our cute octopus. The energetic octopus makes quick work of the job, and the relieved guy shakes hands with its tentacles.

I had worked out a background-projection setup that enabled me to combine the prefilmed actor and car with Octo while I animated. Holy Harryhausen! I was doing it almost like my idol!

The sales rep wrote some copy and finished the spot by giving it a soundtrack. A few days later, the rep called. The guy had seen it and didn't like it. It just wasn't what he expected. The rules of speculative enterprise are harsh. I had to "eat the project"!

CHAPTER 5

Ka-Boom!

The summer of '76 was coming up and with it an opportunity to make a chunk of cash to start an animation business. Rick, my brother-in-law, worked as a crew boss on an exploration-drilling rig. I would be one of two roughnecks under his direction. We set out to several spots in the Western states, where prospecting companies wanted to see samples from down below. Rick drove the rig, and I followed with a Kenworth pipe truck.

Our first job was in Yuma, Arizona, where we tried to help an old married couple realize their lifelong dream. For years, they had prospected for gold on their claim with only coyotes and sidewinders for neighbors.

Stick by stick, we stopped to thread another pipe and resumed advancing down the hole with a medieval-looking cutting tip called a *tricone* bit; it looks like three spiked cones, all pointing toward the center, like menacing whirling teeth. Cuttings were constantly flowing up, mixed with water and drilling mud. I'd catch a sandbag full of sample cuttings every 5 feet and mark it for depth.

While we were there, Rick taught me to arc weld and to cut with oxyacetylene. We were constantly rigging something or fixing stuff. I loved it.

Rick picked up our third man on-site, Bob Rider, a desert-rat type who showed up looking for a job. Rider was a genuinely nasty, people-hating hermit who lived in a shack way out in the desert. He drove a beater VW bug with no battery. "Can't trust batteries; they're all shit." He parked on hills so he could start by coasting downhill.

Rider's sour milk of human kindness extended to the dog casually living around his shack. Name? "Don't need a name." What did the dog eat? "Whatever he can catch."

I'm sorry to say we didn't find the gold the old couple was hoping for. They were stoic, but you could see it in their eyes: busted dreams. Even Rider was a little sympathetic. At no charge, we drilled them a 200-foot water well. Rider disappeared, and we moved on.

Next stop was Silver Peak, Nevada, formerly a wealthy mining town until the silver veins dried up. Now it was pretty much a ghost town. This customer wanted us to see if there was a worthwhile deposit of lithium. Silver Peak did indeed have lithium down there, and there's a mine operating there today. Summer was spilling over into fall, and we were headed to another small mining town, Creede, Colorado, population: not much. Rick found us another gem of a third man: Jerry, a scruffy 40-something who lived with his dogs in a beat-up station wagon, with an open six-pack on his lap.

Situated 9,000 feet high in the Rockies and butted up into a towering, narrow ravine, tiny Creede didn't look like it could get any bigger. There was no room to rent, so Jerry and I shared a tent down by the river. Another couple of thousand feet up was where the customer wanted us to look for gold. He had bulldozed a pad for the rig right on the edge of the mountain.

Jerry would crawl into the tent, breath stinking of sweetish, rotten essence. To escape that, I laid my sleeping bag head-to-toe with his setup.

Once, he cajoled me into joining him so he could chat up a barmaid. I was far from the tippler Jerry was, and I fell far behind his tally of emptied glasses.

Jerry was disappointed. "Hey, man, I thought you were my buddy!"

The next day I learned two things: Hangovers are different at 10,000 feet above sea level, and opening the welding oxygen tank to breathe as it blows in your face is of no great help.

Jerry continued to pursue his hobby, and one day he got angry enough to throw a log at the boss. See ya, Jerry.

At 900 feet down, our luck ran out. A cascade of rock dust caved down the hole, trapping the bit and hundreds of feet of pipe, seized by weight and friction. Rick tried everything to no avail.

Norm, the owner, flew in the next day and resolved to cut his losses. He would "cut" the lowest several pipes with dynamite, and we might be able to retrieve the rest of the pipe. Of course, a guy like Norm could just walk into the right store and buy enough sticks of blasting gel to fill a 25-foot drill pipe.

On a beautiful frosty morning, Norm lowered down a couple sticks wired with blasting caps. Then we dropped them all down the 900-foot tube.

I'd seen too many *Road Runner* cartoons. "Don't you have to hook up to one of those plunger things?" No, actually. You just touch the wires to the truck battery.

Norm looked at me with a grin and pointed at the battery. "You wanna do it? Let's go. Do it now!"

I pressed wires to terminals. Nothing. I kept them pressed in place, wondering what went wrong.

Whoa, did the ground just bump under my feet?

A few seconds later, a low whine emerged from the open pipe. It got louder until it seemed like a dozen banshees were screaming out the hole. For half a minute, we had to yell to be heard, and then it was quiet.

No doubt we had vaporized a couple pipes, but almost all of them remained irretrievable. It was great fun, but three months on the road was enough. On the bus trip home, I planned to knock on Harry's door. Maybe I could get my old job back at KZAZ.

CHAPTER 6

Film, Folio, and Frogs

A week later, I showed up early on my first day back at KZAZ. I apologetically told Harry I'd had another offer. Alex Hankocy had just offered me a job, and it would be all kinds of production—some video and a lot more film. I'd be using pro filmmaking gear: Arriflex cameras, upright Moviolas, the real deal. Harry was mad, but he understood. This was as good as film jobs got in Tucson!

My primary responsibility would be running a crew of students shooting University of Arizona football and basketball games for the coaches to review. It had to be 16 mm film; few schools were set up for video in '76. Schools had to trade footage with each other if asked, and film was the common denominator. We'd set up an Arri-16S camera high in the stadiums, with four 400-foot magazines of film to get us through the game.

One obvious perk was traveling with the team on away games—not that we could hang with the superstars; we were dweebs with a job to do. For some of the crew, it was their first chance to be in a new city unsupervised. Another perk was the chance to get nimble with pricey pro camera gear.

Home or away, as soon as possible we ran our film to Arnie's Movie Service, which processed the film and made us two black-and-white prints. We spent the night cutting it all up into three copies of the offense plays and three more of the defense plays. Bright and early, the coaches had their film.

My bread-and-butter job wasn't all that in terms of creative satisfaction, but there were other opportunities. The film department was awkwardly intertwined with the local PBS station. I was working part-time and available for more. KUAT-TV assigned me to producer/director Dave Gallagher's *Folio*, a weekly look at local artists. Each episode featured a short film of an artist doing his or her thing. I was Dave's cameraman and assisted him in editing.

This was an incredible chance to practice filmmaking. As Dave said, we made a 10-minute film every week. The shoots were always on location in the artist's workspace. We shot no talking-head footage. Dave's consistent directive was to get a lot of interesting shots, specifically shots that we could string up to illustrate the artist's technique. Audio was recorded later; this was usually the artist's introspective monologue as he or she mused about beginnings, motivations, frustrations, satisfying moments, whatever. The format worked well. It was basically *Industry on Parade* meets *Deep Thoughts*.

Painting was the most prevalent subject, with traditional forms of sculpture right behind it. At some point, we found ourselves delivering shows that looked too similar. Those close-ups of brushes dabbing paint or fingers squeezing clay had to be augmented by something else.

One unique sculptor created instances of enclosed space, which I mistook for Plexiglas boxes. Next, please.

So how about a nice close-up of a buzzing tattoo needle, skin oozing blood? And the tattoo is a Frank Frazetta warrior babe walking her saber-toothed cats? That tat was big enough to cover the customer's whole back. The episode was big, too, judging by viewership statistics.

Let's not forget the sweet old lady who played the organ and sang in her good ol' Southern Baptist church. On this episode, we *did* record sound. She had herself an organ at home and belted out one hymn after the other in the lively key of good 'n' loud.

Way into it, she gave her all in a high point, and her dentures popped out, apparently called to Glory on their own. Was she embarrassed? Nope; she quickly put 'em back in, turned to the camera like it was her trusted friend, and explained, "Sometimes I get a little excited."

Time passed, and I learned more about the boss. Alex had grown up in war-torn Hungary and saw too much for a little kid. He was a big NRA booster. It turned out that Chuck and Ron, the filmmakers I visited while in high school, were NRA guys, too. We went out to the desert so the new kid (me) could try Alex's vintage Thompson machine gun, a.k.a. his "Chicago typewriter." It looked like it was right out of *The Untouchables*. It was fun, actually, spraying a lineup of empty bottles. I doubt you'd be allowed to do that now.

I think my Polish surname made Alex see me as a comrade, as well as an employee. We could both skip the formalities. When I shot off my mouth on subjects Alex knew better, he'd growl in his thick accent, "I regret to inform you that all roads don't lead to Warsaw."

Alex's department made nicely produced educational films in addition to the athletic stuff. I participated in a few. One odd piece was about how a certain species of frogs goes about reproducing. A biology professor had shot considerable footage of the cute, little amphibians and asked Alex to make it a short film. Alex threw it to me—nobody else wanted it—and I became the editor. Alex suggested a title: *I Am Curious Green*. Not a chance.

I went through all the footage, just as I did for Dave Gallagher on *Folio*, but this time there was no prescribed story, so I assembled everything into a basic narrative. The professor had a look and wrote a voice-over script to work with the shots we had. Once I had an NPR announcer record the script onto mag film, I was ready to transform it into something watchable.

In a bit of luck, I was in award-winning filmmaker Harry Atwood's edit room. Harry counseled me on technique beyond the mechanics: "Good editing is like music. It's all about the line: It goes up; it goes down. Energetic, then relaxed. Cut fast, cut slow. Make it the rhythm of your story." The guy was an artist. Of course he'd equate film and music; he was a musician, as well as a filmmaker.

Reproductive Habits of the Mexican Green Leaf Frog was indeed cute, but it didn't really have the range to benefit from Harry's advice. Nevertheless, I've used his advice several times since.

06:29

Jack Laments in the Graveyard

Alone with his ghost dog, Zero, Jack walks in a graveyard under a starless black sky.

No stars? It happened to work well visually, but the budget was what kept us from rigging dozens of tiny lights in hundreds of shots. Behind most exterior sets was a black canvas with artfully sprayed-on mist. We really needed that ground fog; dark objects would have blended into the background without some contrast.

Good news! Dean's little boy cried when he saw Jack take off his head! Dean had taken home a work-in-progress videotape for the family; at this point, it was filled mostly with storyboards. The news had us high-fiving in celebration of the first proof that we could reach an audience.

Zero would always be a see-through ghost, enabling us to use simple in-camera effects. I enjoyed the dog shots as individual puzzles to be worked out. Most shots allowed us to simply wind back the film after animating Jack and then animate Zero against a black-velvet background. We put a strong fog-effect filter on the lens anytime we filmed Zero, giving him that ghostly look.

Sometimes, Zero would be seen reflected in a 50/50 see-through mirror. That trick was used by stage magicians before movies were invented. It had its limitations; the mirror could get in the way of the lighting, animators, and camera moves. But it was worth the trouble when Zero had to touch objects; looking through the viewfinder, animators could accurately position the dog right where they wanted him in the background.

There's a nice example of the trick where Zero retrieves one of Jack's ribs. Step-frame the shot on your DVD player, and you can see the bone is removed from the background and popped into Zero's mouth. I like to think of the maneuver as a Harryhausen "sword substitution."

Later in that shot, Jack walks away from camera, followed by Zero. This one had to be shot on two different setups: Jack on set and Zero on a moco rig. They were combined in an optical composite.

Eric Leighton and I did that one because it had a low "glory index," and nobody else wanted to do it. The shot was just a "dog on a stick" to the camera guys, and some animators disliked working with Zero because he was mostly sheet lead covered with white cloth tape. Eric and I joked that such menial work was only fit for supervisors.

Animator Rich Zimmerman was among the few who seemed to like it.

CHAPTER 7

Kong in Tucson

Dino De Laurentiis's version of *King Kong* was in the theaters, and I saw the hype as a way to get the ape into a commercial. Mark Schwartz of KTKT radio was just the guy to pitch. I scratched out a storyboard and paid him a visit.

First up, I showed him the octopus storyboard, then flipped on my projector so he could see how stop-motion brought the boards to life. Mark got the drill right away and enthusiastically asked what I had in mind. Out came the storyboards:

Kong would appear in downtown Tucson, roaring and beating his chest while a panicked crowd ran from him. Kong would pick up a rock 'n' roll cutie, who would bash him with her radio, which was blaring tunes from KTKT. Kong would lose interest in the girl, plant the radio at his ear, and start snapping his fingers, a much happier giant ape.

Mark called some guys into his office and took over my pitch. He started selling his own employees on the idea, which made my job a lot easier. There were lots of questions. Who would play rockin' Fay Wray? Well, right over there was Toni Stanton, voice talent on the morning show, and she was a cutie. The deal was done right then and there.

I needed to film a crowd running down a street in downtown Tucson. Make it a Sunday morning; we'd have it all to ourselves. Mark could get me that. He had a radio station!

The night before I was to meet a throng of KTKT listeners at a certain intersection, I called the Tucson police with a much-played-down notice of the activity planned. I didn't ask permission, just told them what was going to happen. "You guys might want to send an officer out just to be there—or maybe not." Just being a good citizen.

On Sunday morning, Mark's on-air invites bore fruit. The crowd looked college age—no surprise—and they were extremely cooperative.

"Run this way, but look back there. Here's a picture of what's chasing you. React to that."

I got multiple takes on most shots, usually to get faster running. When I had what I needed in crowd shots, most of the players took off, but a few stayed to be in Toni's close shots. No mishaps, no drama, just fun all around. A cop did show up, very low-key about it all. He didn't even get out of his car. My only angst was waiting to see the film, but it came out just fine.

The Kong puppet was a labor of love. I carefully sculpted his head to evoke the original not-exactly-gorilla face from the classic. Late into the nights, I made the best armature I could with a hand drill, vise, hacksaw, file, tap, and hammer. To embed rods into drilled steel balls, I slid the rod through, then hammered the end until it was deformed just enough to get stuck when I hammered the rod end back into the ball. Walt, the retired machinist, let me use his acetylene rig to braze everything nice and sturdy.

Casting the puppet in foam latex got a nudge up in quality. Instead of casting two sides in bowl-like plaster molds, I made a two-piece mold that could self-align when pressed together. I fit the armature into one side and filled each half, Kong's front and back, with foam latex.

Unlike the injection process (which I hadn't yet learned about), I slightly overfilled both sides, waited until the foam was about to gel, and then slammed the molds together. As anticipated, excess foam shot out from the crack between molds. Outdoors is the only place to try that!

After some quality time in the oven, I had a one-piece Kong in need of trimming off the flash, the excess foam sticking out. I finished him up with medium-brown makeup hair, short clumps of it pressed into brown rubberized paint as glue.

This Kong was about 12 inches high and had a matching Toni Stanton, more like 3 inches, with a simple wire armature inside. The ape was my best critter so far, and I was looking forward to animating him.

The shooting setup was similar to the octopus spot. Both used a projected-background process called a *front-projection effect*. In essence, camera and projector optically share the same line of sight by way of a 50 percent see-through mirror.

The background screen is specially made to return most of the projector light to the camera. The camera can see the projected background and the actor, who is lit by regular movie lighting. When the setup is tuned right, the actor covers his own shadow on the screen.

I animated for a few days, turning a little crank on the projector and advancing the background action a frame as I animated the puppets another increment.

I was living the dream. I shot a couple extra shots just because they were cool. When it was all shot, I took advantage of Alex's Moviola and the sound mixing setup at work. Long ago, I'd read in *Famous Monsters* about how Murray Spivack created Kong's unique coughing roar. Of course, I followed that procedure like a monk copying a precious manuscript.

Mark Schwartz was a happy man and booked plenty of time for his new spot. I got some valuable recognition among local ad agencies. Money? Good thing this was a labor of love, because the $500 I'd quoted Mark didn't seem so much when I came back to reality.

Back at my real job, we had a new film to make: documenting the innovative Multiple Mirror Telescope being built on nearby Mount Hopkins. Six Cold War hand-me-down telescope mirrors were donated to the university's optical-science department. They were big, each 72 inches in diameter. The idea was to align all six mirrors on a massive frame to work as a much bigger, single telescope. That was clever and audacious.

I shot an opening montage of astronomical images, slowly spinning on a barbecue motor while I zoomed in. Ted Offret, the producer, said it was a little too theatrical for a "serious" documentary. He was the boss, and he'd told me to shoot it static. Didn't he think a little motion would be appropriate for a film about a daring project, never attempted before? I sounded snotty, because I was. Ted bought it, but he was cranky about it.

We shot footage at the site on Mount Hopkins, and, there, it went more smoothly. The MMT, as they called it, was indeed a unique instrument. A computer constantly adjusted each mirror, keeping them all in alignment. That was practically sci-fi at the time.

Ted got his creative groove on when several of us went on location to shoot a reenactment of Galileo or Copernicus looking through his telescope. Somebody in Tucson actually had a Renaissance-style balcony we could shoot on. It was a good chance to use some genuinely artistic lighting. I noted that Ted was leaving more stuff unlit than lit. That might've been my first hands-on lesson in *painting with light*.

The Kong spot was generating interest among advertisers. Jeff of Jeff Nordensson Advertising called and showed me a storyboard: an elf dressed in fairy-tale clothes delivering a tag line. The little elf was the store's logo, formerly cartoon art in print. Could I animate that for them? Sure, were they seeing it as a stop-motion job? I was glad to hear that, yes, they *did* want stop-motion.

The job was more straightforward than the Kong spot: no live action, no background projection, just a little elf asking an unseen Carpet Giant, "How do you keep carpet prices so low?" A giant hand clomps down on foam letters spelling out PRICES, and a voice rumbles, "It takes a giant to hold down carpet prices!"

I'd be animating lip sync for the first time. The agency supplied the voice, and I did my first "track read": roll the mag film back and forth, listening to the dialogue, mark each syllable on an animation dialogue sheet, and, while animating, refer to that sheet as a guide to which taped-on mouth should be used for the next frame. Seeing and hearing it all in sync was kinda fun—another bit of movie magic!

Another job popped up, a spot for a real estate company. They had an idea involving the Three Little Pigs and their houses of straw, sticks, and brick. They wanted traditional cel animation. I was game and drew some characters that worked okay, but character drawing was never an aspiration or a strong suit of mine. To do a decent job of filming the cels, I rented the film department's rarely used animation stand. I liked the rig; it had an air of an earlier age, maybe the '30s or '40s. That's a pretty old design, clunky but charming in its own way.

You may not be familiar with animation stands. In short, a *downshooter*, as it's called in the trade, is a camera support that holds a camera aimed straight down at an attached table holding the artwork. Most are rigged to move the artwork east to west, north to south, and in rotation. The camera can be moved lower and higher above the table to allow moving shots. You don't see many downshooters at work anymore because most cartoon animation is digitized as soon as possible in the process. Anyhow, it occurred to me at the time that I'd have to put together a similar rig if this freelancing continued.

Back to the Three Little Pigs: The wolf blew at all three houses, proving that some houses are better than others, as per the realtor's message. The spot did the job, but it didn't quite light my fire.

Motion Control Discovered!

The July 1977 issue of *American Cinematographer* came as a radical stimulus. I had seen an early trailer for *Star Wars*, but it didn't hold a candle to the production stills in *AC*. That robotic camera crane resonated in a way I'd not felt since seeing the photo of Harryhausen and his Cyclops.

There is something you should know about cinematographers: A majority of us are dyed-in-the-wool gearheads. Just consider the tools of our trade: Mmm, camera-gear oil! Threaded fasteners? Yes! Precision-ground optical glass—exquisite!

I know a lot of people who got a jolt from their first look at the Dykstraflex. It wasn't elegant; it was honest, a mix of precision parts, custom-fabricated subsystems, and found objects from surplus stores. That single photo told the whole story: its genesis, its purpose, and its capabilities.

I saw the value of those precision linear bearings and rails, which were better and simpler than any previous solution. Likewise the use of stepper motors. If nothing else, those components would give my downshooter a shot of Dykstraflex DNA.

Why do it? *Coolness* was reason enough. Motion graphics—the style in which logos came to life by Robert Abel's streak photography, glowing and streaking out of distant star fields, leaving ghostly trails behind—was getting popular. I figured there would be interest in that flashy stuff, along with traditional cartoons. So, my partly completed downshooter did get those Thompson rails on the vertical axis and on the north–south. The camera's single-frame drive was a stepper motor. Everything else was hand cranked.

When *Star Wars* came to town, Mark Schwartz and I agreed it would be smart to make another spot, one more about spaceships and less about giant apes. Again, I boarded a simple story: Cute robot somewhat similar to a trash can with a squeaky speech defect beams down to a desert area. It flips open its communicator and tunes into several parodies of Tucson radio stations. The robot hates 'em all. "No! Nooo! No-no-no-no!" Then the robot finds the rockin' and jammin' sounds of KTKT and goes crazy with happiness, steam shooting out of its head as it boings up and down.

Oh, yeah, and the robot's serial number was K2T2.

I could crank that out fast enough as a simple cartoon. That was important to Mark, so we went that way. KTKT produced the soundtrack, probably handled by on-air talent Ed Alexander, a good man.

The new downshooter's maiden voyage was a success, and I had a new assignment for the MMT. Ted wanted a burn-in graphic of the mirror array over live footage of the observatory. The best way to line up the two images was to use the camera in a rotoscope mode.

Rotoscope is an old process wherein the camera is fitted with a lamphouse, making it a temporary projector. It can be used to trace live-action frames, the way some animation is made. That's where you get this term: You exactly trace an image—by rote—using the camera as a scope.

In my case, I just had to project the live footage down on the table and slide the graphic artwork around to fit. Shoot it there, and it'll line up when printed with the live footage. My Bolex wasn't made to allow that maneuver, but Harry Atwood's ancient Kodak Cine Special II was. He sold it to me for $100, and it became my main camera. Modifying it to rotoscope was as simple as filing a square hole in the pressure plate and mounting a light bulb in the magazine.

I learned a lesson worth passing on: In setups like this, it's easy to get a fingerprint on the back end of the lens. I reshot some titles three times before checking the back glass! It looks like the lens is out of focus. I never did it again!

CHAPTER 8

Time to Go Freelance

B ack in basketball-game films, one of my guys hit his own snag. Typically, one 400-foot magazine lasted us through a quarter unless the quarter had a lot of starts and stops. There was no time to reload during a quarter. One night, my guy rolled out of film during a controversial, game-changing moment.

The next day, I was surrounded by the head coach's assistants, who were glaring at me like a kingpin's goons. The coach demanded proof that we hadn't cut and sold the crucial footage. I showed him the film edge numbers, but he didn't give a shit: "I just want my f***in' *film!*" Truth be told, none of us film nerds cared about basketball, and even if the earth-shattering footage did exist, we couldn't recognize it if there was a loaded jockstrap aimed at our heads.

It was good to know the football guys still liked us. In fact, they found one of us *too* likable. Diane was the first-ever coed to film football. She caught on fast, worked harder than most of us, and radiated enthusiasm. Her only shortcoming was being a head turner. The jocks were losing their focus. And it wasn't just the players. I was surprised to see some assistant coaches falling over each other to give us completely unnecessary details about what they'd be doing next. It was funny until the word came down from the head coach: The girl had to go. We all felt crappy. Diane was maybe a little misty, while the rest of us struggled with survivor guilt.

Folio finished its season, as did the athletic games, and there wasn't much else to do but a little assisting on a short film. But the pace of work in Tucson had never been so fast! With little to do, I felt like a caged squirrel in an exercise wheel.

It was a good time to go full freelance with the animation stuff. I was getting calls, enough to suggest that this could be a real business. Alex was gracious, and we would stay in touch.

People doing film in Tucson were a small group, and we all knew each other. I'd met several my age while working for Alex. Mark Headley was doing a historical piece, actors in costume, and making commercials. He lent me his editing gear more than once and was himself a source of info. Rick Rose had an up-and-coming business, Film Creations, and I worked for him on one or two industrials. Dave Graves had some fun, creative stuff on his reel, primarily live action. He'd also done a clever in-camera effect of flames shooting out from behind a Spanish-language radio station's call logo. That popped on with the announcer saying, "Caliente!" We all had our niches, some overlapping, and we were really, truly supportive of each other.

In my niche, people wanted cartoons. I was no cartoonist, but I could draw well enough to animate simple stuff. Within those bounds, I churned out half a dozen or so animated cartoon spots. You'd only see them in Tucson: a train whistle blowing with all his might, a coin jumping into a nice bank teller's comfy hand, a dopey caveman in a cart with square wheels pulled by his friendly dinosaur, an ailing house getting healthy, and a carpet-steaming machine with a vivid Brooklyn accent.

KTKT Cartoons

Meeting Dave Fitzsimmons was a stroke of luck. He had a great take on caricature and drew funny faces on cue. He was interested in animation and grasped the design requirements in making a face that could be animated.

We collaborated on at least five commercials, beginning with a magician's cartoon rabbit. Dave nailed his design first try. I asked for a face-on view and a side view of the rabbit's head. I could in-between well enough from there. Dave's work always graced my TV spots for KTKT radio.

Mark Schwartz and I had a blast cooking up a new spot. Mark wanted a new spot during Arbitron ratings sweeps, a survey that determines how many ears were listening. Our self-directed assignment was simple: Make a spot that's fun to watch and ties into KTKT's product—namely, fun Top 40 music. With Mark, it was incredibly easy to get into a brainstorming session and come out 20 minutes later with an idea that promised silly, good-natured fun.

Our first new spot was Mark's idea: A well-known sports announcer asks several celebrities, mostly unlikely picks, "What's your favorite station?" Each celebrity names KTKT in his or her own style of speech. For example, President Nixon, shown in a basement operating a tape recorder, replies, "Make no mistake about it: KTKT."

Dave Fitzsimmons's caricature talents were the main event there, along with Ed Alexander's skill in getting seven impressionistic voices on tape. Mark liked it enough to pay for a blow-up (transfer) to 35 mm so he could play the spot in movie theaters.

Around Halloween, I came up with "Disco Frankie," wherein Igor and Dr. Frankenstein throw the switch and their creation comes to life and dances the Spanish Hustle. Dave came up with another great set of characters, and I did some prep for animating Frankie by taking disco lessons. Let's just say John Travolta had nothing to worry about.

I wanted to get some atmosphere into this spot, and sought the help of a guy who was into airbrush art. He made a nice laboratory background and a spooky castle-on-the-hill exterior to be the opening shot.

To juice it up a little, I made the opening view a multiplane shot. The artwork was layered, separated into foreground trees and castle and background sky, and finished with airbrushed lightning effects. Each layer was on a piece of glass, and these were stacked about six inches apart. That way, when the camera pushed in and moved a few inches north, we would see parallax shift, giving a sense of depth.

For the next spot, I came up with a takeoff of a retro TV Anacin commercial. You may recall a pseudoscientific diagram with bolts of electricity, a hammer banging an anvil, and a rope being twisted into a knot, all inside some unlucky headache sufferer's head. We turned those symptoms into rock radio sins: "chatter and confusion," "too many commercials," and "the same old music." KTKT offered "fast, fast, *fast* relief, better music, fewer commercials, and the best morning show, with Ed, Toni, and Tom!"

It wasn't the best, but Mark thought "Fast Relief" could be remarketed in other cities. We'd been talking about teaming up as a company for just such a purpose. The company would be called Excitable Boys Productions. We never got that far, but later, in 1979, we were indeed excited when Mark sold "Fast Relief" to an outfit in Texas that shopped such spots around. It would have been like free money when a check came in the mail.

Motion Graphics

In between spots for KTKT, I had a full plate of noncartoon work. People wanted logos. Bob Abel's candy apple neon motion graphics were the coolest stuff on TV, and I wanted to offer a slice of that look to Tucson clients.

One could blow a fortune gearing up for that stuff; Abel had a computer-controlled, horizontal animation stand and all the trimmings. Nobody else had that stuff, except George Lucas. I had to pare things down to a few modifications on my homebrew rig. Three crucial items would suffice.

First, I built a light well under the stand to backlight the artwork. Paint alone on cels didn't provide the contrast and lighting effects you could get with even backlight coming through colored gels.

Second, the signature streak-photography process required the camera to travel smoothly and repeatedly down the vertical rails. That was the trick of those moving letters leaving streaks of light. Also, you needed a means of opening and closing the shutter as the camera traveled. There would be no computer control. Instead, a simple gear motor and chain drive raised and lowered the camera. In its travel, the moving camera bumped microswitches that controlled the shutter.

Third, the focus had to constantly change as the camera moved closer to the artwork. "Auto follow focus" worked as a mechanical linkage between the lens and a long, bent, aluminum camera shape.

The new image-making tools turned out to be a fun challenge. Unlike painting cels, you can't see what you're laying down on the film; you have to visualize what you're building up on the negative. The exposure sheet didn't have just one column of dialogue, but many as well, full of adjustments on each pass of the same piece of film going through the camera. The first look at the results was always a surprise; even though everything on the exposure sheet was spot-on, seeing it all together was cooler than I had imagined. I compared it to what a pyrotechnician must feel when his preparations come to life as Fourth of July fireworks.

I clocked eight or so motion-graphic logos in that period, enough to justify the preparation and learn some new tricks. Simple jobs included a logo for Rollers Moving and Storage. In five simple passes, I rolled in three Os and parked, followed by the rest of the letters. That's it!

John Roller was one of those big-as-all-outdoors, amiable straight shooters, the kind of guy you wish all businessmen could be. I was in the trailer he used as an office, showing him storyboards and explaining how it would look. He liked everything. I told him about the runtime for a typical logo: "You might think it would be too short, but on TV, five seconds is plenty long."

John shifted back in his chair. "I was an ex–bull rider, and I can tell you that seven and a half seconds can be a god-dang *heckuva* lot, so I reckon five could be, too." We sealed it with a handshake, and the check showed up early.

Several storefronts wanted the glitzification treatment, like this logo. My fave was a twinkling, curved rainbow raining golden musical notes over the glowing entrance of Car Stereo Pad.

While the 1970s high-style streaking logo effects were in vogue, Jeff Nordensson decided he wanted a new Carpet Giant stop-motion elf. I was happy to retire elf #1 and was apparently not alone. This knave had been well disliked for several years. This time, the elf had a less squeaky voice, wore work clothes and a baseball cap, and drove a forklift. Forget the annoying chubby one in a jester outfit. This was Tucson, not Camelot!

Industrials

Paul Karr, who made commercials, industrials, and educational films, called me one day. He was another straight shooter, like John Roller. Paul wanted to hire me to stand in for him and film a jet-turbine generator on the test bench. Sounded like fun, and it was.

After meeting Paul in Phoenix and prepping the gear he wanted me to use, I drove off into the desert. It was quite far from any towns, as the mission of the facility was to collect engineering data while driving jet engines to self-destruct.

One of the guys took me to the test bench. A genuine jet engine sat at chest level, attached to thick steel bolts embedded in the concrete. The test subject itself was a part of the engine, a generator spun by a portion of the engine's exhaust. I learned that such generators are what power all the electrical devices in most planes. In this test, they were going to let it spin faster and faster "until something happens."

We found a good place to set up the camera and ran a power cable from the camera motor back to the blockhouse. Upon startup of the engine, I would plug the cable in a wall socket and just let the camera run.

There was going to be a delay while the engineers tweaked their instruments, so my guide took me around the area. The guy suggested I might like to see the "bird gun." I didn't know exactly what that meant but played along.

There was a test bench with a 20-foot-long tube mounted with one end within a foot or so of the bench. At the other end of the tube was a large pressure tank. And an empty wire cage.

I began to understand that this "bird gun" was not for hunting game. I wanted to hear him say what I was thinking. "So, how does it all work?"

No doubt you've heard of airline flights being endangered by what they call "bird strikes." Well, this setup was where they test engines for durability, like when a plane flies straight into a flock of birds. "We use special-bred chickens, good-size birds."

And the gun?

"Load your bird and lock 'im in the breech. Gotta be pointing down the bore, or it's not legal."

Sure. Just like reality.

"Bird's not gonna move, he's in there snug enough."

The bird is alive?

"Lawyers. A dead bird wouldn't be legal: no muscle tone."

I was learning a lot.

"So, you wind up the engine, trip the pressure bottle valve, and the bird's at 600 miles an hour when he hits the fan."

After *that* moment of discovery, the test I was there for sounded more civilized.

And it worked without a hitch. Several minutes into the test, a very short event took place, and the subject was instantly motionless. The test generator seized but didn't fly apart. Good. They had the readings and our film. At the speed things were going, I'd bet they had one or two frames of the event, before and after.

Some weeks later, Paul Karr and I met with a guy who was writing treatments for a series of educational short films. Our trial lesson was a short piece on the unusual aspects of the planet Mercury. In my detached garage, I built a 4 x 8–foot miniature landscape of the planet's surface. The script described an odd sunrise that had the sun going up, then down a bit and then up again. It was easy to rig using a light bulb on a motorized vertical track.

I embellished the shot, adding a camera move using a second motor, tracking slowly sideways to create a sense of depth. I also included mountains that suggested low gravity, skinnier than you'd see on Earth. Finally, I added a model spaceship sitting on the ground.

The writer-producer didn't go for the skinny mountains and the spaceship; he wanted us to stay away from space-opera imagery, a respectable goal. I did another version of the landscape, this time making it more like a moonscape. That won a much better response.

Karr had asked me to make an interesting logo for his company, and I went for a simple streak-photography effect: blue-outline letters rising up into frame, unreadable until the very long streak that trails behind them collapsed into flat art. You could say I got the idea from the opening titles of *Superman*, and you'd be right. Paul liked it.

Word came back that the science series was not going to happen. It could be a chance to look around Los Angeles. Yes, I'd been thinking about it for some time. This freelance work was okay, but it didn't excite me the way those *American Cinematographer* articles did. The visual-effects golden age was gaining momentum, and I wanted to be there.

The fact is, I'd already taken such a trip.

CHAPTER 9

Recon in LA

E arlier, in the spring of 1979, I had taken a reconnaissance trip to Hollywood. Certainly, I would have been happy to find a toehold in the business, but this trip was also for the soul; it was my pilgrimage to Movie Mecca.

My calling card was a nine-minute reel of my better commercials. I'd been "plussing" my freelance jobs with just such a trip in mind: Gotta have something to show. I took the real 16 mm film, no video transfers. And to be sure nobody would miss a viewing, I also took my projector.

I also came armed with a copy of the pertinent section of LA's yellow pages. It contained many names, some I recognized:

Jim Danforth (heir apparent to Ray Harryhausen) picked up the phone, just like a mortal. He invited me to come by his home and show my reel. I knew my work was kindergarten stuff compared to his accomplishments, but Jim gave encouraging comments and especially honed in on the Kong spot.

He told stories about his past projects and showed me artwork for a feature he was trying to get financed, *Timegate*. With a title like that and Jim at the helm, you could bet there would be dinosaurs chasing chrononauts. He handed me his T. rex armature for the show. It was a real work of art, so much so that it was a shame to cover it with dino flesh. He's quite the effects Renaissance man.

Howard Anderson III showed me around the family business, located on the Paramount lot. His granddad started the Howard Anderson Co. in the 1920s—lots of history there. In the '60s, they had shot most of the effects for *Star Trek*, the original TV show. When I visited, they still had some setups for *Superman*, which had come out in 1978.

There were only three (or so) other proprietary special-effects companies in town, and they were doing most of the work not being done by studio departments. Practically every movie and TV show had one or more of them listed in the credits.

There was Joseph Westheimer, owner of the company named after himself. He took time to look at my reel and really studied it; at the point when the octopus was shaking hands with a live actor, Mr. Westheimer looked at me with one eyebrow raised. He knew what it took to get that shot.

Then there was the Van der Veer Photo Effects Co. Greg Van der Veer gave me a tour of their family business as well. Nobody was offering jobs, but Greg grilled me on my rotoscope skills to the point where I probably could've gotten some work—except that I lived eight hours away.

I also visited a couple of companies that specialized in opticals, Cinema Research and Modern Film Effects. You don't hear the term *opticals* in today's digital world; the closest synonym now is *composites*. It was great to see all those optical printers clacking away in well-lit cleanrooms.

One gentleman took me aside and confided that he was about to quit so he could follow his aspirations, and I could conveniently jump into the vacancy. Sounds like a no-brainer, but my sights were on stage work, filming miniatures. I was in town to get away from piloting a downshooter, which was somewhat similar to running an optical printer. This opportunity could get me into a pigeonhole. Eyes on the prize.

I called him later and gave him the same rationale. I was in some serious turmoil, wondering if I was tossing away my big break. He thanked me for my candor, and we wished each other luck. Today he's an A-list, well-respected visual-effects supervisor.

Time was running out on my trip, but there was one guy I couldn't skip meeting if at all possible! Linwood Dunn and his partners, Donald Weed and Wally Gentleman, ran Film Effects of Hollywood. Among *King Kong* effects contributors, Mr. Dunn was the last man standing, at 75 years old. He was well known in the industry for excellent work and for developing the Acme-Dunn optical printer. Unlike the proprietary home-brew printers in major studios, Dunn's brainchild was for sale as a standard product anyone could buy.

Incredibly, I spent several hours at his studio, showing my reel, absorbing his advice on how to improve my techniques, touring the studio, gawking at miniatures I'd seen on the big screen, and soaking up his stories from Old Hollywood. One tip from Linwood: Set focus on the background screen, not the monster. It'll make the monster a little soft, and they will look more like each other.

Linwood and his partners were putting together what he called a "motion repeater," his take on the robotic camera rigs popping up in a couple new boutique studios, but not so much in the old-guard companies.

Linwood had an exceptional level of energy for his age, spotlighted by his vigorous New York accent. He said, "Let's get some lunch," and we briskly strode to a nearby McDonald's. "I like this place," he said. "They're quick; you don't waste time. And you always know how it's gonna taste." This guy was all about the work, not the tinsel.

Linwood had retained mannerisms from a more genteel era. When he was going to show the company reel, he invited me to "step into the loges." And when I referred to one of his partners as "Don," he corrected my overly familiar speech. "That's Mr. Weed to you."

At the end of my visit with a legend, Linwood suggested I contact some guy named Phil Kellison. He was running an effects studio that specialized in the stuff I was interested in. I tried, but time and Kellison's availability did not permit. Not to worry; I would return.

Back in Arizona, I reminisced about all those exciting moments with friends, family, pets, and just by myself. How to relocate to LA and find a job? How would it affect all of us? There was lots to obsess about. Meanwhile, there were commercials to make!

Three months later, it was late August—time to visit Phil Kellison.

Meeting Mr. Kellison

I had funds to stay two nights in a funky motel. The bed had been recently occupied, and there was a nearly new condom to accent the floor. Two nights would be enough to ensure an interview with the main attraction.

I'd written Phil Kellison, dropping Mr. Dunn's name, telling him of my two trips, and promising him a phone call when I arrived. Attached was as much résumé material as I could fit in a 9 x 12 envelope, photos included. It all worked out.

Kellison was top dog at Coast Special Effects, located in North Hollywood. Coast was the effects arm of Coast Productions in Hollywood. As I walked into the front office, I smiled. Large photos of the Pillsbury Doughboy and other stop-motion characters hung on the walls.

Phil and I had a lengthy chat at his desk, joined by Joe Rayner, a British expatriate director-cameraman. I ran the reel for them, and Phil especially liked it. He looked near Linwood Dunn's age and clearly had a lifelong fondness for stop-motion. I noticed a few old props on his desk and asked about one in particular, an 18-inch wooden model of Big Ben. I had a suspicion, and Phil verified it: It was used in the opening titles of George Pal's *The Time Machine*, which I'd seen when I was nine.

No doubt about it, this was a place I could get to like.

Phil showed me around the shop and the stages, where I met several guys, mostly around my age, making model props, setting up cameras and lighting. One guy, Laine Liska, was animating "Little Softy," the character that represented a brand of toilet paper. A movie star!

After a lengthy tour, I walked out smiling, resolute that I would find a way to get a job there. As I started to get in my truck, Tom Scherman, one of the prop makers, asked if he could have a word with me.

Tom had heard I was from Tucson, and he knew of a certain movie prop that was wasting away in a Tucson restaurant. Could I visit the eatery on his behalf and negotiate a price for the prop? Sure, but what would I be negotiating for?

He'd seen a door from inside Capt. Nemo's submarine in *20,000 Leagues Under the Sea*. Tom was sure it was the one; there was nothing else like it. Tom would be happy to swap with them, offering a much better door he'd made himself, plus some cash, for the treasure. I understood perfectly. That Victorian submarine was Tom's Monster Totem! What would I give for Ray's Cyclops?

In return for my efforts, he promised to keep my name uppermost in the boss's mind. I wouldn't see a dime from this, but that rivet-studded door could open onto a new career.

Though the Coast interview was my primary goal, I still had a few more places to visit. At one downshooter service, the woman interviewing me began with, "So, do you streak?" There was definitely a smirk on her face. Somehow, I got into a door at Universal and made it as far as some rejectionist, who only wanted to know what union I was in.

After several more dry holes, I met up with producer James K. Shea, who turned out to be a very pleasant guy. He'd made a fun B movie in 1977 titled *Planet of Dinosaurs*, which ought to speak for itself. He started out about his work; this was his biggest piece to date, as "I mostly make X'ers."

James remained candid through the interview and while watching my dinosaur film, my regular reel, and some other material. "Your dinosaur stuff is weak, but the space shots are pretty good." I'd shown him some Paul Karr science-film outtakes, some fooling around with a spaceship flying by the camera, and a commercial with jewelry doing the same. He spoke well of his cast and crew, especially the effects guys. James was another guy I hoped to work with someday.

07:52

Zero Floating against the Moon

How were Dave Hanks and Mike Bienstok going to make the ghost dog visible when it was against a luminous background? When Zero is eclipsing the yellow moon, he should look like a 40 percent smoked glass plate.

Dave set up a rig to raise and lower Zero and wrote a motion script that would double expose each frame, one with Zero in and one with Zero out. That same rig was also programmed to make Zero fly while Tim Hittle animated Zero's flapping.

To hide Zero's rig, Dave stuck on a small piece of retro-reflective screen and adjusted it to match the moon. If you look carefully, you can see the strip of retro-reflective material just under Zero; we never quite got a perfect match.

As Jack walks down the uncurling branch, it looks too spindly to hold Jack's weight. We didn't use invisible wire or any postopticals. Tim Hittle preferred to animate with a beefy armature inside the branch, just like another puppet, attached to Jack's feet.

CHAPTER 10

Getting that First Job

Back in Tucson, the owner of the Kon-Tiki Restaurant was happy to take Tom Scherman's new-door-for-old offer at face value. I gave Tom the good news and sent him a self-promoting poster. Tom pinned it up in the Coast Effects men's room, a spot where it would have a guaranteed captive audience. Ironically, the poster read, "Pete Kozachik makes it *MOVE!*"

To help them remember me, I sent a fusillade of résumés on a regular schedule.

During that period in the seventies, Linwood Dunn came to my house in Tucson. How did *that* happen?! Mark Headley, a born mover and shaker, as well as a filmmaker, had been encouraging famous Hollywood cameramen to meet with us Tucson filmmakers. Mark's first soirée was a wonderful get-together with cinematographer Lee Garmes. He'd shot 136 films. *Gone with the Wind* was in the middle of his filmography.

Mr. Garmes showed up at Mark's house, an awkward moment. We were all milling around and froze when he appeared. He said, "Hello," and nobody responded or moved. I guess the *Gone with the Wind* guy from Tinseltown was just too intimidating to us. *We're not worthy!*

I felt for the guy, all eyes on him as though we were waiting for him to perform. I crossed no-man's land to Garmes, shook his hand, and thanked him for coming. During the long, memorable evening, he was a gentleman, patient with our questions and generous with lighting tips that he'd probably devised before most of us had been born.

The guest at the next event was Linwood Dunn. Mark knew I'd met with him in LA and asked if I'd open my house to Mr. Dunn and the group. But of course! Dunn proved to be as informative as he was inspirational. At that moment, he was the face of the industry walking among us. I was inspired, and that night, I resolved to move to LA.

In late November 1979, Jeanne invited my film buddies for a farewell get-together. That's a very powerful way to self-motivate. I've used it often: Tell a lot of people your plan, and peer pressure keeps you on task. So I sent Phil Kellison a final note, saying I'd call him next week from a local phone.

I'd been told by everyone I interviewed with in LA, "You have to *be here*." Lots of jobs are short term. Opportunities often pop up at the last minute. Nobody wants to deal with your relocation, which is often messy. They don't want to be responsible for you. They want to try you out before committing. If they have to get rid of you, they don't want the guilt of stranding you there.

It is so important that I know a number of people who have cell phones with LA area codes but live out of state. That's not an incredibly great idea; it'll bite you sooner or later. It's just an illustration of the need to be there.

What about that résumé and your reel? They're good for getting an interview, and that's when they find out if they can stand to work with you. They also ask questions about your reel, like, "Why are you putting my work on your reel?" DVDs and personal websites are far better than the Stone Age media I used. Make sure that it's your work, not someone else's, and burn your name into the reel.

The efficient "breaking into the business" ploy begins with setting up a situation where you can hang out in LA for as long as possible as cheaply as possible!

Hollywood Bound

In mid-December, my traveling companions were a suitcase, a sleeping bag, the projector, and $700 cash. My immediate destination was a couch near Santa Monica that belonged to a guy I had worked with in Alex Hankocy's department. When I got there, it appeared his roommate had just been informed of that. That was a little awkward.

In the week I spent there, things moved surprisingly fast. Phil Kellison had nothing for me, nor did the other contacts I'd met. Not much gets done around the holidays, but dumb luck came my way: Gene Warren, one of Kellison's lifelong friends and collaborators, called me just before Christmas. Warner Bros. needed a quick holiday introduction to its coming year's lineup, so they *had* to get on it. Gene needed an assistant right now. Forget the interview; if Phil liked me, Gene was willing.

My hosts were impressed. Two days and I got a job? That's crazy! Yeah, I was very lucky, but it was nothing to depend on. Maybe saturating the coast with my letter bombings helped a little.

The next morning, I showed up in my ill-fitting, fake leather jacket (the dorky '70s cut) and met Gene Warren Sr. and Jr. Their business was named Excelsior! Animated Moving Pictures, and they specialized in stop-motion and related crafty special effects. They had a couple of freelance guys and an optical-effects cameraman. He had his own optical printer on-site. Cool!

My first job was to clean up their short strip of La Brea Avenue's sidewalk. It needed a little sprucing up; a VIP was coming. I jumped into the job, and it was a piece of cake. Years earlier, I'd learned the art of sweepery from my boss, Oscar Segura, at the grocery store. "Take the broom and swing it around like you're dancing with a beautiful girl! That's right—a whole lotta *shakin' goin' on!*"

Picking up bottles went at a slower pace, but I got 'er done before the Warner guy showed up. Gene Jr. thanked me. I hoped he'd get the message: This guy's no prima donna. He's willing to do anything. Passing grade!

My next task was taking down a miniature setup. The setup was an airplane's view of ships plying the Atlantic. A shallow, glass-bottomed pan was high above the model ships on a solid blue sculpt of the ocean surface. They had thrown light through rippling water in the pan, casting wave effects on the ocean below. Clever.

While stowing away lights, stands, sandbags, camera gear, and handmade pieces, I got my first look at a Mitchell 35 mm movie camera. It had 30–50 years' worth of battle scars.

Opening the camera door, I found the magic, the movement, with its register pins, cams, and pressure plate, polished to protect film from scratching. It even *smelled* good. I could be smelling that camera oil for years to come.

Someone had painted a jungle scene on one of the stage walls, a leftover from the Saturday kids' show *Land of the Lost*. Animator Pete Kleinow had done the scenic painting.

Later, I opened a drawer in the shop and was greeted by 20 heads, which I instantly recognized as the Pillsbury Doughboy. They had been sculpted mouthing vowels and consonants and could be swapped in during animation, following a dialogue track.

With a clean stage ready, we got into the Warner job. The boards showed a fancy, round box drifting down from black into a brilliant spotlight, then opening to reveal a shiny film reel. I started on the set floor, a piece of milky Plexiglas. We'd point a light straight up, under where the box would land, for a bit of magic: light from the floor!

Gene Jr. had me spray-paint black outside the area to be spotlit.

The "milk-plex" was new to me. Everything was new. I'd never seen the lighting instruments, at least not in person.

We rigged a 2K Fresnel above and below the set floor and hit the many facets of the box with separate, 200-watt "Inkies" with snoots. Then, we were going to hand-animate the camera on a Raby camera dolly.

I started by rigging the dolly so we could make calibration marks for all the axes, from floor wheels to pan, tilt, and focus. In that task, I learned how to use such indispensable prop-shop tools as a band saw and hot melt glue.

Gene figured it would take a couple days to shoot it, and off we went. Gene worked the camera, Paul operated his box mover, and I adjusted lighting dimmers. Gene would call out the frame numbers and we'd all move to our marks. Gene shot a frame, and we continued over and over, like animating a puppet.

About two-thirds in, the box support rig broke, and Paul sang out a single "Goddammit!" Gene pursed his lips and sighed. Admirable. I kept my mouth shut but vowed to follow his example in the future, to be cool and soldier on. In our case, it was rerig and restart!

The Warner guy liked the result, and my first gig was over.

I'd been couch surfing with my sleeping bag from one pad to another during that first job. At the end, a fellow expat from KZAZ called me at work and offered a couch with a longer end-date. His girlfriend had split, so there was room at the inn. Generosity like that can be a game changer. I was very grateful and still am.

During my first job, Gene Sr. had been promoting a TV movie about passengers marooned in orbit in the first commercial rocket liner. I approached him with some sketches of a camera rig that could be computer controlled specifically to shoot models for the project. He was interested enough that I spent some more time on research and design, but Gene Jr. gave me a valuable piece of advice: "You should be looking for other work." The TV movie could take many months to come through, if ever.

This began a long dry spell. I spent time refreshing old contacts and meeting the occasional new potential employer. Dry.

Six or eight weeks in, my time was up on the couch. I went out to the post office late at night to send Jeanne a letter. The only other person there was a crazy old lady yelling at a line of payphones on the wall. She didn't see me, just the phones. I told myself I'd better get used to wackos if I was going to live here.

Jeanne was getting antsy, and said she was coming out West right away. I couldn't blame her, but it was going to be awkward with three cats and a large dog in the dinky efficiency apartment I'd just found. Shortly after that, we found a slightly larger place in Los Feliz. We could afford it for a month with what we'd saved.

Miraculously, Mark Schwartz called about another radio-station spot. He now had a companion station, 96 Rock, brand new and in need of a strong introduction to the good people of Tucson. What I could realistically deliver under the circumstances was a spot based on motion graphics. That fit Mark's needs perfectly.

Mark's spot showcased the heavy-metal fare they played, dropping lots of band names in hyperkinetic, streaking graphics with a badass track. I told the viewers just exactly who was coming to town: *96 ROCK!*

That paycheck kept the household afloat long enough for the next lucky break: Phil Kellison called from Coast Effects.

CHAPTER 11

Coast FX

Coast Effects had quite a pedigree. In its many previous incarnations, especially Cascade Pictures of California, it had been the birthing place of many key effects guys on *Star Wars*, including Dennis Muren, Ken Ralston, and Phil Tippett, plus luminaries like Jim Danforth and Dave Allen. Right then, the company was taking on new blood.

Like most small shops, everyone had several skills and pitched in when needed. Most projects were short, overlapping, and diverse. My first two years at Coast were a great way to learn a lot.

The Invulnerable Flying Saucer

I was hired as a model maker to make the interior cargo bay of a space shuttle and a satellite to fit inside. Very quickly, I was in over my head, worried I would be let go for not knowing a simple operation like slicing a long, Plexiglas tube lengthwise. Tom Corlett, the senior model maker, showed me how to rig the band saw to make a clean cut and retain all my fingers.

Coast made its money primarily on commercials, but this project was for a movie, *Hangar 18*. Besides the model making and studio photography for the movie, most of the crew were preparing for a big pyrotechnical climax. The titular secret government hangar, housing an alien spacecraft, would be blown up by a Learjet crashing into the building. We would see the spacecraft undamaged in the flaming wreckage.

My next assignment was to make the invulnerable flying saucer, a 3-foot concrete mockup of a smaller plastic model. It had to withstand a real pyro explosion and sit there with blinking lights in the midst of gasoline flames. Two of us worked on it.

Meanwhile, others were making the miniature hangar, which was maybe 2 feet high with a 10-foot or 12-foot-square footprint. Recent newcomers Chuck Miller and Dwight Shook were rolling industrial aluminum foil into 1:16-scale corrugated panels and gluing them to a frame, just like a real steel building. Forrest Leathers, another recent hire, was finishing up his Learjet model, and Monty Shook was helping Forrest and working on other models. Everywhere I turned, somebody was doing something I'd never seen before.

Ernie Farino was working on some graphic effects, running between his stage setup and the model shop. Back in Tucson, I'd read Ernie's excellent fan magazine, *FXRH* ("Effects by Ray Harryhausen"). Ernie was from Texas; I was from Arizona. Both of us had freelance experience back home. Instant bond!

On stage, Bob Ryder was filming models, assisted by John DeChene. Rollin Swan oversaw the activity in his role as production manager.

On the day of the pyro shoot, we brought everything to Hansen Dam in the northeastern San Fernando Valley. We had all day to rig things up, as the shoot would be at night.

The pyro guy was Mike Sullivan, who had learned his trade in World War II as an underwater demolition diver. When I had my concrete spaceship wired up and cemented in place, I watched Mike making his bombs. Vermiculite soaked in gasoline would be contained in a strong plastic bag. Setting it off electrically would blow flaming streamers all over. It was weak in destructive power, but spectacular on film. He rigged several such bombs for the festivities.

As evening turned to night, it got chilly. We had a generator running several large movie lights, which provided a means to see and would simulate moonlight on film. Bob Ryder, John DeChene, and Joe Rayner set up four or five cameras to run at high speed. I think the maximum was 120 fps (frames per second), five times the normal rate.

Mike Sullivan was decidedly old school. When I asked him about his safety record, he held up his hands and said, "How many?"

Huh?

"Fingers. How many fingers?"

Oh, yeah, 10 fingers. I got it.

Then he picked up a couple of cigarette butts and twisted them into his ears. "Ear protection. Works fine."

As the big moment approached, I noted that most if not all of the company was on-site for the show. This would be an important time to look sharp. I found a push broom and the small axe I'd brought to detach the spaceship and joined my colleagues.

The ritual of a high-speed destruction shoot is shouted in terse shorthand. The director calls on all operators to roll camera, and you hear a lot of whining camera motors. As each camera's tachometer hits the proper speed, the operator yells, "Camera A—speed!" and so forth. At the instant the last camera is at speed and everyone has run to safety, the director yells, "Action!" That cues the pyro guy to do his thing.

Mike punched his detonator buttons in the agreed-on sequence and blew the living shit out of the hangar, bam-bam-bam-BAM! His sequence was very fast, as the cameras were running fast, too. Suddenly, the night chill was banished by a cloud of exploding gasoline. For a few seconds, the radiant heat felt hotter than desert sunlight.

The crowd cheered when the cameras turned off and fire extinguishers came on. I ran out with the axe and severed the ship from the dam (still blinking!), then laid into the debris with the broom. The next day I got a little chiding about sweeping like a madman, but the bosses were smiling.

Umbrellas and the Old Guard

On the heels of *Hangar 18*, Phil set me on a more finicky task: machining a pair of umbrella radio antennae for a model TRW communications satellite. I didn't know Forrest well yet, but he told me he'd wanted that job, and I'd better do it well!

The umbrellas had to slowly open and close electrically. There were some other moves the satellite had to perform, more like armature joints, but this was the trickiest. In each antenna, I fitted a tiny planetary gearmotor. It turned a skinny leadscrew, engaging linkages to each rib. The fragile rigs worked okay, just barely able to stretch the gold-painted netting taut enough to look like umbrellas. All the rigging was enough, and I passed the model making itself to the gentleman I'd worked with on the last job.

I took the finished satellite to Bob Ryder and John DeChene, waiting to film it. In the middle of my spiel about how to operate the prop, Bob said, "Don't dump it on me. You made it; you're gonna run it." With that, I started helping Bob and John on the shoot.

Bob was a kindly effects cameraman from Old Hollywood, around 80 at the time. He was the hands-on guy at Howard Anderson's during the original *Star Trek* TV show. He'd be filming the *Enterprise* while the rest of the company was leaving at quitting time, reminding Bob, "Don't stay late, but get it done." He usually finished after midnight, turning around at 9 a.m.

Computer motion control was a dozen years in the future when Bob was shooting the *Enterprise* cruising by the camera. His method was to mount the enormous model on a Worrall geared head, a support for heavy cameras that was fitted with cranks for pan and tilt. He motorized the cranks with slow-running gearmotors and did the same for the camera itself. He'd run the whole system very slowly while the camera rolled at a slow frame rate.

That was the method Coast was using, too. They had more motorized widgets on hand, rotary tables, cable winders, pipe tracks, all simple components, all driven by Bodine variable gearmotors. They were very simple to rig, inexpensive but unable to repeat a move.

Using that system, Bob and John did a great job, a montage of close-up satellite parts opening to finally reveal the whole spindly model in all its glory.

John and I enjoyed Bob's tales of yesteryear, which conjured images of how things were done when we were just little dudes. Bob's stature leapt in our eyes the day he casually told us of his dalliance with Marilyn Monroe—in his convertible, no less. "She was just a starlet then. No big deal."

Another story? Sure. Bob told Howard Anderson Sr. the job was killing him, and he needed a raise.

"I don't have money to give you a raise. I'd have to fire somebody."

Bob pointed to a guy sweeping the floor. "Okay, fire him."

Anderson walked over to the guy, said something to him, and the poor schmuck dropped his broom and left.

Hot for New Tech

You could say Coast Effects was not looking to improve on its motion-control capabilities. The bosses were not about to dive into an R&D project like the one their recent graduates had undertaken in nearby Van Nuys, home of Industrial Light & Magic (ILM).

By contrast, Phil complained about Phillips-head screwdrivers. The old, flat drivers should be good enough for anyone! And all these overblown new adhesives! In his days working for George Pal, they had one big pot of rabbit-skin glue cooking in the shop, and that stuck to everything.

I was hot for the new technology. One could create much more nuanced animation than what we were doing. But I lacked any practical background. ILM's system would remain a proprietary secret for years to come. But I was the new guy, just hanging on, not looking for a confrontation.

Besides the Bodine motor system, Coast had elevated the multiple-crank system, better described as "team stop-motion." A typical moving-camera setup had six of us, each with a crank to advance each frame. Keeping everyone on the same frame number was like Abbott and Costello's "Who's on First?"

We really did use baseball terminology. "171 shot, 172 is up!" meant "We've just now shot frame number 171, and everyone should move their cranks to position 172." Who's up? Kaline's up. Simple? Apparently not, especially at 2 a.m. It was typical at that time of night for us to discover we were not as synchronized as the Rockettes; John's on position 12, Pete's on 11, Chuck's on 13. Forrest, perhaps because of his tour in the Marines, would blow up and take over in his Georgia cadence: "Nobody move! From now on, everybody just do exactly what I say!" And it worked better.

Even doing the whole job alone was a challenge if the rig was too sloppy. On a promo spot for Carl Sagan's *Cosmos*, I used an ancient, wobbly rig, trying to overcome slop with dial indicators. Rick Clemente, a recently hired producer with some motion-control background, pronounced the ancient rig a "wonky piece of shit." We decided to rectify that then and there.

We had some precision rails, the key makings of a decent motion-control track. Clemente specified a simple 6-foot track, and I built it as a clandestine foot in the "moco" door, disguised with a hand crank on the leadscrew.

Coincidentally, Joe Rayner presented me with a basket case of a stop-motion motor project to fix. With a little shifting around, I could put together a single-axis stepper motor like the ones at ILM. Clemente got behind it, and I got in over my head.

At the least, a stop-motion camera motor rotates once and stops in the same position it started from. That's what Rayner was hoping for. I upped the ante with promises of variable exposure times, shooting two frames at a time, running forward and reverse, and a big digital frame counter. This would involve electronics but not a computer.

I'd read a Radio Shack booklet on TTL (transistor–transistor logic) circuits, and it appeared that one could just hook up various logic chips, and presto, there would be the final product. My design was logical, but I'd not yet heard about the devil in the details. Now was the time.

After two weeks of weaving a rat's nest of wire-wrap connections, I flipped the device on. Oops! It was erratic, occasionally shooting more than one frame or stopping with the shutter open. Those flaws were fatal for an animator. I took it to my high-school buddy Tony Wechselberger, now an electrical engineer in San Diego. He gave me pointers. "You really need a scope to check every step of the way so you can catch the error." Or, more universally: In any complex project, divide and conquer.

So the camera motor was not successful as advertised, but I had immersed myself in the realities of stepper-motor technology, a crash course that would prove useful in the near future.

Making and Animating Models

Rick Clemente had a fun spot coming up: The camera approaches a group of computer chips and dives into a channel in one of the chips, kind of echoing Luke's point of view when he attacks the Death Star.

I made a large chip model, around 2 1/2 feet square, covered with small pieces of Masonite connected with flat strips of rubber. When painted, it looked a lot like a microscope's view of a real chip. The background chips were vacuformed off the original.

To get into the 3/4-inch channel, I mounted a medical endoscope to the camera. All the camera motion was hand cranked, but it needed to be more precise than usual because of the extreme closeness to the subject. Our new 6-foot track helped a lot.

I'd hoped to work with Laine Liska, the staff animator and puppet maker, and got a few opportunities to do so. Under Laine's direction, I cast new Doughboy heads and sculpted those vowels and consonants into them. One piece of advice regarding those replacement heads: If you keep the head moving, the inaccuracies between heads won't be caught. Tom Corlett showed me how to run the spray gun so each head got the same paint treatment, and Laine showed me how to mix realistic flesh color for those plaster-cast hands that poked the Doughboy.

Tom, by the way, kept a stock of used X-ACTO blades and carefully resharpened them. He also had the phone number for a UFO hotline pinned over his workbench. Regularly, there were differences of opinion between Tom and others on that and other subjects. Once, Tom warned us that the Tesla Society was getting very powerful. Chuck wanted to know what the hell that meant.

Later on, I asked if anybody had a sharp X-ACTO blade. Chuck grabbed one of Tom's dulled blades and formed a pyramid over it with his fingers, warning, "This might take a while."

Among my odd jobs was assisting Laine during animation. That turned out to be incredibly boring. If you can't see what's going on in the animator's head, there's not much else to look at. And you ought not speak while they're working.

Some years before, Laine had animated Santa riding in an electric razor while several ad-agency guys looked on. They kibitzed throughout the session, pointing out individual poses they wanted changed. Everyone could pick at the shot. Laine caved in, as he tried to make them all happy, and animating by committee resulted in a shot of Santa flailing his head and arms in terror. It had to be reshot, but this time, Laine set out a pile of girlie magazines to keep the armchair animators distracted. Since then, anytime clients wanted to observe a stop-motion shoot, out came the men's-room library.

Later on, David Allen came on to do some animation, and I assisted him, too. Dave was happy to explain everything he was doing, and I soaked it up gratefully.

Phil asked me if I was up to animating a puppet, a milkman representing a dairy company. I leapt at the chance. This wasn't quite the big time, as it was for a regional audience, but it felt like a heavy responsibility. Phil knew I was into stop-mo, and he told me about some of the movies he'd worked on. *The Giant Behemoth* was one I'd seen, and there were also *Jack the Giant Killer, The Time Machine, Dinosaurus!* and effects for TV's *The Outer Limits*. I'd be honored to take direction from anybody with those classics on his résumé.

Phil asked if I was another member of the "Kong Cult," his teasing name for those who were obsessed by the big ape at an early age. That included Laine, Dave Allen, and a boatload of other guys in the business, now including me.

During the daylong animation session, I bumped a prop and didn't know about it until the next day's dailies. With more than a hundred precious frames at stake, I suggested an optical fix. No-go, according to Phil's ethics. He sent me back to reshoot the whole thing. I think he was partly giving me a lesson in being careful and was also being cheap, as my day rate was considerably less than the cost of a film optical.

Bonding Sets and Friendships

Because John DeChene and I had a little welding experience, Phil had a "Phil-O-Gram" for us. A Phil-O-Gram was a cartoony diagram, his style of direction for how he wanted us to rig a special effect. This 'gram showed a phone booth, the enclosed kind that Clark Kent would find useful. The front was normal, but the rear was considerably wider, maybe twice as wide. The sides splayed out to join the front to the back. This was to make room for stuffing in more people than could fit into a normal booth. At the right camera distance, the front would exactly cover the rear, and it would look like a regular rectangular booth.

Building that phone booth jump-started my friendship with John. Both of us were mostly camera types, and we worked well together. Johnny D, as most called him, got well into the welding, singing about himself, "John Henry was a steelworkin' man." It was real bonding conditions.

The job was a Dr. Pepper spot, one of the series with Dave Naughton singing, "I'm a Pepper," and so on. John and I delivered and assembled the booth on location, an iconic concession stand on Santa Monica Beach. We adjusted the seat for Naughton's height. We were a little starstruck working with a well-known character who didn't have an armature inside him.

As it turned out, I had another task: chasing winos off from the area and especially from Naughton's seat when it was unoccupied. One bum in particular sat himself down on the seat and started singing and bouncing, entreating everyone to use him in the show. When I sent him off, I noticed he'd fouled the king's throne. I took care of the bum's accident while Naughton wasn't looking.

John and I were even more struck by Stacey Nelkin, the second star in the spot. She chatted with us during downtime, maybe because I recognized her as the cutie in *The Serial.*

Monty Shook became another buddy while we collaborated on several jobs. Among us twenty- and thirty-somethings, he had the longest history at Coast. Monty introduced me to sculpting in hard foam, thinned Bondo and fiberglass—all the smelly materials. He knew the technique exceptionally well, as he was a committed surfer and made surfboards just that way. My first use of the process was making a Doughboy-sized Santa sleigh.

Monty said I should learn to surf now that I was in SoCal. It wasn't long before he and I were looking for good waves up and down the coast as a weekend ritual. I was "totality stoked" when Monty gave me one of his longboards. I maintained my newfound zeal for surfing for a year or more.

After Hours

One thing everyone on the Coast crew enjoyed was the open access we had to the studio, letting us use the facilities for our own projects. Any weekend, you could find several of us there, working on our own projects. Some were for the soul, like Monty fixing a cracked surfboard, Ernie machining an armature, or Forrest making a found-objects sculpture. One of Forrest's pieces was based on a dog skeleton he'd found. He mingled machine parts, typewriter parts, and so on, with the skeleton. He called it a "cybernetic organism" or something like that.

We could moonlight, too. I shot my last KTKT spot there. This one was Mark's idea—that the TV game show *Funny Fud* was hot in

Tucson. We came up with current celebrities to be the contestants, Dave Fitzsimmons drew caricatures, and Ed Alexander produced some great voice impressions.

Instead of regular cel animation, I sold Mark on a "2 1/2D" look (not 3D) for the spot. I made a tabletop set that mimicked the show's set and peopled it with two-dimensional cutout characters. I figured this could be a more flexible way of getting a multiplane effect.

Time was short for me and for Mark, so I had to shoot it on a work night. I was able to get 30 seconds overnight on the other KTKT spots, mostly flopping cels, but this setup might take longer. Best I could do was get prepped during lunch and dive into it at quitting time. The soundtrack was read and on several pages of dialogue exposure sheets, and I'd worked out a nice dolly shot to match the one in the real game show. This spot had to be cut while shooting—no time for post-editing.

The shoot went very smoothly. I knew when each cut had to be made, right on the exposure sheet, and I moved to another frame at each cut and kept on animating. I finished just as the crew was showing up. It was a fun way to close that era.

Learning to Make Puppets from a Pro

I was not a staff employee at Coast; it just felt that way because jobs often overlapped. That didn't always hold true, and I think it was a good thing. I learned to save for those inevitable dry weeks and continued to make use of the facility for my own projects.

With Laine Liska there on-site, I decided to fill some downtime by making a stop-mo character under his mentoring. No, it would be two characters. I already had a human-figure armature on hand and sculpted a skinny alien over it. Big head, giant brain, spare body, scales—whatever was interesting.

Laine showed me the foam-injection method; he had made a gargantuan syringe out of a Plexiglas tube that was maybe 6 inches in diameter and 2 feet long. Output funneled down to a clear plastic tube, about 3/8-inch. You could close your plaster mold, stick the tube in a hole made just for the purpose, and pump foam in until it came oozing out. If all went well, there would be a complete cast of your critter.

It's all prep, getting everything ready for the magic moment when you inject. You must do it *now*, before the foam gels and can't get through the tube. Finally, after all those lesser methods, this was the gold standard!

Critter #2 was to be ridden by the alien guy. I sketched some unlikely creatures, each with too many elbows and a head you couldn't relate to, so Laine got into his take on practical creature design.

You might think it's creatively restrictive. That's what went through my head at first. Then I grew up. Laine's counsel was that, first and foremost, the audience needs to identify with your character. It should be a body that looks believable, like it evolved into a simple, efficient form. Like us vertebrates, it should have no more limbs than necessary, bilateral symmetry, one head, and a balanced body. That would work better than what I had drawn.

So, my critter became a spiny reptilian bulldog, the devoted protector and powerful steed for the alien guy. I made a sturdy armature for lizard-dog, with a hole in his head where I could stick in a key to open and close his massive jaws! Dave Allen happened to see the skull and liked the mechanism.

Another practical tip from Laine: Don't work so hard in sculpting individual scales. Instead, sculpt the overall smooth musculature and maybe detail around his eyes and mouth. The rest you can do after casting. Sure enough, Laine had a plaster mold he'd made from a large iguana who'd met his fate in some low-budget dinosaur movie. Sad.

I painted liquid latex into the iguana mold and peeled out thin patches of really great scales. I could rubber cement them over lizard-dog like a mosaic. All that critter makin' was huge fun. Now, what to do with them?

Off in a small area of the stage, I began setting up a *Kong*-inspired jungle scene. This was going to be an exercise in glass foreground painting, with all the expected twisted vines and roots on glass and model trees behind. There was lots of atmosphere.

Phil lent me his Acme process camera, a favorite among animators for the clear viewing. He liked it for another reason: The viewfinder pointed up, and he was extra tall.

Good for Phil, but not for Mel, a snit-picking director who was . . . um . . . extra short. Mel wouldn't ask for a ladder to reach the finder, so he was unable to mess with Phil's framing.

I was having the time of my life putting the setup together. Clay bas-relief tree trunks on the glass, streaks of mist airbrushed on back of the glass, raking light on background bushes, painted sky. It added up to one of those in-the-zone experiences!

Shooting Model Missiles and Blowing Up Things

Bob, Johnny D, and I were back together on another feature, *The Man Who Saw Tomorrow*, a somewhat embellished documentary about Nostradamus and his predictions. Coast was hired to envision World War III. For us, it meant nuclear missiles launching from underground desert strongholds, flying in space, and blowing up New York City.

The first scene was a great example of Phil's ability to get the most out of a limited budget. We would build an outdoor desert set on higher-than-normal supports. That would make room for model missiles rising out of the ground, raised by vertical track rigs.

Engine exhaust was as simple as bare 1K bulbs mounted under the missiles and diffused by CO_2 fire extinguishers blasting up through the launch openings. Like many things, it was all about the prep. We all did our things, working toward the same goal; I was working on the rigging, where several of us would manually raise the missiles as quickly as we could.

For what it was, it looked pretty good on the first take, but after all the prep, we shot more takes to justify all our work. On screen, Phil's trick was amazing. I'd expected a cheesy B-movie effect, but the boss obviously knew what he was doing.

Then it was back to the stage, where we camera guys got out the Bodine gearmotor erector set for the missiles-in-space shots. As this show had no budget for opticals, we had to get it all in-camera. That usually means a lot of black velvet to hide the rigging.

Bob would describe a dog-legged missile support in the air, custom for each shot. John usually welded the contorted assembly of square tube right on set. Then we'd rig the missiles and CO_2 hoses, wrapping it all in black velvet. It was pretty much the same trick as outdoors but smaller and filmed at quarter speed, not five times overspeed. When backlit, the cryogenic gas jets looked great.

The destruction wreaked by the missiles was boiled down to two shots, as dictated by the budget. The Statue of Liberty and the Empire State Building took the hit as large model shots. Forrest sculpted the top half of "Miss Liberty," as he called her. The bosses insisted on a very short schedule, which gnawed at his artistic sensibilities. He worked through the weekend, trying to capture the Lady's essence in clay. Monday was his drop deadline. We came in that morning to find Miss Liberty on her face, apparently having fallen over during the night. Now Forrest would need more time for the repairs. We kidded him about the convenience of the mishap but never found out whether she fell or was pushed.

A hollow wax casting of the sculpt was artfully blown apart by Mike Sullivan using a compressed-air gun spraying BBs out of an array of tubes. It looked good in slow motion.

We only needed to create the top half of the Empire State Building. It was built as an 8-foot model, assembled out of foaming plaster casts of walls. The intent was to blow it away with Mike's rig; it would come apart in chunks and a little plaster dust.

The budget allowed us one go, and that was stipulated in the contract. Unfortunately, we loaded up too much dust and debris inside. Even with the camera running at top speed, the model was there in one frame and was a dusty white-out two or three frames later. I, for one, wished we could have a second go, but deals had been made.

As I mentioned, it was commercials, not movies, that kept the doors open at Coast! The company owners tolerated feature work to keep Phil happy, but commercials were more profitable. So there were a lot of short-term commercials going, usually more than one at a time.

There's no use trying to cover all the ones I worked on; I can't recall most of them, anyway! In the first two years I was at Coast, my assignments were an even mix of special-effects rigging, model making, and stop-motion that mostly didn't involve puppets.

You might presume puppet work would be the most popular, but working out unique tricks, like perfectly poured floor polish or animating through an endoscope, was as much or more fun and challenging.

Coast began to enter an extra-slow period, and Phil gave us freelancers the word: "This layoff is not good-bye, but *au revoir*." He was classy in his Gilded Age way.

CHAPTER 12

Introvision

I'd worked almost continuously from early 1980 to late 1981, long enough to lull myself into a sense of security, but I was still a freelancer. Among colleagues, I called the layoff "chilling." It was a good reminder of the erratic nature of the film biz.

Jeanne and I had taken out a mortgage on a house in Van Nuys, which was a concern, but we had no regrets. Jeanne had started working as a flight attendant, and I had a few freelance projects, including a pair of robot arms for a model spacecraft that would be used in an IMAX show.

Dave Allen also had a short job for me: rigging up a synchronizing device for his stop-mo camera and projector. Then another model-making job came along that led to many more friends and coworkers—and ultimately a staff job.

Model maker Gene Rizzardi was calling for freelancers all over LA; he was putting together a model shop for Introvision, Inc., the outfit making visual effects for Hal Needham's *Megaforce*.

I walked into the stage on the Raleigh Studios lot that Rizzardi had converted to a model shop. Chuck Miller was there, along with a lot of new faces, including Steve and Charlie, the soon-to-be-legendary Chiodo Brothers, and a couple dozen others. The project at hand was a large power station that was destined to be blown up.

My job was to mount lots of tiny aircraft panel lights to the structure. These lights had been sourced as the best choice, as the 14-volt bulbs were extra durable and could take up to 40 volts for a short time, giving the high-speed cameras more light. That task took a couple of weeks, and then I started working with other people painting model vehicles.

John Stears was the visual-effects supervisor and would be the pyro guy as well. If that name is not familiar, think back to the Aston Martin in *Goldfinger*. You know: Bond's trick-wheel spinner comes out and cuts Tilly Masterson's tire. That car was John's brainchild! I was 13 when I doctored a slot car to do that, so, of course, I indulged in hero worship at age 31. I complimented his creation, and he seemed pleased (in a British sort of way) to have some recognition.

On shoot day, John showed me how his low-tech nail board pyro controller would guarantee no mistakes when blowing up the expensive model. It was a real board with real nails in it. Wires ran from each nail to individual bombs in the model in the sequence he wanted them to go off. When he dragged a ground wire across the nails, the performance went off as planned. He said he didn't care for preset timers. Sometimes, he had to change the plan in the middle of things, and his nail board made it simple. Sure enough, Stears played his nail board like a musical instrument, holding back while one explosion took a little longer to go off.

Usually, the model crew didn't go to dailies, but this time the boss, Tom Naud, allowed it. We were a big crowd for the small screening room and got comfy on the carpet while the long reel ran. Five or so cameras running at high speed can generate a lot of footage in no time; I recall it adding up to 50 screen minutes.

Apart from the overhead black cloth catching fire, everything worked perfectly. There was a lot for the editor. Naud seemed grumpy. We got lukewarm compliments, followed by, "It cost me $400 for you to see this." There were pressures on him, no doubt.

While we were building the three main models, we got the word that everyone needed to stay late. Coming up was a night-shift relocation of the model shop. Apparently, they'd got word of a union bust the next day. We were a mixed group, and I was among those not in a union. We did our best to prep all the little details, but when the time came, so came one of our own, driving a forklift. Anything without wheels went up on the forks and then rode to our new secret stage and model shop. The mood was pretty good, camaraderie among us all.

Our next model was the bad guys' desert compound. From my point of view, it was all about the barbed wire. We needed lots of miniature barbed wire, and for some reason, it had to be real wire. Several of us took on the task of twisting the tiny barbs onto 8-foot lengths. It was a great setup for daylong yap sessions, as the task required minimal brain activity. We were constantly puncturing our fingertips; soon, nobody reacted to our monosyllabic curses.

Introvision was the name of the company's signature process, a highly developed front-projection process. The whole idea was to film live actors in projected environments like the models we were making.

Some 14 years earlier, *2001: A Space Odyssey* had used front projection in the opening scene, showing actors in ape suits against the African desert. Introvision added the ability to put foreground images in front of the actors and background behind them. Just out of curiosity, I spent my breaks in the stage where they were filming the actors.

There was Hal Needham, the director. He must have been great to work with. He'd been a stunt man for years and had a "been there, fractured that" limp and plenty of stories about broken bones. He was upbeat, joking with his actors. I figured all that physical anguish he'd endured must've eclipsed any angst from directing.

Barry Bostwick played the hero, much changed from his role in *The Rocky Horror Picture Show*, and Persis Khambatta was a charming leading lady, having grown back her hair since playing the bald alien babe in *Star Trek: The Motion Picture*.

My tour of duty in the model shop was coming to a close when Bill Mesa, Introvision's director of photography, asked me to shoot some single-frame material. He'd heard that I did that kind of stuff somewhere. The job was quite simple, just clicking off frames from a computer display. But that created a right-time-and-place opportunity to get a job.

Unfortunately, the job was replacing an assistant I knew who had just been fired for a trivial offense. Bill Mesa made the offer; they needed a camera-savvy person to maintain and operate the system. He asked me a couple times, would I really want to do the job? Sure, it was a neat trick, albeit only one trick. I'd enjoyed making much cruder background-projection setups back in Tucson. This could be pretty cool.

Being cool was Bill Mesa's standard operating procedure, as I had seen. The company head of production, Elliot Rosenblatt, strove to keep things moving, pushing Bill to finish making adjustments by announcing, "It's showtime!" Bill silently carried on until he was satisfied that we had a shot that would make the company proud. The pair made an effective operation, despite their headbutting; nothing would get done without both of them.

Introvision was getting noticed; several reps from Disney came to see Tom about future work. Tom, bless him, had the fabled Old Hollywood producer's bravura, which was probably not what the mannerly Disney guys were expecting. He ushered them in to see the reel, promising, "This'll make you piss your pants!"

Directors could work with their actors, seen in their background. One day, I opened a door to the waiting room, and there was Orson Welles, waiting for a meeting. His stage presence was that of a god! I stopped and stared like a startled woodland creature, just long enough for Welles to mercifully break the ice with his sonorous rendition of the word "Hello."

Raleigh Studios remained the company's base after *Megaforce* wrapped, and I spent my time either organizing all the fiddly stuff that composed the system or working with Bill Mesa. We took on a couple of commercials, one featuring a very nice model car flying loops in a European countryside. Channeling Coast, I hand animated the camera-projector rig for that shot.

From the beginning, the boss was concerned about our trade secrets getting out, but I don't think there was much to be worried about. I mean, we had the agency guys on set with the rig in plain sight; they could watch a beam from the projector winding its way through beam splitters, lenses, and retro-reflective screens. What did the agency guy ask me while looking at live video from the camera tap? "Is this all done in *software?*" In 1981, that was a hot, new buzzword. I pointed to the rig and explained, "It's done with mirrors."

Our next destination was the Disney lot in Burbank, where we would add live pirates to a beached model pirate ship. The model had already been shot and was destined to play in a Disney park in Japan.

This was going to be a big setup; the 30-by-60-foot screen was at one end of the stage, and we set up near the other end. Our first test came back with the live actors looking too big for the ship. Bill and I tried all our pirate-shrinking options with wider lenses, moving the rig right up against the rear wall. No-go. The pirates still looked like Baby Gojira. Luckily, Disney's stages were lined up so we could join two stages, doors open, with a lot of canvas bridging the gap. That got us double the throw. Finally!

Then again, no. Nothing was going to work except a bigger screen. Unless . . .

Tom Naud jumped into action and called around town for "all the midgets you got" and a special request for a "stunt midget." I doubt he ever used the more politically correct term, "little people," but the recommendation was made. This time, the test shot showed sufficiently small pirates—in fact, maybe a little too small. We could fix that by moving the rig closer to the screen.

A lot of little-people-sized pirate outfits showed up a day later, and we were ready to go. Every pirate, including the stuntman, had some business to do in the shot. The stunt pirate's job was to fall off a yardarm and land in a hidden water tank. Nice work if you can get it. He dropped over and over, all afternoon, at $200 per dunk.

Before moving on, I met Peter Anderson, well respected in visual-effects work. He showed me around the studio, and I got an eyeful. Going up and touching the original multiplane animation stand was a cosmic moment. After that, I looked at the ACES motion-control rig, the one they'd made to shoot models for *The Black Hole*. It was partly disassembled, the camera lying on the floor. It didn't seem to have the respect the ancient multiplane rig was still enjoying.

Next stop was Culver Studios, a.k.a. Laird Studios. Look it up, and you'll see 10 or more names the studio has carried. My favorite was RKO, the company that gave the world *King Kong*. Yes, Fay Wray was in the stage next to us, but I'd just missed her by a scant 50 years. I could still detect a trace of her perfume.

Director Marvin Chomsky (ever see *Roots?*) needed a scene for his TV movie *Inside the Third Reich*, about Albert Speer, Hitler's architect. Chomsky had a few rare photos taken inside the Reich Chancellery shortly before it was destroyed. He wanted those photos to be Introvision environments.

To get the photos into the system, Bill had some 4 x 5 glass transparencies made to fit the still projector and painted them with dye colors. When all the gear was in place, two of us worked together in separating foreground areas in the plate that should cover the actors. One of us would keep an eye to the viewfinder, guiding the other to precisely black out foreground objects with black tape on a very large piece of glass mounted 10–20 feet in front of the camera. Then we'd do the exact opposite on another piece of glass, blacking out everything except the foreground image. When these mattes and countermattes fit together, the patented optics combined them with the actors right in the camera.

Depending on the complexity of the cutouts, this could take 20 minutes or a full day. One afternoon, Charlie Chiodo and I were cutting mattes for a wide shot with lots of detail in the foreground, and it was going slow. The actors would be showing up in the morning, so we had to finish it no matter what.

A young production assistant came to me, popping her gum. "I'm supposed to find out where you want your cot."

"Whatd'ya mean, my cot?"

She popped her gum again. "We already know you're gonna go all night on that shot, and you won't have time to go home, so you have to sleep here. Where do you want your cot?"

The logic was inescapable, but the unilateral decision, well, it would've been a lot more palatable if they had at least tried to fool me into thinking it was *my* idea.

"You can put my cot anywhere you want because I'm sleeping at home tonight."

In response, she blew one more bubble and . . . pop!

I showed up the next morning with two hours of sleep, fired up the rig, and checked in with Bill and the assistant cameraman (AC). There was Marvin Chomsky on the minimalist set, talking to a couple of actors. I couldn't see the actors' faces, but it was easy to recognize Rutger Hauer from behind; we'd been working with him for a few days already. I walked over to meet the new guy, who turned around just as I imagined I saw a spitting image of Adolf Hitler. Freaky!

On another day, better rested, I noticed the AC had a lot on his hands, and I took a film magazine off the camera and downloaded it for him. I would've been doing Johnny D a favor at Coast, but this guy was trembling as he told me to never, ever, blah-blah . . . A tip for camera-crew hopefuls: Canning up someone else's film is a major territorial gaffe.

Back to Rutger Hauer. He was called "the Dutch Paul Newman" in Europe, a full-on movie star. You might know him as Roy Batty, the white-haired replicant in *Blade Runner*. In Mr. Chomsky's film, he played Albert Speer. I noted that he navigated the invisible set with apparent ease. Working with live actors was a rarity for me, a special treat.

Mr. Chomsky was a treat to work with, appreciative and flexible. At the end of the shoot, he gave a brief address to the troops, ending with something like, "Thank you all for a week of learning and movie magic."

Thank *you*, Mr. Chomsky!

I'd been working with Geoff Williamson, the camera machinist who built the Introvision rig. It was never considered "finished," but rather an ongoing process of refinement. To me, it was a great chance to see this world-class craftsman at work. Another of his projects was the Wilcam high-speed VistaVision camera. He'd gone all out to achieve 300 frames per second, making the spinning shutter of beryllium, a very light, strong, and toxic metal.

Geoff showed me how to sync camera and projector with an oscilloscope. Knowing how to use that instrument was the key to making a much more reliable animation motor than the one I'd fabricated at Coast. I soon had a project going at home, intent on improving my first motor.

Jack Discovers Christmas Town

Standing in the circle of holiday trees, Jack reaches for the Christmas door, and we cut to a shiny brass doorknob. We can see everything reflected in the knob. This was a single-use 360-degree set built around the small knob. If we can see everything, where is the camera hiding? For a clue, step-frame as Jack's hand covers the knob.

Jack's first view of Christmas Town includes the only stars in the movie. We built a dozen or two: a black card with cutout pointy stars taped to clamp lights. Pressed from behind a blue muslin backing was a night sky with movable stars.

More subtly, we rigged up the Aurora Borealis in motion. Wrapping a basketball with crumpled aluminized Mylar was the key; we mounted it on a moco rotator and hit it from two sides with spotlights. The light that bounced onto a rear-projection screen became the effect.

The same shot has dozens of flagrantly glowing Christmas lights. We double exposed them into the animation. Step-frame on that shot, and you can see the lights punch right through Jack as he somersaults in the air. This was just the beginning of our use of tiny colorful light bulbs as "practicals." We'd use hundreds of those 14-volt aircraft panel lights I'd used on

Megaforce. Model makers Gretchen Scharfenberg and Aaron Kohr would have a lot of soldering to do.

Fitting an ultracolorful Christmas scene into a Halloween-style movie might appear to be somewhat tricky, but no. If there was any trick, it was about pools of light and shadow setting up a suitable contrast for the mood. To begin, the entire scene was night. Some shots were dark enough to throw shadows from legit sources like the cozy fireplace, where Jack appears peeping in the windows. Or there was the oil lamp, creating Jack's shadow as it approaches the sleeping children. And elves appear in silhouette on window shades while up light throws Jack's stretched shadows.

This was when I brought in monochrome contrast glasses for everyone in my crew. Looking through the dense yellow glass helped us evaluate how strong the contrast would be on film.

Have you ever seen an overhead projector? In predigital 1991, a lot more people had seen one in their school classrooms. That's what we used to throw Santa's shadow on the snow. Huddling under the set, the animator flopped cels as if working on a downshooter!

CHAPTER 13

A First Taste of Moco

I n the spring of '82, Phil Kellison called and inquired about my availability. I felt a certain loyalty to both companies, but it was clear that Coast offered much more variety. I'd been obsessed with making a motion-control system, which didn't have much use at Introvision. There was the decision.

Back at Coast, my first job was to mechanize a talking roll of toilet paper. The prototype puppet was a thin casting in latex foam. Phil wanted a remote squeeze handle to operate the mouth like the brake handle on a bike. I found some useful parts at a bike shop; you can save a lot of time in rigging by taking advantage of what's already out there.

Meanwhile, a couple of guys were supposed to be improving the look of the puppet, but they were shifted to other jobs. The agency back on the East Coast inquired repeatedly about our progress, and our producers stalled them. After several weeks of promises, the agency said they would fly out in two days to see what we had so far.

Suddenly, a number of us were on the prototype team, charged with making as many failed puppets as we could crank out. The lead agency guy saw right through our big box of rejects and announced it was a "fuckin' disastah!" But eventually, we finished the job to everyone's satisfaction. And the rant about our "disastah" became a memorable quote for future applications.

Then we were back into short, overlapping, and diverse projects! That included moonlighting, armatures and camera-track widgets, and especially meeting Jim Aupperle and Randy Cook. They were on *The Thing*, shoot-ing stop-motion performances that the live-action animatronics couldn't do (which wasn't very much, with Rob Bottin on the job). All they needed was a replacement for the lower backbone in an already-made puppet. It needed to have room for a tentacle or something to shoot right through the unfortunate puppet's gut.

Simple, quick, and cheap. That's what they got, and that's what Randy pointed out to his producer, enthusiastically complimenting my work. I appreciated that.

Dave Allen needed a gizmo to give his hand-cranked camera track a little motion blur for the film, which was *Q*, as in Quetzalcoatl, later subtitled *The Winged Serpent*. His final shot reveals the eggs of the van-quished creature hidden in an attic. Incredibly, I found just the right widget at a surplus store in Pasadena. Call it a continuously variable transmission; whatever it was made for, it was also good for incrementally reducing the travel output from a constant-speed motor indexing one full turn. The rest was easy.

Dave was happy with the rig, and I was in awe of C&H Surplus. Pardon a little name-dropping; the outfit was a source for parts to the Dykstraflex.

Work activities had plenty of variety for a while. One day, I was hand animating a flying model car for McDonald's, and the next I was animating that milkman character. Then it was flying a Kodak logo and, later, flying a Bank of America checkbook. There was a lot of flying going on.

At lunch, Chuck Miller pointed out my distracted expression while I was flying my food around on a fork. Forrest predicted we'd soon be film-ing tampons "gracefully floating in space." That actually happened later on. There was a flying-merchandise fad in the commercial world on the coattails of the *Star Wars* films.

This seemed the perfect time to lean on the bosses to dip their toes into motion control. There was an ad in *American Cinematographer* for a turnkey system. It was an entry-level system based on Radio Shack's TRS-80, running a program written in BASIC, controlling up to six AC stepper motors. For each motor, the move programming consisted of typ-ing in start or stop frames and positions, plus optional ease-in and ease-out frame counts. Hardware limitations allowed stop-motion only, starting and stopping each frame. To a contemporary motion-control operator, these specs would be completely unacceptable, but for someone accustomed to the Coast multiple-crank system, it would be a significant jump forward. This was the starting point I could sell the bosses on!

We had a great candidate for upgrading the system: *Airplane II*. As with *Hangar 18*, we'd be flying a space shuttle. There were obvious motion-control shots in the boards, plenty of high-speed crash landings and uses of the Bodine system that couldn't be done any other way.

That was a good thing, because Phil wasn't exactly thrilled at the prospect of the new puppy replacing his tried-and-true methods. He'd want old school whenever possible. I, the self-appointed motion-control advocate, would soon find we didn't have enough time to squeeze all our shots through the fledgling moco system, which was merely a computer with untested software. You could say it needed a lot of development.

Among the shots earmarked for moco, I picked one that would require the most mechanical prep. We would work toward that shot, learning the program and building the mechanical components while shooting the simpler shots.

Some of us were moving between two or three setups as needed. One day, I was sent to rig Monty's 3-foot space shuttle to skid around backward in a crash landing on the moon. The trick involved a hidden slot in the outdoor set and some steel linkage. As this was shot at high speed, the fiberglass model had to survive several abusive takes. That it ended up in one piece was a testament to Monty's experience making bulletproof surfboards.

Indoors, I was mostly working with Bob, Johnny D, and a new face, Catherine Hardwicke, who had just come from Texas with an arty take on model making. That turned out to be quite useful when we had to arrange Styrofoam asteroids in a maze of very fine tungsten wires to shoot Bodine setups of the shuttle flying through an asteroid belt. Bob could work us youngsters under the table. We figured he knew some way of pacing himself or had just been hardened over time. He was mild mannered but could keep us neophytes in our place.

Lighting under Bob's direction, I officiously informed him, "You know, Bob, there's no fill light in space."

He responded, "What do you want to do when you grow up, Pete?"

One of our "'roid shots," as we were calling them, was a close-up of oncoming 'roids battering the shuttle's nose. Phil specified a high-speed setup, camera sideways, with 'roids rolling off an endless belt onto the upended shuttle.

The rig didn't behave at high speed, spraying 'roids every way but down. Monty and I were on this shot and didn't want to tell Phil that his Phil-O-Gram didn't cut it. Monty said it would go better after lunch, as Phil, Bob, and Joe were going to Boardner's, their favorite watering hole. We threw together a hopper that would drop 'roids right where we wanted and prepped through lunch.

Sure enough, Phil came in as we were shooting a take and inquired, "Why have you not done what I told you to do?"

Monty got snappy. "If we thought it would work, we woulda done it."

Those martinis did the trick. Phil just grumbled, "Carry on."

Tom Scherman was 20 feet away, making a moon base for *Airplane II*. He'd exhumed my oversize computer chips and massaged them into his moonscape, creating the impression of many buildings connected to each other.

My moco crusade inched forward as shots required more capabilities. We had a decent 8-foot track, like the 6-footer, plus rotators and a camera drive. We were almost ready for the trickiest moco shot.

I needed a rig that could rotate the shuttle in three axes—pitch, roll, and yaw, in aviation parlance. I found a Volkswagen universal joint and built the rest of the rig around it. The gag was to emulate a skidding, 180-degree turn performed by the shuttle, which makes it just in time to avoid getting too close to the sun. It took a while for me to understand what Bob was asking for. He used the term "button-hook turn," which didn't mean anything to me. After a few trials, he explained it as a turn initiated by locking up a car's rear wheels, spinning around the front wheels.

In the same stage, Phil was setting up the sun element for the same shot. Picture two disks about 18 inches across cut from textured Plexiglas shower-door material. He'd mounted them to slowly counterrotate with Bodine motors. With yellow and orange gels backlighting the gag, it looked a lot like the roiling surface of the sun. When the optical composite came back with shuttle and sun together, it was a testament to complementary methods.

Producer Howard Koch was on-site for the film's opening shot: the shuttle crashing through a *Star Wars*–inspired introductory title crawl. A 4 x 6–foot tempered glass was roto painted with the last frame of the crawl, then mounted on one end of a dolly track. We planned to run the 3-foot dolly-mounted shuttle into the glass, filming at high speed. We wanted this shoot to go flawlessly for Koch.

He was apparently hard to please. Once, after screening some "finals" we'd sent him, he called back and said, "Stop sending me test shots."

Safety glasses on, we pushed the shuttle with all our might. On contact, the mount bent the shuttle, the dolly climbed up the glass, and the glass bent into a horrifying curve. You could just about smell the pent-up energy in that glass. Everyone got the hell away from it ASAP. After several uncomfortable minutes, the glass gave up the ghost with a loud bang. Koch silently turned and left for the day.

Hands down, *Airplane II* was our favorite feature to date. We crew went out to see it in a regular theater and felt proud of our contribution to such a fun show. Monty said it was the first job where he didn't sneak out early to avoid meeting people he knew. I was especially glad we'd broken the moco ice!

CHAPTER 14

Doughboy and the Lizard People

L aine was getting overbooked and overworked. He was a superstar in stop-mo. Agencies requested him, and he was a draw for puppet business. A solution to not having enough Laine was to have a ghost animator. That turned out to be me.

It was great fun. Phil would give me direction in a brief pep talk, leaving the details to me. Mostly, it was Doughboy shots: Keep him moving, make gestures go with the dialogue, don't overanimate, and—an extra important directive—use your best judgment.

Typically, I'd set up an angle, shoot a lighting test, read the track, and scribble poses on the dialogue sheet. Then I'd come in the next morning and start animating with a clear head and a loaded camera. The next day, I'd meet up with Phil and the editor, Reese Woodling, and we'd run the shot through the Moviola twice. Reese commented on clean animation and synchronous voice with mouth movement. "No hitch in the giddyap" meant it was smooth. Phil generally concurred. There might be a special performance detail he wanted to check, but all in all, that was how shots were bought.

Phil was in on the inception of the Doughboy character in 1965. He had the drill down to a fine science; we were billing a modest $6,000 for most shots and still making a profit.

One special performance had the Doughboy conducting a classical symphony; Phil wanted stronger motion than usual when the puppet was wielding his baton. I threw in a Beethoven-ish, passionate scowl sculpted with a little white clay on his plaster face. Protocol mandated I ask about it beforehand, but Phil was secure enough to take the surprise gracefully and kept it in the spot.

I finished the first take in midafternoon and asked the producer, Nancy Evelyn, about shooting take 2 the next morning. Nancy responded in her Texas-gal tone, "Honey, I thought you wanted to work with us. Now you get back there and finish the job."

I had another version to shoot. The agency wanted a certain shot to be animated twice, once for domestic use and once for international use. The French version had the Doughboy winking at a boy off camera. No problem. But the American version had a girl off camera instead, and it was deemed too risqué for the Doughboy to wink at the girl.

I whined, "What can the little eunuch possibly do, anyway?"

V

Shortly before the end of 1982, Coast joined several other effects houses on Ken Johnson's TV miniseries *V* (for *victory*). The story concerned Nazi-fied humanoid reptiles from space who were bent on crushing the human race, and they needed a lot of model spaceships to do the job. That's where we came in. Dreamquest and David Stipes Productions were two of Coast's partners on the job. There may have been more, but a lot of well-known freelancers contributed as well.

Joe Rayner was the boss on this show, and he gave me considerable control over how we'd shoot it. I started with several angles on an emissary ship descending onto a skyscraper landing pad. On the first shots, there was considerable rigging to be done, as the ship was pretty big and heavy. The shot was to be a down angle on the ship, and I figured we should mount the camera track vertically to scaffolding. The ship itself would be mounted on a Worrall head rotating slowly.

New Year's Eve split up our rigging with a nice party at Johnny D's. The next week, I was back on the scaffold, and Joe asked me why I was so cranky. I told him that Jeanne had walked out on me. This seemed a reasonable explanation to Joe.

She had a good reason for leaving. I was pouring all my time and energy into the business, leaving little for our marriage.

Back on the scaffold, we were shooting elements, typically fighter ships to matte into live-action backgrounds. To compose the ships correctly, I had to see both elements together. Usually, I could slip a background frame into the viewfinder, looking through it to see the ship. Sometimes, it took several frame clips if the background was moving.

I got into the habit of shooting a black-and-white test move of the ship and sandwiching it with the background in the Moviola. It was sloppy looking, developed in the darkroom as a negative, but it gave you the feel of the shot and how it all lined up.

Right down the street was Warner Bros., where Ken Johnson was shooting pickups, among other things. I would show up with my little test roll, find a Moviola, and show it to Ken. To his credit, Ken could look past all the light stands and other junk in those tests and visualize the finished shot. He was always excited to see the "slop comp" and would usually give me the go-ahead to shoot it for real.

What's the difference between a motion test and a real element? A motion test is shot as simply as possible, whereas shooting an element takes considerably more time and finesse.

There was no digital compositing in 1983, so what I shot was put together in an optical printer. Blue screen would've made for easier shooting, but Coast hardly ever paid for the process because a photochemical blue screen optical was pricey. The bosses figured we could do better by shooting multiple passes, filming the same moco move two or three times, each with a different purpose and lighting. Typically, there was a "beauty pass," lit the way we wanted it to look on screen and shot against a black background. Then we'd shoot a "matte pass" with the model softly lit evenly, with white tape covering dark parts of the model. This was the silhouette cutout element that could have been more expensively derived from a blue background. Often, we'd require a "light pass," which was shot in a darkened stage with only the small practical lights on in the model; this was shot through a fog filter to make those lights glow. The result would still be an optical composite but less expensive.

Sometimes, on those visits, I waited for Ken on stage and watched the shooting. It was a good chance to see how quickly TV shoots go. Once, there was a slight delay in getting makeup or some such thing tweaked, and they filled the five minutes by shooting an insert. All at the same time, grips put a slab of blacktop on the floor, lights and camera aimed at it, and a prechewed piece of gum was placed on the asphalt. Roll camera, slate, actor's shoe steps on the gum, walks out of frame. Cut and move on.

On another visit I was directed to a music recording session, which was a great place to wait. The orchestra was playing Beethoven's 5th, the upbeat, inspiring part near the end, and the producer introduced himself with a wink: "Who wrote this shit?"

V was broadcast over a week in May 1983. It went over great, especially with my half-siblings back in Michigan. Eileen, in her early teens, wanted to know what would happen with the interspecies teenage lovers in the next episode.

Her mom asked what I did on the show. I told her proudly, "I worked on the special effects." She sounded disappointed: "That's okay, maybe you can act in the next one."

The show went over well with me, too. The challenges and creative opportunities were excellent, and Ken Johnson was a pleasure to work for. He really showed talent for making people feel appreciated, and we paid him back with interest.

Toward the end, Tim, a freelance model maker, asked me, "How's life?"

I just had to say it. "Well, my wife left me, and my dog died."

Tim busted into guilty laughter. "Nice country-western song! Is your pickup busted, too?"

I realized nobody seemed surprised. Breakups were a common occurrence in the biz. If you aspire to work in film, be aware of the inevitable pressures, internal and external, you're signing up for. To my mind, choosing a significant other who is also in the business will at least ensure mutual understanding. Also, think twice about having kids or dogs. Will you have time for them?

Pete animating Dough Boy.

CHAPTER 15

Contrails, Weak Knees, and Rusty Bones

The next movie job was *Deal of the Century*, a satire about military contractors. Several model makers made a great miniature set featuring a billboard that proclaimed, "Arms for Peace."

My assignment was another moco shot. Ironically, Coast had won a bid for creating about 45 seconds of wireframe graphics of a jet fighter flying. What was ironic was that the low bid, ours, was going to be a model shot using a real wireframe made of steel wires brazed together. I can only guess that computer graphics were a lot more expensive in 1983.

Dwight Shook built it and painted it with green fluorescent paint. I mounted it on the same rig used for *Airplane II* and shot it under ultraviolet light to get that glowing-green monitor look.

At the same time, Johnny D was setting up the cleverest trick in the show. The boards called for high-altitude contrails. John built a Plexiglas tank about 6 feet long, 1 foot wide, and 3 inches deep. He mounted it high off the floor so the camera could look up at the clear bottom, and then he rigged a Bodine motor to move a small nozzle underwater the length of the tank. He loaded the nozzle with skim milk that he could squirt from a squeeze bulb. When everything was tuned and running, his underwater "milk rocket" created a realistic contrail. Bravo, Johnny D!

Shortly after that, we got a destruction model shot for the TV movie *Samson and Delilah*. It was nice to shift gears to a couple of non-moco assignments and work with Monty and a couple of relatively new guys.

Dave Sharp came on as a model maker, and he had carpentry skills as well. He introduced me to the wonders of battery-powered zip-screwdrivers. Suddenly, driving screws was as fast as hammering nails. Oh, brave new world! Chris Burton came from Wyoming with fine-art sculpture talents and rigging know-how.

They built a temple to Dagon and a statue of the deity, all destined to fall when Samson topples the giant idol. My job was to come up with a means of supporting the heavy statue and then cause it to fall on cue, making the rig disappear before the temple could collapse and reveal it. It was just what you'd expect: When Dagon was halfway in his forward fall, he'd trigger bungee cords to swing the rig out of frame and continue his fall unsupported.

Dave had a talent for mimicking actors chewing the scenery with famous lines. While we were carefully stacking the blocks and columns, Dave chose his Edward G. Robinson voice. "Where is your god *now*, Samson? Nyach-nyach!" We stifled laughs as we tried to balance the precarious setup.

Monty introduced me to the "weak-knee" joint on this job: a setup that can hold a lot of weight as long as the weight is bearing straight down. Give a lateral tug on the joint, and the weight will force the joint to collapse. Envision two sticks standing straight up, one on top of the other, with a simple hinge joining them on one side. That's approximately what Monty was using to hold up the temple.

About this time, I figured out there was a dichotomy in film-biz lifestyles, and similar types do better with each other. I'd started dating again, beginning with a comedienne. It didn't take long to hear that she'd described me as "a little scientist." Others worked out better, notably those who had nonglam jobs in the biz.

Talking to a woman at a high-end party, I identified myself as a cameraman. She asked, "But do you want to direct?"

"Not really, no. I really like camerawork."

At that, she glazed over and disappeared.

A Run on Armatures!

Little Softy (the toilet paper puppet) needed a new armature, said Nancy, and I told her that we weren't tooled up to improve on what we already had. That was true, and it was also true that I was interested in getting a small milling machine. The addition would make my garage a serviceable facility for such jobs. I offered Nancy a fixed price, which saved her worry about going overtime, and covered the cost of my new toy. In retrospect, it was interesting that we could have two separate business relationships at the same time: staff employee and freelance contractor. Nobody bothered to question it.

One problem with armatures was rust. The sulfur in the foam latex would attack steel and brass, making joints rough after carefully lapping them in. Jim Danforth had shown me the chrome plating he used instead of the spray paint we used to stave off corrosion.

I checked in with a local plating company, and the boss steered me to another material: bright nickel. Softer and more durable than chrome, it was more appropriate for the job. Touring the shop during a hot day, I was concerned about how much metal and acid the workers could inhale safely. I like most industrial smells, but all those open, steaming vats made me breathe as shallowly as I could. When I asked the boss about it, he said something philosophical and fatalistic.

Fortuitously, that new mill was in the garage. Ernie Farino called about a Randy Quaid armature he needed for *Dreamscape*, a sci-fi where the good guys and bad guys battle it out in each other's dreams. It was nice to see Ernie again. The last time, he and I were doing weekend projects at Coast, and he cut a tendon when his hacksaw slipped. I befriended him just driving him to the hospital.

Right on the heels of that moonlight job came Bill Mesa from Introvision. They were making effects for a TV movie called *The Night They Saved Christmas*, and they needed four reindeer armatures. Peter Kleinow was going to animate, and I met him for the first time. He was a very nice guy, maybe half a generation older than me, with two remarkable careers running in parallel. Animation was his day job, and at night, he was "Sneaky Pete," master of the pedal steel guitar for the Flying Burrito Brothers.

The armature job was an exercise in interchangeable parts; all four critters would be cast from the same mold. Just because I liked Kleinow, I threw in a breathing mechanism on one of them.

Our "trainer" moco system had made it through flailing spaceships only because it wasn't required to be precise. But more challenging motion designs were showing up in storyboards.

Here are two assignments that were interesting technical challenges:

In one spot, the live-action unit had filmed a very long dolly shot, backing through a house and stopping when they came to the end of the set. Phil wanted me to continue the move in miniature, pulling out of a window to reveal a whole neighborhood. It took days to massage the hookup between dolly shot and moco rig. It would've been a breeze with two or three key frames, but curve fitting was not in the system's entry-level capabilities. The payoff was the houses wearing fire helmets, the logo of our insurance-company client.

In another spot, an egg grows to an enormous height while a live chicken sits on it. Live action filmed the chicken riding up on a Bodine-driven rig rising up from the nest, and Phil asked me to film a real egg and make it appear to grow by moving closer to it. The challenge was to keep the bottom of the egg stationary while the top of the egg always lined up with the bottom of the chicken. I used Phil's ancient Bell and Howell 2709 camera, because I could roto project the chicken footage right onto the egg, lining them up. This also would've been a job for key framing instead of trial and error, and I told Reese, Phil, and Nancy exactly that when they asked why it was taking so long.

Reese said it as plain as could be: "You're working with the wrong tool." They all saw the light and asked me to find something better for next time. I had the perfect solution already in mind.

18 : 0 9

Sally Makes Soup

I liked setting up the establishing shot of Sally traversing her kitchen. It was a simple moving shot; we track with Sally as she turns from a bright window and walks across the room.

The fun started in adjusting the compositional elements. "I want the hatchet closer in the foreground and to be here when Sally is there." Then it was a matter of placing pools of light in the gloom just so. Get some light above the stove and make a hole in the floor for Dean's sickly green swamp gas, right under the hand pump. Make another hole under the stove for some blue gaslight. We also needed a blue practical *inside* the stove. And set a hard-light right over Sally, a little brighter than all the other lights.

After animator Trey Thomas finished up his performance, I double exposed in cartoon steam, projected on a scrap of white card, right over the boiling pot. In fact, for each shot in the scene, Trey animated Sally with another invisible cartoon in mind. After a few shots, I had to pass the scene to Jim Aupperle.

I liked our "daytime dungeon lite" atmosphere, but we couldn't play the same card too many times. Right upstairs, Dr. Finklestein has a yellow-green look from his ancient fluorescent light table.

I liked everything in this simple lighting plot except that live-action close-up on Sally's bowl of soup. Henry and I agree it has been a thorn in our saddles since it was shot. Suddenly, we're not watching *Nightmare* but looking at a TV cooking show. It wouldn't be hard to make it look more like stop motion, but we had to move on.

CHAPTER 16

The Music of the Stepper Motor

B ill Tondreau, one-man band, had won my recommendation over the other two contenders for turnkey motion-control systems. He'd demonstrated his system, skipping any fanfare. He showed that he knew, as an effects cameraman, what people in my job would need.

He'd literally wired up the whole computer himself, starting with a Z-80 microprocessor, and wire-wrapped a motherboard that boasted 256 kB of RAM, running on the CPM operating system. Those modest specs allowed double the axes I was used to, and they were *real* DC stepper motors, capable of running a move continuously while I looked through the viewfinder. On one 8-inch floppy disk was the program. Another such floppy disk was set aside for moves in the form of lists of positions for each frame, for each axis. The program offered key framing and editing commands, and on a second monitor you could see a position graph for a given axis.

Bill had made what they call a "teach pendant" in the industrial moco business: a handheld remote control for jogging motors, taking key frames, and so forth. He called it a "jog box." I could look in the camera's viewfinder and move motors at the same time.

There wasn't space left in the RAM for user interface. To invoke a particular routine, you'd tap one of several dozen two-letter codes in the

DOS command line. For example, *JB* meant turn on the jogbox. *MM* was to move a specified motor a specified distance. *IN* let you insert a key frame and position, and *RE* was to refigure the curve fit through key frames.

Bill had removed the passenger seat in his van to make room for a tall, enclosed rack assembly containing the whole system. He delivered that, several sizes of stepper motors, and cables for $20,000. It sounds like a lot, but I'd seen other systems where the cables alone cost more than that.

Bill didn't deliver it to Coast Effects, because by the time he finished the system, it was time to use it in a big, live-action setup at the main stage. A spot for Wang Computers called for a huge, vertical tracking shot ascending past several stories of an office building, without the front wall, so we could see the actors acting like happy office people.

Because there was only room for one story in the soundstage, we would have to redress the set over and over, shoot one story at a time, and blend them together with an optical. We had a rigging grip prepare a 20-foot vertical camera track for just that shot. Of course, the blend would require the exact same track speed for each story, which was the task of the Tondreau system.

The day before the shoot, I met with Bill on stage to work out the kinks of the rig. Everything worked as planned except that the track needed another 6 feet under and over the elevated set to get a clean entrance and exit in frame.

I took the camera back to the shop and made a stepper-motor-driven camera-tilt axis. That would add a little tilt throughout the move, just enough to extend the track's shortcoming. Next morning we tested that, and I felt some relief when it ran as I'd hoped.

Having never operated a Tondreau system, I didn't think this was the right time to learn by trial and error—not with a full crew and lots of actors burning money while I fiddled. I asked Bill to hang with me for the day, and he happily agreed. The guy was a gentleman and a lifesaver.

Knowing now what I needed to know then, I can tell you with certainty that going solo would've been a "fuckin' disastah!" Instead, it was a great day for the whole company. Bill joined my short list of all-star-level friends and heroes. I gave him some payback in the form of glowing word of mouth.

A Deal for Progress

The Tondreau Era at Coast Effects quickly gained momentum, and I was hot to make it my baby. After a Saturday night date, I'd skulk into the studio on Sunday to polish my skills on the machine.

The bosses were asking about the system more and more while writing bids, and I was getting a lot of experience. I proposed we set aside a budget for developing the system. Sometimes we had to scramble to prep for a trick that we should have seen as inevitable long before.

I ventured the cocky notion that I keep an eye open for probable future needs and have a "moco development" box on my time card for time spent beefing up our capabilities. The bosses were positive and never challenged what I was doing. Anytime I needed something to do, I drew on a list of "we ought to have" capabilities and made the widget on my own recognizance. If it were something big, I'd run it by Nancy.

Small stuff would be an overdriven camera motor for stall protection at 24 fps or more. Other small stuff included a number of small and medium model movers, as well as lighting dimmers controlled with stepper motors. After Laine had repeatedly unplugged the system to plug in his hot-glue gun, I realized we needed a few hardwired cable-drops on separate breakers just for the moco.

The big stuff was in the range of heavy precision floor tracks. Done right, the welded frames had to be stress relieved in a large kiln, then planed flat before mounting the precision parts. We couldn't do that in the shop, but such a service could be rendered for a price. I was pleasantly surprised to get a quote of $1,000—until the vendor called to set up delivery. He'd meant that number for one track, not all three. I passed that new info on to Nancy. No, Nancy wasn't going to cough up $3,000 just because some guy messed up on his quote. I was to be the one to finish the dickering myself. It ended with Coast paying only a third of the regular rate and the pissed-off vendor saying, "You can come down and haul 'em yourselves!"

We got a flying-pizza job, just what we needed to pull out the stops and show what we could do! Admittedly, I was hungry for another crack at flying a spaceship, and I overanimated it, flying in from infinity, doing a pirouette, and settling onto a platter. In my zeal, I managed to fill up most of the stage with a full-capability rig doing it. This was a beauty pass/matte situation, where you spray-paint it after the beauty pass.

I joined the bosses and the clients to watch dailies on the Moviola, and they liked it. Forgetting protocol, I opened my yap and said, "I hope the matte fits." Reese grabbed me by the shoulder and marched me out of the room. "You don't say *anything* around clients! You wanna shoot this again?" Actually, I would have. It was fun!

Dave Allen happened to visit before I struck the setup, and I proudly ran the move as fast as it could go, about 4 fps. He wasn't exactly thrilled, and the motor sounded like bad synthesizer music. "What am I looking at? What's all the noise?" I backed up and explained why it was so freakin' cool, but he wasn't buying it.

Phil wasn't exactly a convert, either, but he liked the motor noise, likening it to "a steam calliope." If you've not had the privilege of hearing stepper-motor tunes, it's possible to imagine: The motors change speed in jumps, not smoothly, so you get the effect of notes after notes in cadence. They change speed once each frame, "Da-de-do-de-doo!" In a complex move with lots of motors, it sounds like soulless chords on a mighty Wurlitzer pipe organ.

CHAPTER 17

Lost World Teaser

Shortly after the pizza spot, I found Tom Scherman crumpling and stretching out large pieces of industrial aluminum foil. What he was doing promised to be a very exciting job for us dinosaur freaks. Tom had discovered that a TV network was considering making *The Lost World* as a TV movie. Phil happily let Tom use the studio to make a teaser with the hope of winning the effects contract for Coast.

Because you're reading this book, you probably know about Sir Arthur Conan Doyle's classic story of dinosaurs found on an isolated plateau in South America. At that point, it had been filmed twice already. Tom was diving into miniature set-making, using heavy crumpled foil to simulate the rocky walls of the plateau. Staple it onto the wooden frame, hit it with spray glue, toss a little sawdust at it, and paint it a rocky color—looks just like fractured slate.

Tom's talent and imagination were cooking. I was pleased that he was already hoping to enlist me and Laine. I would have paid *him* to get the job.

Tom wanted to make a wide shot of a dinosaur walking near a plateau edge. It was pretty but not very attention grabbing. We agreeably came up with something more ambitious.

Open on a jungle scene, with a carnivorous dino catching a small mammal as the camera wanders away, slowly approaching Tom's cliff. We'd see a brontosaurus menacing two explorers on a fallen log, bridging to another promontory, just like in the book. This could be a super-cool show-off shot, the kind I got into the biz for!

The boss reminded us that we were here to make money on commercials, and this joyride was secondary. That would lengthen the project, maybe to the better.

I got fired up over a fancy moco move idea: The set and creatures were going to be in two scales, the first part about three times bigger than the distant view, so why not scale the movement to fit the big and small sets? I rigged up an animation table on a moco track so it could add to the camera move going by the bigger-scale set.

When Tom had to peel off for another job, I had a great time dressing the set with jungle foliage. It felt like following in O'Brien's assistants' footsteps. Staying in those footsteps, Johnny D and I filmed two of Coast's best, acting the roles of the cowering explorers in silhouette. We would project the explorers on a card on the fallen log as a separate pass.

Harry Walton would combine them in his optical printer. Harry was a multitalented stop-motion animator who also did opticals at Coast. This was getting complicated, but it was fun!

Laine and I ended up sharing the animation. He did the tricky part. Then, he left me to do the distant brontosaurus while he stepped away to work on a commercial. It all came together looking great!

That is what I call "the pure experience," where everybody gets to contribute, find creative satisfaction, and even learn something. But even a lesser situation, like my next assignment, can be a learning opportunity. That's why I still appreciate it!

Definitely Checked It

Since the first live-action moco spot, I'd become capable enough to take on one by myself, but that didn't mean I knew it all. There are more skills in play on a shoot than just running the machinery.

A new assignment was simple from my point of view: Program a pan–tilt–zoom move starting close on an actor, then swing to a wider frame. It would reveal a point where we'd add an animated logo next to him.

The evening before filming the actor, I rigorously tested the rig and programmed the move. Somehow, I managed to drive the zoom lens just a little past its end stop, twisting it slightly in its mount. No problem. I twisted it back to what felt about right. If it wasn't perfect, I'd refocus for the actor.

On shoot day, everything was ready to go, and we could shoot take after take without delay. The only slowdown factor was the actor flubbing his lines. I was sympathetic, having made a fool of myself making impromptu announcements back at KZAZ. At one point, I told the assistant director, "He can blow one more take, and I'll have to reload." Unfortunately, the actor heard that, and I'm sure it rattled him even more. He registered it by giving me the stink eye.

The next day, we had dailies in a regular screening room, and all hands were present, including the clients. As the takes ran by, we noticed the image going soft during the camera move and then sharpening at the end of it. It wasn't motion blur; it was something going on in the lens. How strange. I knew damn well what was going on but didn't offer details.

The director of photography turned to me with a steely glare and asked, "Of course, you checked the lens at the rental house, *didn't you?*"

It wasn't really a question.

I'd been in random thought: *Wow, that flange-focal distance is really critical in a zoom lens. This DP has shot a lot of famous movies, and I'm letting him down. They can't fire me until after the job is done. How much would a reshoot cost? There's a lot of people here who want me to blame it on the rental house. I should just tell 'em I screwed up. Wouldn't the actor be glad if I did?*

Considering all that, my response came with the greatest of ease.

"Yeah, definitely checked it."

The uncomfortable exchange over, we silently made a gentlemen's agreement that it didn't look so bad. People chimed in, willing it to be true.

"Can't hardly see it unless you're staring at it."

"Looks just like motion blur."

Anyone who might've seen otherwise knew better than to open his or her pie hole now.

So, I'd learned something about lying. I wasn't proud of telling them what they wanted to hear, but I recognized the value of considered use of that technique in this imperfect business.

Playing Doubles

Our next live-action spot could be a more sensitive situation, because the talent wasn't a seasoned actor but the tennis star Chris Evert. She'd probably be nervous, and there wouldn't be a chance for retakes or a dialogue-dubbing session. It really had to go smoothly.

But first, we had to win the job. Studios were bidding around town, and we needed something extra to win. Joe Rayner asked if we could shoot a test of the trick. Evert was to be seen playing doubles, with herself on both sides of the net.

We had to pan, tilt, zoom, and rack focus to follow the action. That would greatly increase the complexity, timing, and coordination compared with a locked-off shot. I was enthused by the challenge and secretly glad to shoot a test for my own self-confidence.

Johnny D and I would set up in the outdoor stage area. The idea was to shoot a split screen in-camera, with the same moco camera move on each pass. After a lot of timing and rehearsing, I had the move programmed, and John had left- and right-side mattes cut to tape on the matte box. We put two Barbies whacking the tennis ball on the same piece of film by winding the film back and reshooting. It worked surprisingly well, with the Barbies in perfect coordination, and it won us the contract. Joe was very appreciative, and we high-fived.

We would have to silence those lovely stepper-motor sounds, as Evert had lines to speak in close-up. The simple solution was to make a massive sound blimp that would encompass the camera and the Worrall head. The first trial was still noisy, so we lined the box with lead sheeting. That worked pretty well, but in terms of weight, the setup was a big, fat pig.

When we got set up at the tennis court, the director of photography nixed the glass window in the blimp, because it could catch reflections we'd never see until dailies, plus it had a slight green cast. I'd have the same concern about reflections if somebody dropped such a clunky thing in front of me.

Ultimately, we nixed the blimp, which was fine by me, as I couldn't see what the rig was doing in the box—not a safe situation. We hung a lot of stage blankets around the camera to dampen the motor noise.

Moco was getting unpopular in live action, because it upset the conventional workflow. The assistant cameraman seemed dismayed when I hooked up the focus ring to a stepper motor. "Well, I guess you don't need me to pull focus anymore." I explained that it had to be the exact same move each time, starting and stopping on the same frames. He was a good sport about it and sighted in the lens positions for me.

The director, by comparison, was a pain. "Hey, how long does it take for you to reset?"

I'd need about 20 seconds to be ready for another take.

"Oh, God, get Chrissy out of this nightmare!"

Was that sucking up to the star or just being a whiner?

I ended up being the guy calling "Action," because he didn't want to hold the small stepper motor I'd programmed to vibrate, cuing him to trigger the scene. He might have liked it.

The actual shoot was smooth sailing. We shot pretty much like the test procedure, only with much better preparation and without having to wind the film back. Evert was a good sport, too, and got into the process with ease; she could adjust her timing in small increments and duplicate her performance, take after take. My main concern was that when she moved to the other side of the net, the timing of Chris-2's return would be out of sync with Chris-1's serve. With the camera move, we couldn't slip sync if it was off, but, apparently, world-class tennis players have some baked-in expertise in the physics of tennis balls, finesse the rest of us will never possess.

Unlike studio shooting, the lighting crew had to chase the sun throughout the day, although they had some heavy-duty HMI lighting to help out. Also, unlike effects work, we started and wrapped on the same day!

The Army Way

Months went by, and the moco shots kept on coming. The deal was working as planned. At one point, I'd spent the weekend doing what I had to do after a wishful estimate didn't fill the bill. The following Monday, I was still drained, and I overheard the bosses grumbling in the conference room:

"He doesn't ask for permission; he just comes in alone and does whatever he wants."

"It's like in the army: There's a right way, there's a wrong way, and there's Pete's way."

"He can work the machine, but he is *not* a real photographer."

Each bleat made my ears feel hot. Instead of making a dramatic entrance and giving them a cocky telling off, I slipped away to write an interesting proposal.

It described a new role I'd been hearing about: technical director. I pointed out that I was actually doing that job and would like to continue serving Coast rather than take other offers. What I wanted was a flat yearly salary, double my current full-time rate. The flat rate would save them from inaccurate estimates. Also, I would be recognized as the guy determining methodology in technical situations. I ended the note by saying I was looking forward to a continued, mutually beneficial relationship. I delivered it after hours, figuring it would either work or end my days at Coast.

Nancy was perfectly calm when she ushered me into her office, saying the company owner wanted to meet with us. Her main counsel was, "Don't try to hold him up." I pictured sticking a six-shooter up his nose. No, that was the wrong concept.

The owner said the same thing. "Don't try to hold me up on this."

I explained the great bargain he was getting in my proposal. He and Nancy were skeptical.

"Think about how you will feel when you're working overtime for no more pay, because I'm gonna hold you to it!"

I had already mulled it over. "Don't worry about me. A deal's a deal, and it was my idea in the first place."

With some more reassurances, they agreed to the deal. Maybe there was a quizzical look at that point, but when time came for shaking hands, the owner wore a relieved smile.

Not a lot changed visibly, but I did feel more autonomous in doing my job and noticed a certain respect from the bosses. Assignments continued to be a welcome variety of high-tech, low-tech, and moonlighting. My next assignment was a chance to work with a very sweet leading lady.

Creating a set.

CHAPTER 18

Getting Sticky

I n grocery stores, Mrs. Butterworth is a glass bottle shaped like a grandmotherly cook and full of syrup. But her stop-motion stand-in is made of resin tinted with dark-honey dye. As animation puppets go, she's pretty simple: a few replacement heads for dialogue and some replacement arms and hands. Ball-and-socket joints are sculpted into her neck, shoulders, wrists, and waist. Beeswax held her joints in position; a small amount was placed in the sockets before jamming in the ball ends. She had no legs, of course.

Harry Walton, another animator, lent his single-frame background projector to the commercial. The machine had quite a pedigree; Harry Cunningham had built it in 1949 specifically for filming *Mighty Joe Young*.

A live-action crew had filmed background shots of a little kid talking to Mrs. Butterworth, and I loaded those cuts into the projector. The biggest part of the job was preparation. Several tests for color balance between background and foreground animation and reducing the projector screen hot spot, plus lighting the puppet to match the live-action lighting, took two or three days. Mrs. B's heads had a lot of dye in them, requiring bouncing light into a small mirror behind her head so you could see her facial features. As she moved her head, the mirror had to be animated as well.

The animation turned out to be a snap. With her limited capabilities, especially no walking, it went pretty quick. I noted that those heads had painted-on blue eyes, not a great match with the syrup color. The agency guy explained with some amusing insider info: There was another talking syrup bottle out there, fomenting the same kind of jealousy that goes on between two actresses who show up to the party wearing the same dress: Aunt Jemima. Neither company wanted to be on the same shelf in stores, and just to make sure the distinction was clear, Mrs. B would have blue eyes.

Repurposing History

About the time I was using the projector Harry Cunningham built, I found another of his creations under glass at Birns & Sawyer's. It was a pin-registered film movement removed from a Cunningham Combat Camera, smaller than my hand. A movement is the assembly of gears, cams, pull-down claws, and register pins that move the film into place for each exposure.

I couldn't let it languish there. This shiny work of industrial art was calling to my inner gearhead. Five hundred dollars would be a bargain for the heart of a tiny 35 mm effects camera, something I figured I could build around it.

A little history: The Cunningham Combat Camera was made in World War II to film handheld news footage in combat situations. The design was not popular among news cameramen, because it looked like a weapon. Yes, some unlucky journalists were shot by mistake.

I came home with the little gem and started sketching a body to house the movement. The plan was to make the camera as light and as small as possible so we could mount it on really small moco rigs, maybe just on a wooden two-by-four.

I went a little overboard, making it mostly of magnesium, lighter than aluminum. That was more trouble and cost than it was worth. The design was just big enough to contain 100 feet of film, about the size and shape of a squared-off Bolex. When I finally projected a test shot, I could see a very steady image thanks to Harry Cunningham's efforts some 40 years earlier.

That didn't make it finished. The complete package came later, with a video tap and a lightweight moco pan–tilt–roll head. The whole package weighed 7 pounds.

Were it a little sooner, I would have used the camera on the next spot. We really needed a camera that didn't get in the way.

The Dad Factor

Dole Cherry Juice was a new product, looking for a splashy introduction. The storyboards called for a series of blown-glass shapes (full of cherry juice) to change shape in sync with the dialogue track.

There were no computer graphics then, so the transformations were designed as dissolves between similar-looking profiles of different objects. For example, a flat-disk lollipop rotates from the skinny aspect to the round view. As that happens, a dumbbell shape dissolves over the lollipop.

The props were to be in motion, along with the camera, throughout the spot. The boards were necessarily sketchy, as there was only so much a board artist could envision. We would devise the details of rigging and camerawork, interpreting the boards as best we could.

Our little stage crew was headed by the uniquely talented director of photography Alex Funke. Chuck Miller was the prop guy; I'd be the moco guy, and both of us would handle rigging.

We brainstormed the "how" aspects of the assignment for several days while setting up the normal stuff. Alex finally broke our paralysis by bringing a 45-foot roll of white film leader and a marker. He rolled it out on the floor and marked each transition accurately, and there lay a tangible way of breaking it all down. It also reminded us that it was finite. Alex is very good at finding the way out of a morass.

Tongue in cheek, I rejoiced that "All we need is something that long, but with pictures."

A shot like this would normally be run through several times before shooting for real. We started out that way, but it didn't take long to realize we would be dismantling the set as we moved forward and would never hit the same marks. You know: chaos theory. Serendipity would be watching over us. And, indeed, the first few gags fell together. I'd program the camera and the glass prop to move into a position for transition.

When we had shot that, I glued a jig around the (for example) glass lollipop, removed the lollipop, and fitted the (for example) glass dumbbell into the jig. This position dictated how I'd make the dumbbell moco rig. From there, I could continue programming up to the next changeover. Weeks went by, and we were going later and later into the night, to the point that we'd drive home watching the sun rise.

All that time, I didn't make a mistake programming the motion control—until I did. It was a simple "go to home position" instead of "go to frame 312." The glass prop plunged into the set, and I yanked the power cable just before the lens would've been shorn off. Alex was very calm and said we'd call it a night, even though it was already morning.

It didn't take much to get back in the groove, but entropy had set into us and into the set itself. We were reduced to crawling on hands and knees under the kitchen set, scooping up juice-soaked sawdust while the rest of the world slept.

Chuck had worked with "crazy kids," where he recognized and defined the "Dad Factor." Having an authority figure on-site allows others to release their sense of responsibility. This job was ripe for the Dad Factor. Chuck and I became goofier, as it appeared that we would never be free of this cursed commercial. Alex was there, half a generation more mature, so why not act like morons?

Finally, even Alex found his breaking point. We saw it coming. It was 2 a.m., and Alex was hemmed in by grip stands, trying to make a small lighting adjustment. His normally amiable expression slowly degraded into something more diabolical. With what appeared to be his last vestige of rationality, he decided which grip stand would be the least damaging to throw. He threw it a satisfying distance, and the clatter it made on impact was superb. Chuck and I looked at each other and instantly became responsible adults again.

I threw up this silly-looking rig to make sandwich fixin's magically fall into position. The client wanted the bread to bounce slowly; that had us shooting at double or triple speed.

The spindly rig made it through the shoot. Yes! This job was quick, fun, and painless!

20:22

Jack Returns to the Gate

Ray Gilberti and Chris Peterson had a minor challenge in lighting for rosy dawn, with all those charcoal-gray cobblestones and gate walls to cheer up. Our instincts failed us; this light and that color gel would make it the gates of heaven. All we could get was a lukewarm mud. Ray, the trouper, doggedly chased down the magic solution, trying everything. He got it on the third day and was a hero.

Perhaps more interesting, this scene has Overstuffed Mum trying to keep her little blind boy in check by jerking on his leash. This got the biggest laugh in dailies and has to be the most cringeworthy, least politically correct shot in the movie. Once *Nightmare* was in theaters, I heard two middle-age women gleefully cackling at the shot, noting that "This is really wicked!"

Nightmare set.

CHAPTER 19

Graduation

My buddies at KZAZ-TV always said it was a great place to learn, but you had to decide when to graduate. It hit me while I was animating a talking-toilet barking orders at a platoon of talking toilets that I had done a lot of that kind of stuff in the last five or six years. Would there be some kind of a notice that I'd hit my quota?

Maybe this was a sign. I'd been incredibly lucky to get such an education among such great mentors and coworkers. Now I wanted to bring it all together in high-end feature work. But how could I make the move?

Things slowed down at Coast, just when a couple of freelance armature jobs came my way. In late 1985, the creature maker/special-effects-makeup artist Rob Bottin phoned with a mysterious assignment. I recognized his name. He'd done all that over-the-top, nightmarish creature stuff in John Carpenter's *The Thing*.

Rob came to my house with a half-scale human figure made of fiberglass. He wanted me to cut it up and fit armature joints throughout so it could be posed. He needed to be able to lock off the joints to support heavy modeling clay. It was some kind of design maquette—but for what? This job would proceed on a need-to-know basis, and I didn't need that info.

Rob was one of those guys I'd like to work with again, amiable and appreciative.

On the heels of Rob's mystery project came Randy Cook, who needed a regular stop-motion armature. Not as big as the maquette, but at 2 feet, about as big as an armature ought to grow. Randy had taken on a lot of work as an effects designer and supervisor; he had also animated a multi-tentacled monster for *The Gate*.

While I was midway through making the monster's innards, I heard that ILM was looking for camera operators. I couldn't see why George Lucas's visual-effects company had to look for people to work there. They must have reams of applications from all over the world. Could it be that most of the talent was in Los Angeles and didn't want to relocate to the San Francisco Bay area? Whatever the reason, I needed about 10 seconds to decide that this opportunity was the best I could wish for. Of course I'd throw my hat in the ring!

It's hard to believe now, but very few people had personal computers then, and I was among the computer-less. It would have been so helpful to make a résumé at home, away from prying eyes at work. Instead, I sat down at home and began scribbling one, intending to go looking for a typist for hire.

While I was scribbling, the phone rang, and there was Rose Duignan from ILM. She was asking if I'd be interested in interviewing for a camera-operator job. I quickly turned down the TV and told her I was writing a résumé for her. During our very agreeable conversation, I glanced at the TV and saw something odd about the space shuttle. After the call, I found out what that twisted contrail was. Yes, the *Challenger*, January 28, 1986.

I didn't know it at the time, but Harry Walton had been working at ILM and had dropped my name. I'm still grateful.

Processing Words

The typist I found had an amazing new device called a word processor. She was entirely happy to herd my paragraphs around every which way until that résumé looked impossibly, perfectly laid out in a way I never could have accomplished with a typewriter.

Printing was another wonder; you could actually change the font by swapping "daisy wheels," spinning disks with all the characters on the perimeter, smacked against the paper at just the right moment. She was proud of her up-to-the-minute machine, which would soon be regarded as something from Jules Verne's era.

I was determined to give ILM a good show and prepped some visuals for the interview. An editor buddy at work helped a lot, cutting a reel for me after hours. Having access to all the work I'd done at Coast was crucial. All those production stills I had been shooting since the beginning became the basis of a portfolio. I figured all those behind-the-scenes photos would prove I was from the same stock as my interviewer.

A Stressful Interview

In February, I played hooky to fly north for a day trip, plenty anxious, intent on making the grade. As it happened, the "interviewer" turned out to be all of the company's legendary effects supervisors; they were seated on one side of a long table, and I was on the other side. Rose sat by me and ran the proceedings. I was glad to have her there. Just one of those guys would have been intimidating enough, but there must have been a dozen ready to test my worthiness.

We started with the reel. I'd prepped it to be entertaining, cut rhythmically along with energetic music, but they turned the sound off to concentrate on the images. As it ran, I looked at my work with a more critical eye and felt my humble offerings must look like kid's stuff compared to the wonders they'd created. But nobody indicated that. My own intense desire for this job was doing a number on my head.

The portfolio was big enough that everyone could see most of the photos, which were mainly 8 x 10, without passing it around. (That's a tip I learned when a guy came to Coast with a bunch of slides and a magnifying glass. It didn't work well at all.) There were plenty of questions about the stills, and I volunteered comments when nobody asked a question I'd wanted to answer.

"How long did that shot take?"

"Why did you do it that way?"

"How do you expose a blue screen?"

We were getting into the gearhead realm.

I happened to glance at Dennis Muren and saw a smile and unwavering eye contact. Maybe this was going okay.

One guy had remained silent: Ken Ralston. He seemed preoccupied, as though he wasn't interested in technical stuff. All of a sudden, he grinned. "*I've* got a question for you: What is Ray Harryhausen's best monster?"

Stop-mo freaks tend to pose that question everywhere, and there are two universally recognized contenders. I tendered my answer. "It's the Cyclops—the first one."

Ken said resolutely, "You're hired," then got up and left.

Not that Ken had sway over everyone else. Such arcane knowledge doesn't make one worthy of a job at ILM, but at least it seemed to put the "one of us" question to bed.

The questions were running out, and the meeting was coming to an end. I scanned everyone seated across from me and left them with a heartfelt statement.

"We may or may not meet again, so I thank you for all you've done to make visual effects as good as they are now. Most of us in effects owe our jobs to the renaissance you created." Or something less polished.

A few days later, alone one night in Coast, I laid an envelope on Nancy's desk.

Transition

Writing a letter of resignation was both easy and hard. I really liked my bosses and my coworkers. Many of us had been hired around the same time, and six years of bonding like war buddies had created an extended family. It was easy to say nice things because I felt it. Writing the note was hard for the same reason: I would miss my buddies.

Nancy called me to her office. Why was I leaving? Was there something they could change to keep me? No, nothing was wrong. She asked whether I could tell her the name of my new employer, and when I answered, "ILM," her optimistic expression faded. No contest there.

Phil invited me to lunch at one of his favorite spots. We must've been there for two hours, going over the jam-packed years we'd worked together. Phil had brought up many of the guys I was about to work for. He had stories about them, too. Into his third martini, Phil waxed philosophical and sentimental, proud of his protégés.

I'd been nursing a wimpy white wine all through lunch, and Phil growled, "You're *not* a drinking man, are you?" No, I just ordered another glass for fellowship.

Phil let on that he was about to retire, which opened up a career's worth of amusing stories. Here's one:

Everyone shot commercials in black and white in 1950s New York, because nobody had a color TV. But one spot cost so much to produce they shot it in color anyway, figuring it would still be playing when color came along. The commercial's cost? Seven hundred dollars.

After a warm handshake, we walked to our separate vehicles. Phil headed home early. I sat in my truck for a while, waiting for the buzz from that extra wine to dissipate.

At the end of my last day, Johnny D unveiled a going-away video. It featured the crew saying goodbye in their individual ways, some serious, some humorous.

Johnny dressed up as my mom and sat in a rocking chair, reminiscing about how odd her son was. Dave Sharp was quick and deadpan. "Are you going to San Francisco? Be sure to wear a flower in your hair."

CHAPTER 20

Lucas Land

A Galaxy 400 Miles Away

It was only an eight-hour drive to the Golden Gate Bridge, but my first crossing of that graceful span promised adventure in a new world! ILM used a nearby motel to house newcomers. After checking in, I test-drove my commute to the studio. No *way* was I going to show up late on my first day.

Next morning, I was introduced to Pat Sweeney, another effects cameraman from LA. As some had anticipated, work for people in my category had failed to materialize, so I wasn't needed at present. Not to worry, I could learn the ropes as Pat's assistant; that was a better way to start, anyway. ILM was an entity unto itself, with procedures and technology I'd never seen in Hollywood. Pat was an expat from LA, like me, with several years at ILM and a wry sense of humor. He'd steer me straight.

Upon entering Pat's stage, my eyes homed in on a legendary contraption: the Dykstraflex, original shooter of X-wings, TIE fighters, and the like in all three *Star Wars* episodes. I'd been ogling photos of it for years, and this moment was like bumping into a movie star.

"Wow! Are we going to shoot with that?"

We certainly were, along with a lesser-known rig named the Nikonflex.

Pat's stage was long and narrow, dominated by a 60-foot track for the "D-Flex." At one end were a blue screen and a model rotator. It must've been purposely laid out years ago for all those spaceships zipping to and from camera. The other end was filled with a 1:12 scale Brooklyn brown-stone neighborhood. Model makers and scenic painters were still adding their finishing touches.

"What're the buildings for?"

Pat said, "They're gonna be Howard's POV falling into one of those windows."

"Who's Howard?"

"He's a duck."

"Howard the Duck, like in the comic book? That's a great idea!"

Pat wasn't so sure. The underground comics weren't exactly scripted in the same irreverent vein. I didn't care; this was going to be a full-on intro-duction to how the top dogs did effects!

A fellow assistant, Ray Gilberti, coached me in loading the D-Flex. Ray had appeared from behind a long, black curtain that divided the building into two adjacent, skinny stages. He and cameraman Sel Eddy made up a two-man crew, as Pat and I were going to be.

Now, about loading that D-Flex. It was done in the most awkward orientation possible: camera hanging from above, the door facing the floor. With flashlight in mouth, you'd crane your neck straight up, fiddling a 100-foot spool of film onto a spindle pointing straight down. While you were lacing up the film in the sprockets and register pins, the film could easily spiral off the spool and onto the floor. After a few such mishaps, I got the hang of it.

Why the advanced yoga poses? Gearing up to shoot *Star Wars*, they had wisely chosen to film all those effects in a large format, VistaVision, to minimize enlarged grain crawling from optical compositing. VistaVision used regular 35 mm film, but it ran sideways through the camera, not ver-tically. Result: more than double the real estate for each frame, just what the doctor ordered.

That made perfect sense. But, like every other Tondreau disciple from LA, I asked the same question: "Why can't we just roll the camera over 90 degrees to load it?"

Tondreau's key-framed position curves were created mathematically, whereas the ILM Motion Master was essentially a recording device, stor-ing incremental motor speeds, not positions. Without position data, you couldn't tell a motor directly where to go.

Over the next weeks, we shot various objects flying in space. The camera did the actual flying up and down the track, so the objects remained in their lighting setups.

Howard the Duck needed some asteroids for the opening scene. I was directed to a prop vault, where I immediately recognized several 'roids in a range of sizes, some as large as a cantaloupe—definitely from *The Empire Strikes Back*. Not as cool as the D-Flex, but still a magic moment.

After finishing up with the 'roids, we hosted three live animators, Phil Tippett, Tom St. Amand, and Harry Walton. Each came in for a day to animate the same monster, a very twisted version of an Alaskan king crab.

Pat had created three similar moves to make the crabby "Dark Overlords" fall away from camera into oblivion. Basically, we'd do the falling, and the animators would deliver the flailing. The idea of using three animators was to get a different performance for each monster. The guys were seasoned pros; each walked in on his appointed day and started flailing—no testing, no rehearsals, no gauges.

Spending lunches with a realtor and hunting for an affordable rental yielded nothing but a lot of overpriced offerings. In dismay, I asked her to look for something I could buy for the same money. The next day, we visited a modest home, and I was immediately fine with it.

That was too easy for the realtor. "Pete, you can't just look at one. Let me show you a few more." We had different priorities; she had some respectable realtor thing going on, and I just wanted to close a deal so I could concentrate on making movies. The next house looked fine, too. I went back to the first house, for good form. "Vivian, this is the one I'm going with."

Great! Now I could get back to filming a talking duck that flies through space.

The ILM Way

All over the studio, I saw evidence of systematic thinking that led to efficiency and high quality. Cranking out hundreds of shots required things to go smoothly.

The first thing you'd see past the front desk would be sequence storyboards up and down the main hall, each shot broken down into lists: models, artwork, crew, and gear—all the separate film elements needed.

On stage, we used backlit blue screens, a huge time saver compared with the beauty passes and matte passes we'd done at Coast. The optical department knew what a blue screen negative had to read under the densitometer. We were expected to keep the blue screens evenly lit to a couple of tenths f-stop in variance. Sometimes we actually did it.

We always shot a quick black-and-white move test, and I could walk into the optical department and develop the film while Pat was tweaking things on stage. Then I'd sandwich the test film and the background film into one of the custom-made VistaVision viewers. So cool! They must've been pricey to make, because they were made around pin-registered VistaVision camera movements. It was worth it; we could instantly show our supervisor how the elements would look like when put together in an optical printer.

After shooting the real thing, we assistants had to can it up for the color lab in San Francisco. I'd fill out paperwork for the lab, but in-house, we assistants were typing electronic "camera reports," surely the first time ever.

The next day, the screening room was filled with everyone working on the shots. It wasn't once or twice through the Moviola, and it wasn't hoodwinking the client to save a reshoot. The projectionist ran one shot back and forth dozens of times while the supervisor wielded a device that was a dim precursor of a laser pointer. Everyone heard and saw everything—tests, first takes, slop opticals, and, best of all, "finals," meaning finished shots that were ready to cut into the movie. Finals usually got applause.

If there was any weak spot in the dailies procedure, it was overscrutinizing details. Unrestricted, it could lead to things like reshooting a night-sky background so three stars would "line up." Overall, I was thoroughly impressed. All that stuff added up to days saved on shepherding a shot in progress.

The Tondreau system and Motion Master were philosophically divided in a left brain–right brain view on how to create motion. The Motion Master's method was "high touch," with hand-operated speed controls. I didn't like this in terms of efficiency and hated it because of innate boredom. So what was it like to work with?

The first day on the job, I'd heard Ray mysteriously counting out loud from the other stage, "Ten. Twenty. Thirty," over and over for hours. He was calling out frame numbers to Sel as part of the process.

Soon, I was doing the same. Pat stood squinting into the D-Flex view-finder, with a remote speed-control knob in hand. I sat at the Motion Master console, a custom-built array of push buttons and glowing red LED alphanumeric displays. Assign a track to the speed-control knob, start recording, and call out frame counts.

Counting was a subtle form of torture. Your concentration required you to stay on count, which was just above autonomic. But, somehow, you were left no room to safely think about anything else, at least in *my* frontal lobe!

Pat ramps up the track motor, moving toward an asteroid 60 feet away. As he gets closer, he slowly reduces speed, going very slowly as he goes by the 'roid. Then he stops, and I stop recording.

Now we'll work on the pan axis. To get back to the start point, I play back the recorded track data in reverse. Playing the track forward, Pat walks with the camera, this time controlling the pan motor while I call out frames. Pat's speed adjustments are continuously recorded. Eventually, we've recorded all axes on the fly, including focus, model pitch, roll, and yaw. I'm ready to remove the viewfinder and load up to shoot a test or the real shot.

That's essentially how the pioneers (my new bosses!) shot effects on the *Star Wars* trilogy. Perfect for on-the-edge, exciting aerobatics. It was brilliant in 1977 but frustrating to us newbies in 1986. Expectations and capabilities had increased many times over in LA, while ILM's isolated evolution veered off like marsupials did in the world of mammals.

Trekking with Whales

Without a skipped beat, we were done with ducks and moving on to a *Star Trek* movie. This would be the fourth movie in the series, *Star Trek: The Voyage Home*. Our immediate boss was Ken Ralston, and Ken's boss was Leonard Nimoy.

Pat and I remained with the D-Flex, shooting spaceships. I got another brush-with-greatness thrill when the model crew brought the *Enterprise* on stage. Quite a beauty, around 7 feet long, glimmering with numerous miniature lights outside and in. It was originally built for the first film and had a few parsecs on the log.

Doug Trumbull's company, Future General, first filmed the ship detailed all over in overlapping squares of pearlescent paint. Trumbull could film the reflective surface by using beauty and matte passes. It was very pretty then, but the $10,000 paint job had been knocked way down with dulling spray! ILM had used glowing blue screens on the later *Trek* films, and that would've reflected all over those shiny surfaces.

We planted the ship midway beside the track for a flyby shot. The D-Flex ran the full track length, panning all the way, keeping the ship in frame. One other item moved: the blue screen. We had a larger stage crew than usual that day, and they muscled the heavy blue screen around on furniture dollies as we shot.

Pat stayed with the camera, making sure the screen stayed behind the ship. That shot ended up being cut into three pieces, reportedly intended to get three shots for the price of one.

While we filmed other *Trek* models, Ray visited us, flashing a big grin. He was having a great time wearing scuba gear, filming robotic whales in a swimming pool. And for this he was getting paid?

As the show's deadline loomed, Pat and I were split into two units, which gave me a chance to fly some spaceships on my own. Thanks to Pat's tutelage, the transition was smooth, and I was happy to be back as pilot in command.

I got wind of an impending need for a frame-filling view of the sun's roiling surface. Hmm, that sounded familiar. I told Ken about Phil Kellison's sun effect back on *Airplane II* and showed him the clip. Ken made his decision then and there: "You've found the solution." At that, he strode out of the room, calling back to me, "Go see the model guys and do it!"

I admired Ken's quick response—no search for alternatives, no cud-chewing about imperfections, just judgment and experience. He wasn't the only supervisor with those qualities, as I was about to find out.

Innerspace

Forrest Leathers had a great figure of speech: "Grinning like a jackass eating briars." Looking in the men's room mirror, I saw just such a grin—and why not? Dennis Muren had just invited me to lunch! Whether social or business, it would be great to spend an hour with him.

We were barely acquainted, so this was getting-to-know-you time. We exchanged stories about Coast and our shared mentor, Phil Kellison, among others. Dennis had a picture coming up, and he was set on a goal that seemed yet to be fulfilled at ILM. "We're going to do something new: We're gonna bring this in on budget."

The film featured a test pilot in a submarine shrunken down to microscopic scale and injected into a person. No, it wasn't *Fantastic Voyage II*. If anything, that film was going to be our example of what *not* to do in effects.

The film was *Innerspace*. Dennis had in mind three or four camera crews shooting live-action inserts and moco submarines and a lead crew filming set pieces in various water tanks. Dennis wanted me to run the tank unit, a great compliment and upward opportunity, maybe a life changer.

The sane response would have been to gratefully accept, but I felt my long-sought desire about to be sidelined. I'd worked on such crews, where we'd rig up an effect and shoot take after take, hoping for Lady Luck to make it go right. Deep down, my nature was *design, control, and execute*. Stop-mo and moco reeked of it.

I flashed on bypassing that optical-printer job in 1979, which had worked out for the best. I decided to follow that lesson and keep my aim steady.

Dennis was a smart guy. He pointed out the considerable gain of taking his offer, but he totally got my take on it, and he put me in one of his moco slots for *Innerspace*.

The lead job went to a fellow newcomer, John Fante. I was lucky to be teamed with assistant Bob Hill and gaffer Brad Jerrell. They had worked at ILM for years, and their knowledge of the ropes would be invaluable—doubly so, as this was my first go at running a crew. We first met in a detached stage building, where we'd begin shooting some interiors.

Dennis had run me through the stomach battle scene with storyboards depicting shrunken good guy and bad guy duking it out, in danger of falling into the hero's stomach. We were going for an establishing shot located in the back of Martin Short's throat.

I was excited about the scene and briefed Bob and Brad with an art-direction painting of a throat, a huge pink cavern lit like a cathedral. ILM's creature shop had made a beautiful foam-rubber set just for that shot. I struggled more than I should have lighting that first setup. The concept was clear, right down to the "holy light" where the battle begins. Too much worry about making the ILM grade made for too much fiddling and too many tries. The third time in dailies, Dennis accepted it, but he didn't sound pleased. "Okay, we blew it. We're out of time; we gotta move on."

With several similar sets on the way, I sorely wanted to conjure up a quicker, more efficient game plan. I decided to stay late that evening to get a different handle on the lighting. First, I dropped those diagrams full of spot-meter readings. That stuff can be a lifesaver, but it can also be a crutch, addictive if you let it become so. Better to understand the look viscerally and lighten up. Use the Force.

That evening, I was simply training my eye to own the look. I'd do it the same way I'd assimilated the look of *King Kong* some 20 years earlier: staring at stills in *Famous Monsters* magazine. This time I was comparing my test clips against the set as it stood, still lit. How did the contrast differ, the glints, the shadow values? There's a translation between reality and what film delivers, and you can learn that difference.

I went home feeling better prepared, glad to have done the exercise. It worked well in the proceeding setups, well enough that I could light by eye, concentrating on the established feeling of the scene. But no matter what, I always verified with meter checks on two or three spots. It's too easy to drift further with each setup if you don't have a benchmark.

Something called *methyl cellulose* played an important part in the look, too. The viscous compound looked like clear mucous, perfect for slathering on our organic sets. The stuff was commonly used for slimy effects makeup. It worked great at adding a wet look to our giant throat sets, and we had some fun with it, setting a glob to ooze over the ledge leading to the esophagus.

Although it sounds like a noxious chemical, methyl cellulose isn't dangerous. We eat it all the time; the processed-cellulose thickener is common in milkshakes and hot dogs, not to mention its use in treating constipation.

The flesh sets were always in some kind of motion, mostly puppeteers or creature-shop artists performing loosely choreographed twisting and heaving in a manner we surmised guts would do. Some performances evoked the sensual, and Fante would call out in dailies, "I wanna work on Pete's crew!"

My father happened to be visiting from faraway Michigan on the day we did our big peristalsis shot. You know, swallowing, as done by circular muscles around your esophagus. A doctor by trade, Dad was intrigued with our ungainly 10-foot-long rubber gullet. Several stagehands held it with their encircling arms. As the camera was looking down the tunnel, the guys bear-hugged the esophagus in quick sequence. Our first take surprised Dad into weeping, howling laughter. On successive takes, he had a great time playing technical advisor, still chuckling.

Harley Jessup, the effects art director, was cruising a grocery store's produce aisle, looking for useable organic shapes. He scored with green onions; the bulbous ends looked great as cilia, the tiny protrusions that round up dirt and push it out of our lungs. Clever!

We got an assignment to pinch-hit for Fante and work out the details of making cilia move underwater. The creature shop delivered a foam-rubber cast of many cilia sticking up some 5 inches high. Once submerged, water logged and artfully motivated with a garden hose, the cilia performed a tribute to "amber waves of grain."

We gave Fante our findings and began on the background, a cavernous lung interior. I loved how the background looked in smoke: ethereal, soft beams from distant windpipes. It got a murmur of appreciation in dailies, but I had to tone it down to make it look like it belonged in the same movie.

We were changing over to a moco stage, banished to night crew because we'd be shooting lighting effects in smoke that would permeate the whole building. Ned Gorman, the visual-effects manager, would meet with me at the storyboard wall to pick our evening's assignment, mostly featuring a model submarine against Fante's water-tank sets.

Before Dennis went home, we squeezed in evening dailies, a briefing on the next shot, and a review of last night's move tests. Like Ken Ralston, Dennis could make a fast go/no-go decision about a shot. Harley came up with a way to make fat cells by cooling lemon Jell-O in balloons. He'd pop the balloons and load up Fante's water tank with dozens of weightless, yellow blobs. One day, I gave him two test moves of the submersible bobbling among those fat cells, then powering up and speeding away. I'd learned that he liked large differences in versions like this and gave him just that.

"Ooh, that one's perfect. Shoot it just like it is, and shred the other one."

Calls like that made the job go smoother and boosted everyone's confidence. I filed that away for some unknown future. One of my favorite moments took place making a POV shot zooming through a syringe needle and into a miasma of capillaries and cells. We had company that night, Tony Hudson from the creature shop.

The plan was to build the set on stage in many layers and back the camera away several inches at a time while Tony incrementally created another layer of his organic stuff. Then we'd film the move forward, dismembering Tony's creations as the lens passed through them. We worked through the night, Tony maintaining himself with cans of Jolt. And this was just a shakedown test.

The next evening in dailies, Dennis stared silently at the test as it ran back and forth. I couldn't wait.

"Whatd'ya think?"

"Give me a minute. We might have it here."

Nobody made a sound. Damn, did I jinx it with my big mouth? Tony, a stranger among us nocturnals, looked like he could use some sleep, not another all-nighter.

Dennis resolved, "Yeah, this'll work fine."

One intrepid guy who wasn't on my crew elected to join us on night shift: John Knoll, yet another recent hire. He said he could navigate quicker between his downshooter and the film-test developer at night, blazing down the empty hallway on his skateboard.

We became friends, as we were both Tondreau boosters and from Michigan. John was slick with his Apple computer; he'd programmed it to draw two intersecting spheres. The now-ancient machine took all night to render the single image. Who knew? Maybe someday he'd conjure up something more practical.

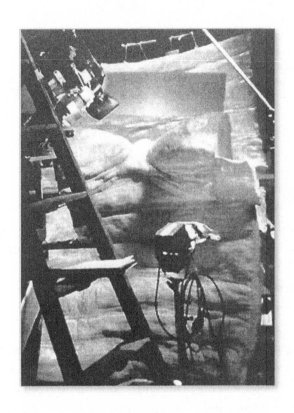

CHAPTER 21

The Butterfly Effect

R ose Duignan didn't choose who to hire and who to layoff, but she was the one to give the news, good or bad.

"You're seen as not the quickest cameraman, which is a concern," she said. "The studio is trying to streamline to be more competitive. We have too many people now, and you're among the ones not likely to get first call."

Sorta direct, but mercifully soft-pedaling, I thought.

"You seem to be good at stop-motion. You really should call Phil Tippett. He's starting a stop-motion studio in Berkeley."

Nuts. I had passionately wanted to be part of the greatest effects house in history. Now stuck up here with a mortgage, I'd take what I could get.

I liked to think I had my plans under control, firmly in my own hands. But sometimes a wild card sneaks in and nudges us in another direction. That leads to another wild card and another and so on.

John Knoll was needed back at ILM right when he was in the middle of a moco job at Colossal Pictures, a Coast-like operation in San Francisco. Could I pinch-hit as moco operator on a Doughboy spot? Sure. I didn't really want to get involved with another commercial house, but I had time to help out a buddy. But without the recent upset of my precious plans, I'd have passed on it.

This job turned out to be a bigger deal than my Doughboy experience in LA: several setups shooting at the same time, several animators doing much more elaborate animation, live-action setups, and a reputable director of photography from LA.

My job was mostly helping animators with camera issues; they were young, fresh from the *Gumby* movie. In fact, they were young enough to tolerate broiling under large, hot lights more suited for live action. I'd worked with several DPs who only knew how to expose for 24 fps. Speaking in subdued tones, I'd translated to animation speed for them. This time I couldn't cool things down for these animators, but just giving my sympathy was enough to bond with them.

Eventually, I worked with the director, using Colossal's imposing moco rig. He wanted to make some kind of interesting camera move, but he was not sure how to go about it.

"So," he asked me, "what can it do?"

"Well, it's made for moving all around in three-dimensional space. The works are separated into three degrees of freedom." (Sometimes I still lapse into science-teacher mode.) I started jogging motors. "We can go up and down, side to side, forward and backward. Rotation is the same; the camera can pitch, roll, and yaw, like an airplane." I jogged tilt, roll, and pan.

"That's pretty much what we've got to work with. Program the right combinations of all six, and we can do just about anything."

Breaking down the contraption into a few elements must've resonated with him. "Say that again, what you just said."

I got more realistic. "Let's say you wanted to start close on the Doughboy at eye level, like this." I jogged into such a frame. "And maybe you'd want to curve up and around into a medium shot to see him against the muffins, like this. That's your A and B positions. It takes some tweaking to make it look nice, but you don't have to do that. Tell me what you want to see, and I'll make it work."

It was time to turn on the creative juices. We spent an hour sketching in several moves, having a great time at it. After the job wrapped, I heard that the director had done mostly cel animation at Disney. Cartoons? That's not my style! He was a nice guy, but there was a slim-to-none chance of working again with this Mr. Henry Selick.

Moco to the People!

"Did I just see that thing go straight to a frame position, not running through the move?"

The timbre of Mike McAlister's voice suggested he might have seen a minor engineering miracle. Mike just happened to walk in on my personal project, hooking up the D-Flex to a Tondreau system.

You might wonder why I bothered, given that my term at ILM was circling the drain. Mix a little optimism with a pinch of denial, and add to that a drive to see it through. I wasn't dead yet.

I was eager to get Tondreau's system on the stages and figured if I could demonstrate it, all would see the light. Bill was willing to come up from LA to make sure it went well, and he brought his new, more powerful motor circuitry.

Anytime I could get a few camera people into a demo, the first surprise was how fast the D-Flex could go—scary fast! It seemed to be more unnerving than pleasing.

The main event, keyframing, was even less well received. It was still seen as too mathematical to make arty moves.

Bill went back home, built an ILM-style joystick, and coded a joystick module into his system. He was always writing special functions on request. Maybe this one would gain acceptance among the camera crew.

It didn't. We had a meeting, and reactions were predictably polarized. I recognized some territory being stepped on, as well as concerns about learning a new skill. But nobody spoke of the obvious: Knowing how to work the Motion Master guaranteed job security at ILM and made it hard for anyone else to get in. It wasn't going to happen, and I could easily sympathize. ILM was effectively the only job option in town. Camerawork was already competitive in this fragile ecosystem; nobody wanted more bodies showing up.

If I really wanted to work with Bill's system, I still could. The demo showed that. For two or three paychecks, I could add a Tondreau system to my kit, along with the light meters and ditty bag.

Can you believe that an XT clone computer cost over $700 in 1987 dollars? Ka-chunking along at 4.7 megahertz, with a miserly 640 kilobytes of memory, it was still capable of running a dozen moco axes at 24 fps. Bill supplied his special circuit board, software, and jogbox for $1,500. And there it was, my own system.

Suddenly, moco was democratized; anyone with a job could afford it. It grew quickly, from ILM's lone proprietary setup in 1977 to dozens, soon to be hundreds, in just 10 years.

Bytes and Pieces

That moco demonstration was probably what got me a chance to spend some time with the Pixar guys. They needed someone to test an Iconix linear scanning camera. As I understood it, they had only their in-house-built laser scanner to digitize film. Maybe this off-the-shelf device could be the heart of Pixar's subordinate film scanner.

Cobbling together a test bed was simple enough. I rigged the camera to look into a projector movement. Scott Squires knew where to find widgets like that. Scott and Dennis had initialed the experiment. The rest of the job was finding what the Iconix camera could do.

I needed help learning the digital ropes. Lincoln Hu, George Joblove, and several others were generous with their expertise. Sometimes, the guys came by just to welcome the fish-out-of-water cameraman. Unix was an easy jump from the Tondreau system command lines, and the fledgling "windows" feature seemed like magic, like having several computers at the same time.

My test camera was interesting, too. It captured one line of a picture at a time as a small motor advanced the linear sensor a tiny bit after each capture. A weird way to take a picture; the process in itself took some time.

Why didn't we just use a normal digital camera with a full image sensor? This was 1986; such cameras were still in development! It would be 10 or more years before we'd see one.

The rest of the setup was slow as well, limited by the tech of the time. I'd capture frames one by one to an IBM PC/AT computer, and I found I could squeeze just a few frames on the hard drive. Nonetheless, I managed to show Dennis a low-resolution 16-frame clip of a man taking a single step. The concept was good, but in order for this to be practical, we had a need for speed. One more click of Moore's Law ought to have taken care of that!

Lincoln said he was glad to have someone from the main building; it was a rarity. The founding fathers of Pixar were isolated in the building next door, just far enough removed that only a few knew what the small cadre was doing. Much like ILM in 1975, these guys were about to make VFX history, tinkering in the nascent stages of digital compositing.

To date, their most remarkable CG was the "stained-glass-man" effects for *Young Sherlock Holmes*. They'd also erased some wires holding Howard the Duck that had bedeviled the optical team; I think this was the first instance of digital rig removal. And they had extracted better blue screen mattes than the optical printers could but left the rest of the compositing work to the optical department.

One setup grabbed me in particular: the pairing of an Evans and Sutherland vector display with a six-dimensional magnetic tracker. In a nutshell, you could move a wand around and see the wand's moving POV, flying through geometric shapes that were only visible on the display. Somehow, I thought, this ought to dovetail with motion control—something for another day.

Like many pioneers, some programmers bore injuries from their efforts—carpal tunnel syndrome, of course, and some nasty headaches, seemingly from the vector display.

Expecting no more than a couple weeks of button pushing, I came away with a glimpse of the future!

Jack Inspires at the Town Meeting

Among several interesting background buildings, a big moon, and six stragglers, Town Hall still stood out, barely. It was the biggest, and its columns pointed to the front door. Our intent was to lead the eye straight to the open door.

Dave Hanks made sure the columns were brighter than the other buildings, and we had some light spilling out the door. I just didn't feel the pull of the door. We inched up that light several times, but not enough. Finally, I over-escalated, calling for "the gates of hell," and this was the ticket! If this was a lesson in lighting, it would say "start with a broad range."

Sel Eddy and Cameron Noble pinch-hit, looking way up at the moon and buildings. We couldn't get all that stuff up there, so they laid the set down and shot.

Inside the hall, my stint was all about Jack talking and singing on the theater stage with conventional lighting: a single spotlight, a curtain warmer, and footlights, plus a practical Christmas tree. But down in the loges, where the motley crowd sat, lighting and camera was less orderly and much more fun. That's when I passed it to Rich Lehmann. We added orange light from wall sconces while the loges footlights threw up green and crimson—just because we needed it to make Jack really scary!

I have to give it to Paul Barry: He knew how to animate molten wax. You'll see the Melting Man dripping through several shots, flawless despite the crazy-making procedure. Paul reposed the puppet on a frame and then fired up his miniature alcohol torch. Gently coaxing the wax with his flame and letting gravity do its part, Paul melted the beeswax head just enough for each frame. A mistake would have been very hard to repair!

When we see Jack's POV as he wades into the crowd, we're looking through that lightweight camera born in my Van Nuys garage. It was time. The pint-size camera needed a matching pint-size moco rig to live on. Two weekends in the shop yielded a Frankenstein of a track-swing-boom rig made of half wood and half aluminum. It was nothing to look at, but it was compact. Ray noted the high-pitched noise from the motors and dubbed it "The Screamer."

Henry was grateful. With it, he could add a few moving-camera shots. Phil also thanked me but said, "Please don't do this again." Both of us knew camera moves took time.

Paul Berry animating on *The Nightmare Before Christmas.*

Paul Berry animating on the set of *Nightmare.*

CHAPTER 22

What's Waldo?

Happily, I was still getting sporadic jobs, and that appeared to be the foreseeable future. John Knoll, working as a new effects supervisor, offered a week or two on *Hudson Hawk*. The assignment was moco-flying a DaVinci flying machine. I was impressed. John did great as a boss right out of the gate.

Then Bruce Nicholson paired me up with David Allen for a few stop-mo/moco shots on *Batteries Not Included*. The times we'd worked together at Coast carried forward, and we got right back into a familiar work mode. When Dave's stuff was done, Bruce had some moco-only flying saucers to shoot.

Looking at another indeterminate dry spell, I was glad ILM allowed employees to use the facilities. I had wanted to try changing out those speed-control knobs on the D-Flex pan-and-tilt axes and replace them with a pan-and-tilt stick, like on a regular tripod. Move the stick, and the D-Flex head would mimic your movements. Wouldn't that feel more connected, sorta like Pixar's magnetic tracker? It wasn't a new idea. Years earlier, ILM, Bill Tondreau, and others had made similar devices for recording live-action camera moves.

After a few days in the machine shop with a pair of digital encoders, I had an odd-looking prototype. Unlike real tripod arms, the shape was more of a dumbbell, pivoting at the center. It had almost no friction; the operator had inertia to push against. The mass at each end would smooth out the operator's twitching hand movements.

Camera engineer Mike MacKenzie showed me how to wire up the encoders to plug into the Motion Master, and the first trial went great. The D-Flex panned and tilted exactly as my hand moved the gizmo. Cool! The D-Flex moved like it was haunted, reminding me of Robert Heinlein's story where a guy named Waldo has gloves that control large, robotic hands.

When the euphoria fizzled away, I found the device was harder to use than expected. Mounted on a stationary stand, it was easy and natural to operate, but when I was walking along, eye to the viewfinder, with the gizmo clamped to the D-Flex boom, it was very hard to move smoothly. As long as the white elephant was there, I'd try it on another kind of motion control.

If you're reading this, there's a good chance you know what *go-motion* is. Just in case you don't, it was an ILM process of preanimating puppets, moved by motion control. Its value was twofold: The performance could be tested and refined, and playing back the program while the camera ran, you'd get a natural motion blur on film instead of the staccato-sharp look of stop-motion.

I wondered if my gizmo could streamline the preanimating. At present it was being done one axis at a time, frame by frame, with a single knob. Turn the knob, the brontosaurus head goes up a little bit. Punch a button to save that position. Turn the knob a little more, and the head goes up a little more. Punch. That's two increments on one axis. Repeat for each axis of each limb and the head.

We're talking about a robotic rod puppet with up to 24 separate axes to program. How many frames, with how many knob turns, in the whole shot? How many versions before we have the take we're going to actually shoot? Wouldn't it be nice if you could just grab some rig, flail it around, and record that head performing in real time? How much time and animator's blood would that save?

That was the beginning of my pitch to Phil Tippett and Dennis Muren. I'd hooked up a two-axis linear slide to the wrist of a creature used in *The Golden Child*. Phil and Dennis played around with my prototype, mostly making the creature describe circles in the air. They immediately understood its potential.

I proposed we expand to a four-axis version, maybe dual-rigs, so the animator could animate two legs at a time, each in XYZ space, plus rotation.

Coincidentally, Phil had a challenging go-motion job looming on the horizon, and he and Rose Duignan got my proposal okayed largely because of that deadline. Better yet, Phil offered me work on that looming job!

Prototyping a four-axis design was trickier than a simple pan-tilt stick, but not too tricky. A different shape, more like a Luxo lamp, and fluid dampening were the main design changes.

Bill Tondreau had already replaced the original Dragon Master (ILM's in-house go-motion system) with a similar system, knobs and all, plus many new features. It would be a snap for him to include support to my input device, but Bill just couldn't spare the time.

Instead, ILM assigned a very capable software engineer who'd actually worked on the Motion Master and Dragon Master systems. To help out, Bill sent his source code and documentation, the key to modifying the new system.

Progress was painfully slow on that part of the project. Several fruitless check-ins went by, and I suspected foot dragging. The ILM software engineer volunteered that he had a conflict of interest; he wanted to make a new system, not embellish the competition's.

I felt like a sucker, a vulnerable sucker. He could drop the ball anytime and did, leaving me with no plan B. Telling Phil the bad news revealed his resilience. He laughed and said we'd just have to do the show with what we already had.

Phil and the Eborsisk

"You camera guys think you're the flyboys, but on *my* show, the *animators* are top dog!"

Phil Tippett's animator-centric pecking order made sense to me. Typically, ILM crews on the ubiquitous "falling men" shots spent most of the day lighting and programming the moco track. Animators were called in later in the day and directed to make the puppet "just flail around."

In Phil's perfect scenario, each animator would be working with a cameraman and an assistant, a dedicated team. The assistant would collaborate with the animator from go-motion programming to shooting, reminding him about upcoming moves and even punching the shoot button.

So, two teams moved into the building across the road where we'd started on *Innerspace* to make about 35 shots of a two-headed dragon for *Willow*. I joined animator Tom St. Amand and assistant Dave Hanks, while Harry Walton did his own lighting and animating with assistant Jo Carson. Harry's move was largely to escape the noise back at "The Joint," as Tom called ILM. (He just liked to speak in the style of old gangster movies.)

Phil had made two dragons around Tom's armatures. "Dragon" wasn't really the correct name; it was the "Eborsisk," a reference to the popular film critics Roger Ebert and Gene Siskel. (I've always thought the name was a compliment, but I've since learned it was the opposite.)

We spent several days rigging 24 small moco track axis sliders from below, from the side, and from an overhead pipe grid. Rods ran from sliders to feet, body, and heads. Those would be preprogrammed, but smaller parts like the mouth and eyes would be stop-mo animated. Two more moco channels would run pan and tilt; those were all I programmed, matching camera moves in the live-action background footage. Lighting was simple: Match the overcast live action.

Tom had a heavier load, so much so that I went looking for something else to do while he was animating. Across the room, I set up a rotoscope tracking rig with my Tondreau system, tracking fiery-breath footage into dragon mouths. It was a great chance to get to know Phil better.

I perceived Phil, Dennis, and Ken as kindred graduates from Coast FX, with much in common. I noted Phil's cost-consciousness right away: "We're gonna treat that fire footage like the expensive stuff it is and not like they do it at The Joint." He sounded aghast at the budget. I didn't have much to compare it to, but $40k every time we saw the dragon on screen seemed pretty fat.

Phil shared Dennis Muren's "one shot, one thought" maxim about filmmaking: Everyone working on a shot should do his or her thing to advance the story. My niche was mostly about lighting to draw the eye and enhance the drama. Like a football coach, Phil would drill the performance into Tom's head: "The story in *this shot* is 'the monster ate the little man,' so what do we want to see?"

Tom: "We want to see the little man."

Phil: "*What* do we want to see?"

Tom: "We want to see the *little man!*"

In dailies, Phil would speak his piece to each of us, and the whole production got to hear our discourse. Once, he was watching a test of my work, keeping the monster nailed to a moving-camera background. I felt pretty good about this one.

"Like it?" I asked.

Phil said, "Look at his foot."

Admittedly, the foot was sliding out of focus a bit, way down in frame.

I blurted out, "Look at his head," presuming that explained everything. I didn't expect to bring on laughter around the room.

Way up in frame, the monster head held a little man in his mouth. The different distortion patterns between our lens and the live-action lens had forced me to pick the most important spot to track. Phil got it, no problem. Still, embarrassing the boss isn't much of a career move.

Our little sequence was a fraction of the effects work in *Willow*, and the optical department was getting overwhelmed. We were making every shot against blue screen, but it wasn't actually necessary. We could invoke St. Harryhausen's rear-projection "Dynamation" technique for many of the shots. Phil offered, and the optical crew accepted.

All of a sudden, I was learning the fine details of my childhood hero's signature camera trick. Phil started me out on blending matte lines with torn scraps of black tape on glass, pretty close to the Introvision system. Harry Walton coached me on balancing rear screen background and rubber monster in front by squinting. It works better than using a light meter!

I came to like RP (rear projection) setups more than blue screen; it's craftier, and you can see small lighting differences right there on stage. The background screen can be used to double expose in special effects—in this case, dragon breath.

"You're not a camera operator; you're a picture maker!" Phil's compliment referred to juicing up several shots by lighting up the dragon with its own fiery breath. That moment still makes me smile.

Best of all, RP shots are completed when you shoot the last frame. There's a sense of authorship you can't get when a dozen other people are going to tweak it after you.

What you can't do with RP is make significant camera moves. That background plate fills your frame at a precise distance, perpendicular to the screen. Long exposure times are another fact of life in RP. The only way to keep a frame safe from sizzling in the projector gate while you animate is to keep the projection bulb dim. That demands a long exposure time.

Our final shot on *Willow* was a very wide shot with the dragon small in frame, making it the dimmest setup on the show. Tom had another challenge in this shot: waiting on 48-second exposures! It cramps the animator's momentum. You can forget what you're doing with all those heads and legs and little men.

Pitying Tom and Dave, I set things up so they could start animating first thing in the morning. They would finish in the evening, and I'd start double exposing the lower background split, flame breath, atmospheric smoke, and so on. Dawn was breaking when I laid the film can on the lab courier's desk. I drove home tired but happy.

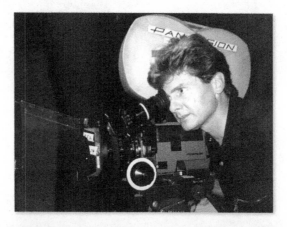

Pete the cameraman.

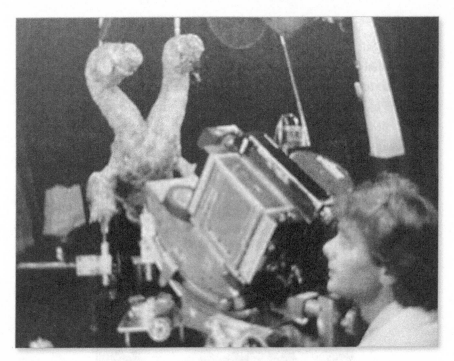

Pete on *Willow*.

Pete on *Willow*.

CHAPTER 23

In Limbo

It appeared that working locally was going to be a luxury I couldn't depend on. The Eborsisk job was a generous two-month bonanza, not business as usual. Short gigs were drifting my way from Los Angeles, and I needed to diversify among them and local jobs. Maybe that would turn out to be a plus in addition to paying the bills.

Bruce Nicholson was my next boss at ILM, and the job was a Japanese TV spot. It was comfort food for a stop-mo/moco cameraman. Flower petals were revealed to be a group of dragonflies that takes flight. It was an elegant idea, classically Japanese.

The agency group was profoundly mannerly compared to some I'd worked with at Coast. They sat all day, silently watching me program dragonfly puppets. There was no verbal communication, just smiles now and then. Finally, I ran a rough move test in real time, and they startled me by breaking out in applause.

A few days later, I was in North Hollywood at Praxis, Rob Blalack's effects house. Rob had done well for himself since winning an Oscar for *Star Wars*. He kept it in his office, positioned so that the client would see it just past Rob's head.

I once got to see Oscar's intimidating presence at work. Two agency guys were unsure about a creative issue. Rob made a suggestion and got vetoed by both. Rob reiterated that it really was the way to go. After some squirming, one guy caved. "See that statue? He must know what he's doing, ya know?" And so it was decided.

I was there to shoot a big, beautiful, model city. A Texas bank wanted to bask in the glow of Lone Star State pride. This ought to do it; the fictitious city featured all of Texas's iconic buildings, from the Alamo to Houston's steel-and-glass skyscrapers. As the camera swooped around the city, lighting would constantly change from night (lit up by hundreds of windows) to a pink-and-gold desert dawn.

Before I'd signed on, someone had rigged a 10K light on motorized cables so we could see shadows creep across the set as the sun rose. The key light's placement wasn't optimal, nor was the moco track, but the money had been spent, and I would soldier on.

The next day, my first day of actual work, I showed up with a nasty muscle pull in my back, making me useless for physical work. The gaffer reassured me. "Don't worry, I'm older'n you, and my back's not that good, either. Let the kids do the heavy lifting." The "kids" were a couple of stage-hands in their early twenties, if that. Years later, one became a top-notch moco operator.

There's not much opportunity to polish people skills while running an optical printer, but Rob had developed his own unique stage presence. It wasn't based on yelling, although he had a compelling baritone voice. It was more about things like the alliterative nickname he coined for me, "Mister Mojo Man." I liked that.

And, he could put you off-balance with a simple Jedi mind trick.

Me: "Hey, Rob, I think we should shoot the matte pass first."

Jedi trick: "What are you telling me?"

Me: "Uh, I just think the matte pass goes first. . . . Or not."

The "truth and beauty" camera move was easy to program. Predictably, details like automated lighting, moving colored gels, and tiny moco'd cars took more of our time.

Homecoming

As we were all patting ourselves on the back for a real purty-lookin' spot, Nancy at Coast FX called with a Doughboy job. Homecoming, that's what it felt like: smiles and hugs all around. Johnny D had already lit the dairy case set. All I had to do was twist a performance out of the "dog boy" (a pet name from David Allen).

As long as I was there, they had another request: Put together another Tondreau system. Now that Bill had made his system fit into a PC, it was easy. With the shop available, I could make them a motor driver box to go with the system. Now I could go back home. Or not.

Sudden Boss

Rob Blalack had another gig: Alex Funke was shooting a spot for some TV manufacturer, and I'd run the moco. It was a cruise for me until Alex was called away for another project. Suddenly, I was the boss!

Unsure of how the crew would take it, I asked Alex to give his crew a thumbs-up for me. No problem. He drew his guys together and introduced me, then passed the torch, telling them to work for me as they did for him. The guy was and is a consummate gentleman.

Besides that moment, my strongest memory of that job was seeing *Director of Photography* by my name on a call sheet for the first time.

The Sting

Okay, now I could go home.

Phil Tippett's studio in Berkeley was compact, shall we say, but it had enough room for a couple setups for *Honey, I Shrunk the Kids*. Joe Johnston needed a few pickups for his ant versus scorpion sequence.

Harry Walton and Tom St. Amand had finished all but one of the shots boarded, but Joe found some gaps where new shots would make the scene flow better. Harry was gone, but Tom was going to carry on.

We started on the last originally boarded shot, a wide establishing shot. Tom had to animate the scorpion among layers of 3-foot-tall model blades of grass, with bridal tulle for atmosphere. Lotsa legs on that scorpion! That, plus the obstacles, made this the first time Tom or I had worked on a two-day stop-motion shot. It was an extra big deal for Tom, who slaved over it.

After that, Joe got into pickup mode. He'd run the Moviola down to a pair of shots and tell us exactly what he needed to patch the gap between them.

"Let's have an ant POV looking up at the stinger. It's about to come done on him. Make it quiver, scary, dangerous . . . Two seconds, then it comes down at us."

We could usually start and finish on the same day. The next morning, Joe typically took one look on the Moviola and told us it was exactly what he needed. What a lift!

Close to the last day of shooting, I hung up the phone and told Tom I was going to Simi Valley. I didn't know much about the job, some underwater adventure thing. It would be just a couple moco shots.

"The girl says, 'We can't pay your lodging, but you'll be doing so much overtime you won't miss that little bit.'"

Tom rolled his eyes. There was more.

"I ask her, 'Who's gonna bring me up to speed on the shots?' She says, 'The guy you're replacing.'"

Dry for Wet

"Are you the new guy?"

That's me!

"They shouldn't have hired you. The last guy was fine."

Dave Stewart was known as a curmudgeonly effects DP, and this was just his way of welcoming me to Dream Quest Images, run by the unstoppable Hoyt Yeatman and his talented associates. They were creating effects for James Cameron's undersea adventure, *The Abyss*.

To his credit, "the last guy" ran me through his formidable moco setup like a gentleman. He only showed distress at the end, when I asked if I could call him about details.

"No, I've given enough help already, considering."

I could respect that.

My job was to run a camera through a 25-foot tunnel full of twists and turns, creating the hero's POV as he is sucked into a huge alien waterway at the bottom of the sea.

I was just a bit player, but this short assignment sticks in my memory as something special. It was a perfect storm of personalities, challenges, and daring innovation. The number one challenge for me was moco programming. The tunnel had a slit all along the way, just wide enough for a snorkel lens. It was those twists and turns, plus Cameron's specific timing requests *and* the crash-prone relationship between a lens and set that made this very nontrivial.

A Tondreau system was the tried-and-true way to plow through this job, but Dream Quest had built another system. Twenty minutes of practicing with the joystick would make me nothing but a bull in a china shop, but spending Sunday alone with the machine actually helped a lot.

The system was based on key frames. Very good. But why did it have to calculate the in-betweens while shooting and not even save them? I could have used a powerful timing manipulation that depended on that missing data.

Monday morning, I asked the system coder why that crippling feature was there. He said it saved disk space, but it was more of a technowank. I cajoled him to code something so I could quickly respond to Cameron's orders.

Off we went. While I programmed, my gaffer mounted dozens and dozens of 1K broad lights, encircling the tunnel. It would be completely lit from outside, coming in through diffused windows with colored gels taped on. The current needed to run all those lights required a dedicated generator chugging away right outside.

My relations with cranky Dave Stewart were still minimal after more than a week. I invited him to join me for some Chinese at lunch. After we were seated, Dave got up for a trip to the head, mumbling to his navel, "Know what I'm havin': kung pao *beef*."

When he returned, it had magically appeared, and he grunted, "Huh, I didn't think you'd hear me."

That put a new polish on things. Dave was quick to fill me in on the embattled show. The visual effects were projected to finish late, making the show liable to miss its release date. There was tension in all camps, blame flying two ways, and perhaps a lawsuit in the offing.

Sure enough, one day Hoyt came through my stage with several overdressed professional types. While he cheerfully pointed out all the cool stuff we were doing, the lawyers just sniffed around like nervous rats.

Just to slow things down a little more, I noticed a lens element shifting inside the snorkel when I rolled the camera. Not good. Hoyt shared his can-do attitude and encouraged me to disassemble the snorkel and somehow immobilize that piece of glass. I don't recall what I used, maybe a wad of tape, but it worked.

My shots weren't the only challenging ones. Every setup in the building was in some way beyond conventional. Most of the six crews were shooting model submarines, some with tiny projectors inside that were projecting live actors into the front windows. Most notable was a set with three such moco-marionetted one-man submersibles inspecting a 70-foot sunken nuclear submarine. That setup may well be the most ambitious and complicated moco rig to date. In any case, deciding to go that way, everything in-camera, was one of those daring but straightforward solutions.

Except for Alex Funke's underwater rod puppets, we all shot in dense mineral-oil smoke to achieve an underwater look. Huge tarps separated our smoke from our neighbor's smoke. One day, my birthday, the girls from the office showed up with a cake. Very thoughtful. They sang "Happy Birthday" quickly and left, as they weren't wearing fume masks. After they left, we heard our fellow crews singing in an ironic tone across the tarps, voices muffled by their masks.

Scott Campbell, another cameraman, found the smoke useful as a sniper's blind. From across his densely smoked stage came the annoying voice of some production guy: "Campbell, where the hell are you?" Scott lobbed an apple into the gloom and somehow clocked the irritant right in the forehead. After some inspired swearing, the guy left, not sure who'd thrown it.

Cameron didn't have a lot of spare time, but once in a while he'd tell diving stories. My favorite was about the US Navy's emergency submarine escape suit, which equalizes your inner ears at extreme depth. Basically, when the high-pressure seawater rushes into the escape chamber, tiny spring-loaded knives puncture your eardrums. You're deaf and scream all the way to the surface, but you make it!

As we closed in on shoot day, Dave advised me that our gaffer had been badmouthing me upstairs, angling for my job. I really needed him on the final stretch, so I confronted him in a kinda nice way. "Willing to let bygones . . . you're crucial to our success . . . blah-blah." It didn't work. He was apparently bent on being fired, so I honored his wish.

My shoot-time estimate predicted more than 24 straight hours, continuously babysitting the shot. Every five frames or so, we'd have to move lights out of the way, getting access to redress the black shroud sealing out light around the snorkel entrance.

I warned my crew about the upcoming endurance run. Prep *everything*, ready to shoot the first frame. Show up well rested in the morning because we are going to "kick some serious motion-control butt!" One young guy latched onto the phrase, repeating it every chance he got.

Tuesday morning, we loaded the stage with smoke, double-checked everything, and shot the first frame at 9 a.m. as planned. We zealously stuck to our drill, knowing that as the hours rolled on, our oil-smoked, parboiled brains would be less dependable, so just follow the checklist.

Sure enough, on Wednesday at 4 a.m., I noticed a light that wasn't turned back on after a redress. I snapped it back on while the rig was running. We had three frames in the can missing that light, just enough to kill the shot if we couldn't fix it right here, right now. It would have been easy enough to go back three frames, turn off every light and burn in the missing light. That is, it would have been easy if I could remember which light it was, but the five of us couldn't agree on that. We were *that* cooked. I had everyone stand where they were at the snap-on moment and recall what he had seen. We triangulated onto the likeliest candidate, and I verified it by feeling its slightly cooler temperature.

At around 3 p.m. Wednesday, we finished. Dream Quest offered a nearby motel for anyone who didn't feel up to driving home, but nobody took it. The company had good reason to make the offer: Recently, another cameraman had fallen asleep on the way home. He was lucky, getting away with just some marks on his face.

The Abyss is a classic tale of adversity, a lot like the real-life reports from the production. Cameron certainly didn't choose to make a movie about two people talking in a room. He stuck his neck out to make an exceptionally difficult film, and everyone on the show felt it. I'm a big fan of the show and proud to have contributed.

Pete shooting a commercial.

CHAPTER 24

Pete & Phil's Moco Rig

Phil Tippett called with a bite-sized assignment just as I got back home and started to unpack. Great. I liked working with him and got the sense I was becoming part of his small cadre.

The job was to insert a huge ghost into the arch at Washington Square Park for *Ghostbusters 2*. We did it with mirrors, if I may say: The camera looks at a rear-projected background, and a 50/50 mirror adds the stop-motion ghost, set up to the side. It was simple, tricks from nineteenth-century magic shows, and I like that stuff.

You might be able to find the stick-frame that caused an assistant's paroxysm of regret. With your DVD single-frame button, look for a background frame that is repeated. Don't get too snarky. It can happen to anyone!

More in-camera fun was coming up, thanks to John Knoll. A mutual friend, Pat Johnson from LA, had made a low-budget sci-fi called *Spaced Invaders*. Now he needed some effects—for cheap. It had been a long time since John was available for such an assignment, and Pat was lucky to get him as his VFX supervisor. John then hired me, along with Cameron Noble and Eric Swenson. All four of us were VFX cameramen with extra skills, most requiring opposable thumbs.

Upon learning the budget he had to work with, John mandated certain conditions. When he sent them a shot, it meant he had approved it, and they must accept it. It was a one-way honor system. We would strive to do our best, and Pat's producers would simply trust us. You don't see that every day.

We all brought any gear we had and borrowed from a lot of friends, plopping it all down in a rented studio space. Our "make a show in our garage" scenario called for a shot a day, and in-camera was the only option. The challenge inspired plenty of Rube Goldberg solutions. It was mostly spaceships, ships on wires, ships on moco systems, ships in 50/50 mirrors, mirrors on moco systems, projected explosions, squirting milk in a fish tank, and hybrids of all the above. Fun stuff!

The producers came up from LA to check things out. It was all good except for the moon. We had a 10-inch photo of the moon cut out and glued to stiff cardboard. It appeared in several shots, hung against black velvet curtains. The main guy insisted a flat disk couldn't look like a sphere on film. John quickly found that reasoning it out didn't work on this guy. At some point, you just have to tell these types what they want to hear.

One weekend I visited John at home, and he demonstrated the fledgling image-editing system he and his brother had created. I especially liked how one could adjust contrast, which was almost impossible in the photochemical world. I figured it would at least be useful to a niche group, but I thought he could surely do better with the name. What kind of a dorky name was Photoshop?

Outside the studio were frequent reminders of reality—gun pops, mostly. Not the greatest neighborhood. Cameron Noble went out one night to find his windshield broken. He yelled into the night, "Next time bring a gun, mofos!" I reminded him he could easily be obliged. That scared the security guy at the front entrance. He quit shortly thereafter.

At the end, we all agreed the job had been one of the most satisfying in memory. I had been shooting for a while now and wanted to get my hands dirty "makin' stuff," as Tom St. Amand says.

In-Camera Fun and Rigging a Rig

Phil Tippett needed motion control, whether he knew it or not. He had a big show coming up, by far his biggest to date. His 2-foot hand-cranked camera track wasn't going to cut it anymore. I didn't need any such thing, but I wanted to make a well-designed robotic camera crane.

Phil was immediately open to my proposal: I would supply the sweat equity, and Phil would open his studio and machine shop to the project. We would both contribute equal amounts of money, and we'd share in outside rentals.

One change Phil requested was the physical design. I was gung-ho for a D-Flex type, a camera hanging from a long boom, pivoting up and down and swinging sideways on the track carriage. Phil was more interested in a small, floating tabletop with three discrete rails going straight vertical, straight sideways, and straight down the floor track. With that, we could mount a puppet or a camera on the table, doing double duty. Phil was envisioning how to track a puppet into a rear-projected moving background. Harryhausen never quite perfected that trick, and almost all of his work had locked-off camera angles. Phil's idea made sense, as his big show would be mostly puppets in front of projected backgrounds. I was okay with it but knew it would be somewhat clumsy in shooting close on miniature sets.

I mentioned the project to Bill Tondreau, and he immediately gave me 10 floppy disks containing a very early version of AutoCAD. "You really should try it," he counseled. The best thing about it was accuracy; bolt holes always lined up, and cut pieces always fit together. The worst thing was its glacial redraw time; rendering a circle was so slow I could count each pixel as it appeared.

Union Machine Works of Oakland was an old-school shop accustomed to big maritime projects. "Machining since 1885," said the sign. I wondered what the company had seen in both World Wars. These guys (and one woman) were happy to take on what I considered "the big stuff," easily a ton's worth of precision steel track frames, counterweights, and a 30-inch turntable bearing. I handed them my CAD drawings and came back a few days later to pick up the lovely bones of our new moco rig.

I wasn't so fast on the small stuff, spending weeks happily drilling and tapping, wiring, machining, and welding the smaller parts. No hurry. I was into the process as recreation, a labor of love!

One fine day the rig stood there by itself. It was a big Cartesian robot, payload close to 100 pounds. It looked cool, sounded robotic in motion, and gave off the sweet smell of machinery. Of all the rigs I'd kluged together, this was my firstborn.

I wanted to establish it as more of a camera crane than a moving stop-mo animation table. Elsewhere in the Bay Area, the *Gumby* movie had just wrapped and was selling off everything. There, I spied a Worrall geared head, made to make smooth pans and tilts by turning two well-balanced cranks. It was easy to motorize and install in the rig, and it would complete the camera mover. And, it was pretty!

Standing close by was Art Clokey, creator of *Gumby*. I offered him four hundred bucks cash.

He looked angry. "No, that's not near enough!"

Then silence, long enough for me to despair the imminent loss.

He maintained a steely gaze.

"I won't take anything under four hundred and *fifty* dollars!"

He was an older guy but seemed to have all his marbles. Was he just having a little sport at my expense? I heard later that Clokey was pretty good at messing with heads.

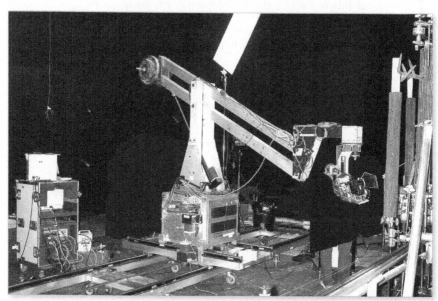

Mr. Lifto moco rig.

25:21

Jack Visits Dr. Finklestein

Featuring the same habitat as "Sally Makes Soup," here the mood was of fellowship as the doctor lends his tools to Jack. With daylight climbing up the stairwell, Jim Aupperle's early-morning shadows had a different atmosphere, in a good way. Warming up the color and aiming the sunlight as it came from the floor made way for more friendly-looking shadows. It worked great, especially as the camera glides over the top banister to reveal Jack, far down in a sunbeam.

The following shot taught us what happens when men spend too much time in small, dark animation stages. When the shot of Sally's legs dangling from her bed came up in dailies, there was a unanimous masculine growl, "Whoa!"

Kathleen laughed. "You guys really have to get out more!"

CHAPTER 25

RoboCop 2!

Tinkering on the new rig could've gone on until I starved, but Phil eventually popped my bubble of creative bliss with a new challenge.

"Hey, Pete, don't you think it's time to get paid for something again?"

Hard to deny. The rig was essentially done, and I could use the dough. Plus, a little variety would be welcome. Some esprit de corps wouldn't hurt, either.

I'd known for some time that Phil was taking on a sequel to *RoboCop*. The original *RoboCop* was a show I'd like to have worked on, but I was having a great time on *Innerspace* during that period.

Wait a minute, I *did* work on *RoboCop*. Well, a little. Remember Rob Bottin's secret project, the half-scale human armature? Belatedly, I learned that was used to design RoboCop's original robosuit; with director Paul Verhoeven's approval of the clay maquette, Bottin and company could move forward and fabricate the real suit.

RoboCop 2 had a different director, Irvin Kershner. Irvin promised plenty of roboviolence, a new nasty robonemesis, and countless rounds of bullets piercing the air. Craig Hayes's design for the new bad bot was a masterpiece. The puppets were just fun to look at!

Shooting *RoboCop 2* effects was going to be Harryhausen heaven for those of us who liked working with stop-mo puppets in front of rear-projected backgrounds. In predigital 1989, Harryhausen's RP trick was cost effective and could deliver good results. To handle the volume of work,

Phil was planning to have six or eight RP setups running, plus a handful of miniature sets, matte paintings, and a lone blue screen setup. This scale was way beyond St. Harryhausen's one-man-band production model: more people, more puppets, and more hard-to-find equipment. We had a lot to get ready for shoot day #1.

My first move was to play hooky. Phil wanted motion-reference film of real industrial robots. Right down the street lived such a robot, wielding a plasma cutter, cutting away excess "flash" from rough castings. The single arm, articulated like a giant human arm, impressed me with its grace and precision and its lethal speed and strength. I'd never seen a movie moco rig that could match that prowess.

I got too close once, and it almost took out my Bolex camera, not to mention my head. Whoosh! The floor was painted like a crosswalk around the machine, and a sign read, "Robot may move without warning. Stay outside of work envelope at all times." The term *work envelope* was amusing, a polite way of describing "the space where it can get at ya and kill ya!"

In addition to the film, I had a simple report for Phil: "These things can do more than an audience would ever believe. Our only concern is looking fake."

I teamed up with electronics expert Steve Raschke on prepping effects lighting. That translated into a lot of puppet-friendly gun flashes, be it ambient flickering or actual flares emitted by a puppet's gun. Steve came up with self-indexing clear Plexiglas disks covered with orange gel and black tape. During animation, we could pump light through the disks and get the look of hundreds of off-screen guns blazing.

Craig Hayes had worked out how to make an on-screen muzzle flash. He cannibalized a photo flash tube, wrapped it with cotton, and stuck it in the puppet's gun. Flash the tube, and there's your muzzle flash.

If only it were that simple. To really do this trick right required a minimum of 13 operations. This is what we were asking of the beleaguered animator for a single-frame muzzle flash:

1. Animate the puppet
2. Shoot a frame
3. Insert flash tube assembly in puppet's gun
4. Roll down a black curtain over background screen

5. Slide in camera diffusion

6. Turn all lights off

7. Open camera shutter by rolling backward a half frame

8. Pop the flash tube

9. Close camera shutter rolling forward

10. Raise black curtain over background screen

11. Remove camera diffusion filter

12. Remove flash tube assembly from puppet

13. Advance rear projector one frame

Shouldn't that be a job for a computer? How about the Tondreau system? Nope. It had a lot of tricks, but nothing so specific. Somehow, I'd run across an integrated circuit that might handle the job. When you sent it two-letter commands and numbers, it would smoothly control stepping motors, sense buttons, and toggle solid-state relays. The possibilities were exciting. Convert our checklist into a small program, and the whole procedure could be automated. This had "cool" written all over it.

For example, this camera was rigged to slide a diffusion glass in and out as part of the whole routine.

I'd have to learn the C programming language. It wasn't as daunting as I expected; it looked a lot like Fortran, the language I'd fiddled around with in college. The program was extremely simple, no options except for adjusting exposure time. The rest was hard coded, which meant you just pushed the button. The routine did the job. And I had a lot of fun learning a new trick!

During the show, I got requests for various refinements, and each go-around pointed to the value of a more flexible system. What if camera operators could select several canned operations, assembling their own do-it-yourself moco routines? No time for that now, but maybe after the show.

Nick Blake was one of those people you should just hire without a job description, which might not do justice to all the skills they come with. Nick's first assignment was to create an environment that we could shoot in with smoke, include rear-projected backgrounds, and keep movie lights out of the smoke. To Nick, that meant building a Plexiglas smokehouse that was 6 x 8 x 6 feet. That was big enough to contain the puppet stage, camera, smoke generator, animator, and two camerapersons—as long as everyone was close friends. Everything else, lights and projector, was outside.

Aside from the *what* and *how*, you might wonder *why* we needed such a facility. Mostly, Phil wanted blinding headlight beams coming from the bad-guy robot. A smoky atmosphere would make the beams show up.

Phil assigned me and my assistant, Matt White, to shake down the smokehouse with animator Justin Kohn. We set up a traditional Dynamation split screen just outside the Plex window; the evil robot would be sandwiched between a live actor hiding among oil drums in the foreground and the murky background.

We knew the smoke density had to be constant or it would flicker on screen. Steve devised an infrared rig to measure the smoke density, and we hired a young "smoke assistant" to constantly check it and adjust the smoke generator.

The air quality was miserable—reduced oxygen, thick and hot. Justin had learned concentration as part of his martial arts. He could take it, but the "smoke assistant" eventually fell quietly asleep. Justin stayed focused while the smoke level rose over several hours. It was imperceptible to Justin. In dailies, we were treated to a perfectly smooth whiteout over the last few seconds of the shot. I continued to admire Justin's ability to focus.

On a later shot, a 5K light blew up like a shotgun report, with cascading, hot glass shards. Justin came to me and calmly reported we might need a new bulb.

As the show grew, we eventually numbered 17 camera people and nine animators. Phil said no matter what the project, it's who you're working with that makes it a good job or bad, and he had picked winners throughout.

Animator Pete Kleinow came on later to join us in the smokehouse. Everybody liked Pete. Remember him? He was the guy who played pedal steel guitar after hours, a real professional crowd pleaser. On Fridays, Pete finished his shot in time to drive 400 miles down to LA for a music gig.

Once, on a crew lunch, a buxom waitress gave him her phone number. I asked him how he could squeeze that into his double-ended-candle lifestyle.

Pete laughed. "Man does not live by bread alone!"

Eric Leighton was another animator working in smoke, but his smokehouse had a 4 x 4–foot floor and was 8 feet tall. It sounds kind of claustrophobic, but there was a rationale: We needed a number of close shots, and the big smokehouse was overbooked.

We set Eric up with a small XYZ moco rig supporting the top half of a puppet. Like Tom on the Eborsisk, Eric preprogrammed the gross movements, leaving himself only to finesse arms, head, and other details. It sped up animation fast enough that the smoke didn't have time to dissipate.

That's not to say it was healthy for Eric in that smoke, but he did get in a lot of deep knee bends, dropping out of sight with each exposure. I worked with him on several other setups during the show, laying the groundwork for a work friendship.

Every morning, each crew pored over their test wedges. Wedges were series of ascending exposures shot with various color-correction gels in our RP projectors. Homing in on a combination that matches the background color and brightness against the puppet lighting could cost a lot of time. To save a second or third day of testing, I shot more variations, only to hear Phil say, "You didn't shoot the only wedge I need." I didn't take it personally; we were all on the same team, and Phil was feeling the pinch more than any of us.

On *Robo 2* we were lucky we had Harry Walton's optical printer.

Cameraman Bob Costa operated by making special low-contrast background plates. This was to counter the normal contrast increase you get when taking a picture of a picture. Credit to inventing that trick goes to Jim Danforth. It depended on a faint black-and-white negative print sandwiched with the original print. This knocked down the contrast in the bright and dark areas. Clever!

Two things flummoxed Bob Costa. Those black-and-white prints often came back from the lab with a flicker somehow built in. It seemed to be due to insufficiently washing the film. It made everyone crazy: all ready to shoot, but the background plate had to be remade. Someone wrote "fuck the flicker" on the bathroom wall. Bob had been keeping a bottle of Maalox close by, and we'd noticed pink stains around his mouth and on his shirt.

Matt, my assistant, was Bob's other tormentor. I sent Matt to camp in Bob's printer room until he got the background plate we needed. Matt did a good job of adding to the pressure. This may be what prompted Phil to call the camera crew together and tell us to quit leaning on poor Bob. The show got big enough that Phil rented another building nearby, and I took on two more setups off-site while carrying on with smoke shots at home base. I got a second assistant, Greg Dykstra (no relation to the Dykstraflex).

A new cameraman, Paul Gentry, took on the smokehouse. I had no regrets there except losing Matt as an assistant. I had to do it; a seasoned assistant like Matt could help the new guy get up to speed quicker.

The new moco rig got busier as the show progressed, with camera tasks like running down an elevator shaft and filming another blue-screen falling man. More interesting were shots where I used it as Phil's floating animation table, tracking models into moving RP backgrounds. One of my favorites was a live-action RoboCop stuntman being jerked around while hanging on a stop-motion bad-guy robot. The live actor was really hanging on a dangerous hydraulic contraption. I tracked the live action and played it back, running the bad robot's body.

At something like eight months, *RoboCop 2* was my longest project at that point. There was plenty of time to bond with our coworkers, as in this familial scene: Catherine, a camera assistant, brought in her nine-year-old kid, who had been taken out of school for fighting. Catherine asked some of us "father figures" to give junior a little advice. He got plenty of the traditional "be nice; fighting is not the way" stuff. But Dave Hanks's advice came in his Chicago accent: "Lead with your left."

There came a day when Phil called us all together for a shock. "I don't have to look at any more shots you guys do. We're out of time, and whatever you shoot is going into the movie."

The Dad Factor suddenly evaporated. Phil wouldn't be telling us what's good and what's not. Our eyes got big as we felt the weight of another increment of responsibility. Right then I discovered the effect of letting someone "own" his work.

Justin Kohn animating on *Nightmare*.

Pete and Robocop 2.

CHAPTER 26

Setting Things Right

After *Robo 2*, it was time to set a couple things right. That abandoned go-motion input gizmo, the one intended for programming the Eborsisk, still stuck in my head. I wanted to exhume it and finally make it work. Same for that nameless muzzle flash routine for *Robo 2*; I wanted to rewrite it as a sushi menu of simple moco actions. Camera operators would string up any combination of selected actions, making custom moco routines.

With Bill Tondreau's help, it was possible. He'd sent floppy disks labeled "RP4 programming guide" to his acolytes. ("RP4" was Bill's name for his program.) The guide detailed how his software worked internally, and with enough study and experimentation, we could write C-code for his motion-control circuit boards. That was a Rosetta Stone if ever there was one!

My first baby step took a week: getting a computer-mouse to move not a cursor but a pair of stepper motors. It was a crude proof-of-concept model of the Eborsisk gizmo. The moment I got it running, Phil happened by and said, "Hey, you cracked the code!" Several weeks later, it had grown to many axes controlled by several digital encoders and was ready to make shots.

I found this kind of programming addictive. Puzzle over a detail, try something, and sometimes get it right. That's your reward and your encouragement to keep at it!

So, the Eborsisk gizmo was validated, albeit too late, as technology was forging ahead. The sushi menu turned out to be more complex, starting with learning how to write a text editor. I wanted camera operators to be able to write out what they wanted in plain English. Then, they could intersperse special keywords, recognized as commands to execute in order. Just call it a motion-control script.

Version 1.0 had a basic set of keywords, enough to move motors, shoot frames, wind film, wait for a button push, wind backward, turn lights on and off, and sync to a Tondreau move. That was at least enough to cobble a moco-script like the muzzle-flash routine.

Seeking approval from the master, I sent Tondreau a copy, and he came back with a pompously official-looking phony certificate admitting me into the "Mystical and Fraternal Brotherhood of the Practitioners and Purveyors of Motion Control Software." The fine print promised the certificate was redeemable for a Jumbo Slushy at 7-Eleven. (Thanks again, Bill. It's still hanging in a conspicuous place.)

I named my program Koz-Mo and offered it to some of my fellow RP4 operators. Only a few were interested; there just wasn't much call for doing in-camera effects with stop-mo in concert with motion control. Besides, Bill had just released the Kuper System, which effectively rendered his own RP4 obsolete.

Oh, well, it was an interesting exercise. Who knew, maybe I'd need that capability someday.

Slow Bob

Phil had just the solution for getting Koz-Mo out of my head: working on his personal stop-motion film, *Mad God*. Eric Leighton joined me and a few others in crafting Phil's dystopian fantasy world. We created some horrific moments, such as an ape strapped on a dissection table, begging for deliverance from model maker Bill Boes's CoreMaster 9000. Later, we filmed throngs of "Shit People," disposable beings in this world gone mad.

Then Henry Selick, the Doughboy director, reappeared with his own personal project.

"Eric says you can do motion control, and you can light, too. Is that true?"

Thanks to Eric's recommendation, Selick was asking me to shoot his pilot episode for his MTV series, *Slow Bob in the Lower Dimensions*. It could be interesting, a quirky mix of live action and stop-motion, all on a shoestring budget. I wanted to help this guy get all the bang possible for his buck; he was clearly earnest about bringing art to the boob tube. More endearing, his wife, Heather, had given up a kitchen remodel to finance *Slow Bob*.

Conveniently, we set up at Tippett's studio, starting with an attic set where Mark Steger played Slow Bob. Mark had some physically challenging work to do, starting with hanging from the rafters like a bat. Early on, we managed to drop him on his head. It was lucky that Mark was exceptionally resilient; he was in a modern dance duo with his girlfriend, Hannah Sim, who also appeared in the film. Mark carried on as a good sport while we filmed him drinking upside down.

But then he really showed his prowess, curling into a pretzel and holding still while Eric animated stop-mo iguanas scampering around him. Yes, it would've been easier on the actor if we'd filmed him separate from the animation, but Henry couldn't afford the optical. At least, that's what he thought.

Harry Walton had given Henry a real-world quote for *all* the opticals. Henry confided, "I need 'em, but I can't spend that much."

I could help there. "Just offer Harry what you can afford. He will understand; he's one of us."

Henry came back pleased, as Harry had gracefully accepted his offer.

Meanwhile, animators Owen Klatte and Trey Thomas animated cutouts on Henry's self-made multiplane downshooter. He'd boiled down the complexity from the original Disney behemoth, leaving two or three glass planes mounted far enough apart that any size hands could get at the artwork in between.

Besides these guys, I was working with several of Henry's Doughboy crew: set builder Bo Henry, puppet maker Bonita DeCarlo, camera guy Chris Peterson, and others.

In a short time, we were almost ready to strike the attic set. Henry and I were just getting to know each other when we learned a little about each other's hot buttons.

Henry wanted some handheld footage shot with his Mitchell camera. We weren't exactly ahead of the game, and the evening had turned to night.

I was still ready to rally. "I'll just get some rope and two-by-fours and rig up a counterbalance for your camera!" When I was ready to mount the camera, I was informed I had to agree to pay for the damage if the rig harmed Henry's camera.

"We won't be using this rig after all," I announced, throwing the contraption as high and as far as I could.

Henry's tone was conciliatory. "So, what do you want to do?"

I got a little nicer, too. "We're going back on the tripod."

Thus began our brotherly bonds of buddiness phase.

Eric and I jumped into the stop-motion puppet work. The lighting called out to be spooky in a theatrical way, and I had a great time doing just that. Most effects work I'd done didn't offer that kind of latitude, so I reveled in it. Henry was all for going theatrical.

The budget dictated all locked-off shots, but it killed me to see that moco-rig collecting dust. One after the other, almost every shot had a good reason for a camera move. Who was going to stop us? Henry embraced the windfall, adding a layer of polish to his film.

Eric was great to work with while doing motion control; he understood the need to hit his marks, meeting the camera at the appointed places and frames. Shot by shot, we developed a usable procedure for blocking animation in concert with moco.

Kuper system.

Moco rig instructions.

CHAPTER 27

In Halloween Town

Tippett Studio had more than *Slow Bob* in the works at the time. Phil was in an early prep phase for Steven Spielberg's dinosaur movie. Animating the Eborsisk was child's play compared to the go-motion effects Spielberg would expect. I was excited because Phil had spoken to me about a job on the show.

And Henry had another show cooking on-site. While I cranked away on *Slow Bob*, Henry was overseeing Jo Carson, shooting a test for a Disney stop-motion feature. I guessed the suits wanted to see what stop-motion would really look like translated from the 2D concept art. It was certainly far and away from a big-budget dinosaur movie. The main character was a dorky skeleton dressed up in a formal tailcoat, waxing poetic in a florid voice. This was Tim Burton's baby, but Tim would be busy on another film and didn't have the time or patience to oversee a feature-length stop-motion film, so Henry was going to direct.

Phil was bemused by the odd mix.

"We've got that weirdo *Slow Bob* here, man-eating dinosaurs there, and over there are Skeletor and his friends!"

Tough Decision

Shortly after *Slow Bob* was finished, Henry invited me to have lunch with him and Tim Burton. That'd be fun; I liked Tim's recent films, *Batman* and *Edward Scissorhands*. Lunch was pleasant, just comparing notes on people, places, and movies and a little talk about ourselves. I didn't take the casual get-together as a job interview, but it turned out to be.

A few days later, Henry told me Tim had seen *Slow Bob*, and on the slim weight of that, he'd agreed with Henry's recommendation that I be the director of photography on *The Nightmare Before Christmas*.

To be sure, the offer was flattering, but it also caused me some angst. Now there were *two* offers I couldn't refuse, with time for only one. *Jurassic Park* or *The Nightmare Before Christmas*? *Jurassic* was the obvious choice: go-motion dinosaurs, Spielberg, big-picture budget, and a secure job doing what I knew best. *Nightmare* could offer none of that.

But just the *possibility* of shooting a whole movie was both attractive and out of my comfort zone. What was a "stop-motion DP," anyway? I'd have to make it or fake it on the job. Did I really need to shoot more rubber monsters, or was I just holding onto my security blanket?

Nightmare could be a whole new adventure, a serious game change. Sounded kinda good.

Phil chided me, appealing to my Y chromosomes. "C'mon, Pete, do you wanna work on a manly dinosaur movie or a kiddie show?"

T. rex was winning.

I approached Henry, intent on telling him about my uncertainty: "Henry, I gotta talk about your show."

He was busy and didn't look up. "Pete, don't worry, you've got the job."

Somehow, that jostled me out of overanalyzing, and I went with my gut.

It's Something New

Henry had his hands full from the beginning. In addition to his directing duties, he urgently needed to find a producer, specifically a line producer. That's the producer on-site, hands on, day by day. Locals were preferable, because they wouldn't be reporting back to Disney every five minutes—at least that was the theory.

We had only so much time to find a candidate before Disney would install its own selection. As the deadline closed in, Henry threw a Hail Mary: Would Phil Tippett like to produce? The guys were too close a match, both creative alpha males. I pictured Henry and Phil at a Hollywood function, wearing the same outfit. Phil's response was candid: "I'd rather sell shoes."

So we got Kathleen Gavin! First day on, she displayed plenty of stage presence. She'd begun in Chicago theater. She had a couple of Disney cartoons behind her, as well as energy, enthusiasm, and the clout that came with being tight with the Disney execs. That made her uniquely able to champion our causes as needed. I liked Kathleen. She had heart and a laugh as big as any Chicago Bears fan.

Up to this point, we were still in Tippett Studio, and we needed to move into a building where we could make the movie. Some of us department heads met Henry and Kathleen at a building in San Francisco's South of Market district. We toured it and loved it.

The building was an empty film studio! Downstairs had a large set-building shop, a screening room, rooms for editing, several offices, parking, and—my favorite—two shooting stages, with more space than I'd ever seen outside of LA soundstages. I told myself we'd never use all that space.

Halfway up the staircase, someone had painted an old industry phrase: *Above the Line*. As it suggested, the second level was full of offices, two large ones and several smaller ones for storyboarding and production design.

Each of us had the same urgent task: get our departments up and running. Hire crew, purchase what you need, and transform your space into a working facility. Also, stay on budget.

The camera department began as me and the stage manager, Jim Belmessieri, fresh off the *Gumby* movie. Hiring crew was not a pressing issue, as we had nothing to shoot for quite a long time. But we could start gearing up; the shooting stage needed power routed throughout. Mark Musumeci, a local electrician, ran numerous outlets from an industrial power regulator. The behemoth would keep voltage constant while nearby factories put dips and surges on the grid. Without it, we'd see jumps in exposure.

Nightmare's budget was $18 million, slim by comparison to the other animated films in production, so we all had to pinch the nickel. Phil Lofaro, the production manager, was good at that; his New Yawk accent meant business. I needed lenses, lots of 'em. Phil gave Jim and me $5,000 cash, and we spent it all at a camera flea market. Our job was to spend it smartly. Nikon lenses had had a good reputation for effects work since *2001: A Space Odyssey*. Stop them down to between f/8 to f/16, and most will hold their sharpness against expensive cine lenses.

I doubt most of us "below the line" supervisor types had a realistic idea of the scale *Nightmare* would encompass. I certainly didn't. As Eric Leighton and I worked on simple character tests in even simpler sets, it seemed most of the time would be spent animating while the camera crew waited. So far, I hadn't seen any boards or a script. Maybe Chris Peterson and I could swap shifts, setting up for animators. It seemed we'd even have time to do commercials in between. That proposal proved Henry had bigger plans. "Get with it, Pete! We're making a *movie!*"

Using what I knew from *Robo 2*, I projected a shoot of six or eight setups tended by two camera units, possibly three. One of those units would consist of me and Chris.

Jim got $70,000 to cover lighting, which about fit with my projection. Working in 1/8 scale allowed us to use the smallest (and cheapest) as our mainstay: Mole-Richardson's 200-watt Inkies.

The cameras were preordained: Mitchell Standards. They may have been archaic museum pieces for live action, but they were good enough for animation. Beat up or not, the going rate was $2,000 each.

And so it went. Be thrifty, practical, and resourceful!

There didn't seem to be line item in the budget for motion control, but I felt any contemporary film needed a camera that moved freely. I told Phil just that and described Henry's taste in camerawork on *Slow Bob*. No doubt such an addition would enhance our film, but we couldn't afford it.

Was this one of those DP responsibilities I'd read about? There's something about fighting for the director's vision. I couldn't shout my way to success, already knowing our limitations, but I did have a semi-rational idea.

What if I somehow made it my problem? Wouldn't Phil like that? On weekends, I could "produce" rigs as needed for zero wages. Skellington Productions would only pay for parts and material. And when the show wrapped, the toys would belong to me.

Lofaro liked it, at least in theory. He called in Kathleen like a car dealer bringing in the big boss. Kathleen seemed okay with it but warned me about ways I could get in trouble. I sensed only goodwill, colleagues who were earnest about making this film great.

My plan for moco was manageable. We'd have three small floor tracks and some kind of pan-tilt head. Certainly, some shots would be too elaborate for those simple rigs. Maybe the cheaper solution for just a few show-off shots would be renting the unit I'd created with Tippett. I'd skip my half of the rent in the spirit of our new deal.

What's This?

Throughout the studio, each department was busily prepping away, isolated islands. We hadn't yet coalesced into a company. That wouldn't happen until we had a tangible point of focus to rally us out of the abstract. That was a tall order. We didn't even have a script.

But Henry had a song. The film's composer, Danny Elfman, didn't have a script, either, but he knew there had to be a scene where Jack Skellington discovers Christmas Town, so he wrote and recorded "What's This?"

That got us going; Joe Ranft and his guys churned out storyboards to illustrate the song, which fed production designer Deane Taylor and his assistants. Henry picked one shot out of the 36 shots boarded, shot number WHA-32. That would be the shot we'd begin the movie with.

WHA-32 was a good choice in my opinion—no pussyfooting around with a simple shot. It was a big one, a big exterior set where we'd define the look of Christmas Town. There would be lots of animation, a major camera move, false perspective, and animation effects in-camera. The shot was our shakedown cruise; it would test all systems. Suddenly, everyone had work to do, work that would end up on the screen! There was another reason it was a good pick: The shot called for just one puppet, the only puppet we had.

You probably know the shot: Jack is riding on a train that's puffing out cotton balls. He jumps off, lands on a toboggan, skis down a hill and past houses, runs into a candy-cane arch and falls back into the snow. A busy shot!

The whole archipelago of departments drew closer. We needed each other. Several departments worked shoulder to shoulder on set, politely stepping on each other's feet. It helped us bond as a company.

Chris Peterson and I were searching for a look that would work for the whole sequence. Snow in moonlight was pretty but looked too austere. We needed more of a winter-carnival mood. We tried punching up the houses with warm special lights. Better! Chris suggested adding colored gels to the specials: red on red houses, green on green, spilling onto the nearby snow. Nice!

Christmas lights were prominent in the production-design artwork, and I'd made sure we got those aircraft-instrument lamps we used at Introvision. They had a long life, just what we needed in animation. Festooned on trees and houses, they made all the difference.

The elaborate camera move really needed the rig I'd made with Tippett, but hiring it for the first shot felt a little awkward. It became more so when I had to replace a burned-out driver. I had a tangle of wires spilling out of the rig when Phil Lofaro appeared on set. He watched silently for a while, then said, "I'm not paying for this."

I just stated a fact: "You're already not paying me for it!"

All in, our first shot took six weeks.

When the set was ready for finishing touches, we shot tests and projected them. The set people liked to see their work in progress on the screen; I liked to tweak lighting and the camera move; and the animators, Eric Leighton and Trey Thomas, studied their rehearsals. Henry presided.

We were developing a procedure that would carry on through the show. First was the big screen, concentrating on picture: paint, light, angle, and dressing. Then a smaller group met in Stan Webb's editing room to refine the performance and for cutting.

When shot WHA-32 was finished, when Trey shot his last frame, we projected it as a loop, literally splicing the film head to tail. The shot ran continuously, over and over. On the first couple runs, the room was silent. I don't know why, maybe some kind of shock, or not knowing if it was good or bad. Then came clapping, and laughing and cheering, like a sports event.

As the celebration subsided, there were murmurs, rolling eyeballs, and silence. Reality was sinking in. We'd spent a month and a half working and had one shot in the can. Anybody know how many shots there are in a movie? This was going to be a big project—really big!

Pete on *Nightmare* set.

Pete's Mitchell camera and Kuper system.

Glam Lighting for Sally

In the same vein as Sally's leg shot, I wanted to push whatever glamour the Sally puppet had to offer. We had a close-up of her just before she jumps out the window. We studied glam photos from movies made in the 1930s and '40s and applied them to that little plastic head.

Let's see: a hard key light hung high, a long focal length, a diffusion filter on the lens, and a special eye light when she moves out of her key light. That was the recipe. We skipped the backlight; it just didn't look right.

Chances were that the effort would look ghoulish, ridiculous, or just overdone. But no, Sally held her ground with the likes of Marlene Dietrich. After the film played in theaters, I ran into several guys who obviously had a thing for Sally!

CHAPTER 28

This Isn't Pinocchio

The story guys might have seen the slow progress on stage as a kindness, but the pace on the floor was amping up. "What's This?" was gobbling up sets at the rate of one new set built for every two shots. We needed more setups working at the same time or we'd never finish. Several new sets were soon in construction. Same for puppets, props, and setups.

Chris and I certainly weren't going to cover all that. I brought in two more crews, including two more camera people, Jim Aupperle and Jo Carson. Welcome to Christmas Town, and meet your assistants!

As we carried on shooting "What's This?" I noted five out of six shots had moving cameras. I was secretly elated; this was going to be a great sequence! But there was a snag: We wouldn't be able to sustain that when we had more sets up and running. I was deeply skeptical of assurances that this sequence was the centerpiece of the show and that we would simplify in Halloween Town. The camera department had to be ready for much more of the same.

I felt a studio expansion was inevitable, and I thought I'd better get ready. I hadn't forgotten that swing-boom rig, the design passed over on my joint project with Tippett. I was about to revive it when I remembered a rig that had more flexibility. At Coast, we had used Roy Tedesto's invention, the Tostado Arm. Picture a giant desk lamp, the kind that has an elbow in the middle of its arm. He'd built exactly that and fitted it with counterweights so a live-action operator could float a heavy camera around with ease. Impressive! I threw together a small model to see if it could be designed to maintain balance well enough for motion control. Result: Close enough . . . probably.

The model intrigued Henry and the producers and helped sell them on a full-size one. Henry was especially into it, maybe because it looked somewhat steampunk-ish.

RoboCop 2 veterans Bart Trickel and Craig Hayes did the lion's share of the building. They didn't get rich on the job; it was more of a "help your buddy" exercise. The contraption was big and scary. "Big" meant we had to disassemble it to get it in the building, and "scary" meant the counter-weights would be lethal if the chain drive failed. Despite a 4:1 safety factor, I never fully trusted all those dumbbell weights overhead, nor the camera way up there. I posted an edict on the rig: Never get under them.

After a few weekends in the studio, the nameless machine was gracefully flailing a Mitchell camera around, flexing its elbow in ways a real elbow couldn't.

Eric Leighton said it reminded him of a Pixar cartoon.

"You know what it should be named?"

I had no idea.

"Luxo Senior!" Pixar's *Luxo Jr.* was a short film starring a living lamp that would later become part of their logo.

Lighting with Paint

I heard Tim Burton wasn't at all happy with the "Scheming Song" sets in progress. He was super busy shooting *Batman Returns*, so any communication was serious. Model maker Bill Boes had lovingly painted interiors with decidedly cartoony details like knotholes. That sort of gingerbread belonged in Christmas Town and nowhere else. Tim's message was short and to the point: "This isn't *Pinocchio!*"

It must've shaken up the bosses because Deane Taylor and I were immediately jetted down to the *Batman* set in LA for a meeting of the minds. It seemed a bit dramatic.

Our first destination was an editorial room, and it didn't take long for Tim to show up via turbo-charged golf cart. Not much time for pleasantries; Danny DeVito, the Penguin, was waiting on set.

Tim seemed pretty wired and got right into it, shuttling film back and forth on the flatbed. His concerns were mostly about getting rid of most of the color and boosting the contrast.

I responded, "Uh-huh, no problem." That wasn't reassuring enough. I could sense Tim's angst. We wouldn't *get* it, and we'd go back and do it wrong again. I really had to gain his trust *now* if this was going to work.

"Yeah," I said, "we can do that!"

Tim turned to another concern: his trademark squiggly spiral lines. He started to describe it, then said, "I need a Sharpie!"

Three or four people whipped out black-ink markers in sync, like kung fu assassins unleashing their deadly hands.

Tim chose a Sharpie. With no time to find a piece of paper, he went straight to the flatbed screen and feverishly embellished it with spirals.

We were out of time and needed some closure.

"Tim!" I grabbed some eye contact with a friendly smile. "I've got it: contrast, dark, highlights, simplicity, less color—everything you said."

He seemed to relax.

I shot him one more reassurance: "We'll go right back and get on it!"

Tim flashed his own smile. "Thanks, Pete!"

And he was gone.

Back at the ranch, Bill Boes might've suffered mild collateral damage to his ego while obliterating his masterpieces in clouds of black spray paint. Having finished the deed, Bill could be heard imitating the sound "Pshht . . . pshht . . . ."

Tim sent a trusted production designer, Rick Heinrichs, to serve as visual consultant. His orders were to maintain Tim's visual style throughout the production. I think most of us "visual" types were a little tweaked by this at the beginning. It could've been a "disastah," but Rick had the people skills to get through to everyone and soothe the bristlier ones. I wasn't sure if all this was going to be all *that*, but Rick won my vote the first time he visited me on set.

For years, I had been accentuating dark shapes by hitting edges with rim light. That's what I think of when I hear the weather-beaten phrase "painting with light." Sometimes, you can't get the light where you want it, or it's not strong enough.

Rick pointed out another way to get that hot edge: Take a white pencil, or white paint, and create the highlight right where you want it.

Why didn't I ever think of that? I felt like the ape-man in *2001* who is inventing the club. This guy Rick had some great tricks, really important ones. I issued white markers to my crew and told them, "If you can't paint with light, try lighting with paint."

There was no ruminating about "If not *Pinocchio*, then what?" We caught on quickly. Despite the walking and talking skeleton at the center of our story, it was obvious this wouldn't be a horror movie, either. A look around the studio, a glimpse or two, proved we were pointed in the right direction.

In the set shop, carpenters were finishing a building for Halloween Town that was as rickety-wonky as something out of Dr. Seuss, but it was prickly with shingles. I just had to rig a backlight and scrape light along the roof. All those shingles, chimneys, and window frames were highlighted with a razor-sharp edge. That was definitely not *Pinocchio*, nor any fluffy, cuddly cartoon world.

In the model room, artisans were making medieval-era implements—puppet scale, of course. The props had their share of prickly items, but all those hatchets and boiling pots had a wonky look, and many were made of modeling clay, which had its own look. The combination made the props look as though they'd been made by mischievous little kids.

Whatever the anti-*Pinocchio* was, it was fun, scary, funny, and sweet. Lighting and camerawork would be influenced by every other craft. All of us, in harmonizing, would make a beautiful movie!

Evolving

About that time, I found some production assistants laying out a grid on all the wall space outside the screening room. Across the top row ran a calendar, and the lower 12 rows represented the individual stages, numbered 1 to 12. The storyboards were crammed with the info that was needed to get an individual shot going: sets, props, characters, crew involved, estimated time to shoot—you name it. We called it "the Big Board," and it served as the one and only call sheet in the studio.

We appeared to be getting organized. Morning dailies were a similar meeting of the minds, with a certain protocol. In the screening room, we concentrated on the image, scrutinizing test shots running on loops. They might be first light from camera and a simple pop through (filming only key poses in a shot) all the way up to a refined dress rehearsal. I'd let a shot loop several times before commenting and then ask for adjustments if necessary. It could be a tweak from camera, paint, dressing, or lighting. Then Deane would concentrate on art direction.

Having heard from us, Henry made his calls. Then he would work with individual animators in the edit room. Usually, the cameraperson and I stood by because a small change in performance often affects camerawork. To make use of the wait, I had a light table set up with an album of reference clips from finished shots so we could check lighting continuity.

It usually took several tests before the animator was ready to be launched. Animators and producers want to hit the sweet spot in the number of tests. Not enough, and you're cruisin' for a reshoot, but too much testing makes animators go stale, another way to trigger a reshoot.

Given the choice, Justin Kohn said he'd rather save his precious bodily fluids for the real shot. When an animator was ready to go for it, there was a checklist for camera to go through. Each item was there to avoid some screwup that had occurred before.

What could go wrong? The animator could kick a light stand. A light could burn out mid-shot. The camera could spring a light leak. The f-stop could be bumped, and moco could surprise us in many sneaky ways. It was a "secure the perimeter" mindset. Hot-melt glue played a big part in immobilizing things.

How would you tell an animator that you ran out of film while he was still animating? We only did that once, but once was enough.

Thanks to a lull in business at ILM, I had the pick of the litter from their camera department. Great! The "Scheming Song" needed a dedicated crew. Pat Sweeney was game for it. From ILM, to our studio, it must have been a jolt. The studio was close to the jail. His first experience with us, he stepped over an unconscious drunk stretched across the studio entrance.

I paired Pat with my main man from *Robo 2,* Matt White, and they bonded immediately. Pat's first shot started us on the first Halloween look and also initiated in-camera visual effects. It included our first use of a process projector, adding a splash as one of the kids was tossed in a bathtub. I wanted the camera to dolly in during the splash. We could've done without adding to the effect, but I felt it was time to get used to camera motion with in-camera effects as standard procedure. Henry's recent history pointed to lots more of the same. The look of the shot wasn't everything we were going for, but we learned a lot. The background was in contest with the foreground action; we could've used just a little more contrast.

As we carried on making more shots, I noticed a difference in priorities among us picture makers. Thanks to mentors like Tippett and Muren, I had clarity and simplicity hammered into my head as our primary mission. Thanks to our extraordinary production design, there was a constant temptation to fill the frame with all those cool props we had at hand. Remember "one shot, one thought"? It seemed "Nature abhors a vacuum" was the art department's countermaxim. Deane and I waged a gentlemanly Kitsch War in dailies. I called for darkening down some distracting eyesore, and Deane called for another wad of lovely props to fill in a naked patch of wall. I felt for my friends in the model shop who looked forward to seeing their creations on the big screen. Sometimes, one of those creations never gets seen. My condolences were decidedly lame but honest.

"What can I say? This isn't a museum display." Or "Think of it as a compositional element."

Eventually, Deane and I saw each other's point of view, but it took a while. Today, I'm glad we had such a lived-in look. It made it warm and organic without suggesting Pinocchio's world.

Set on *The Nightmare Before Christmas*.

Henry Selick coaching animator, Paul Berry.

CHAPTER 29

It's a Different Job

Between dailies, various planning meetings, and checking in with my peeps on set, there still seemed time to get my hands dirty. A new scene, "Sally Makes Soup," was ready for first light, and I lunged at it, secretly glad nobody else in the camera department was available.

Here was our second spooky daytime interior, which we wanted to look a little different from "Scheming Song." Deane suggested having a sickly green glow from below the set. "Green, like it's coming from the sewer," he rationalized.

We were getting better with Heinrichs's paint tricks, and it showed on our opening wide shot. Huge fun! Then Jim Aupperle needed another assignment, so I passed the sequence on to him. Right after that, I did some pinch-hitting for Sweeney on a shot where the Halloween kids exit their elevator.

I found myself running a lot, summoned to anywhere in the studio. Fortunately, no animator was hanging around, waiting for me to finish. Patching holes like that was expected, but it only worked at a certain scale, as I was about to learn.

The next time I took on a scene, it wasn't a one-off shot. A new song, "The Town Meeting Song," would require shooting on three sets, a full-time job. I figured I could handle it if I had an overqualified assistant who could carry on while I was away from the set.

Cameraman Sel Eddy at ILM was profoundly overqualified and happy to come on the show. Plus, he had done lighting at the San Francisco Opera House, so he'd keep us honest about lighting Jack's theater stage!

Sure enough, Sel knew what a "curtain warmer" was. (It's that blob of light on the closed curtains before a show.) That was easy to rig, but the miniature footlights were more challenging; they overheated in seconds, burning the limelight green gels. We fixed it with a Koz-Mo script by keeping the footlights dim except during an exposure. Definitely fun, but it took time.

Our animator was Paul Barry, fresh from London. This bloke was both talented and easy to work with. He had enough reserve that he preferred hand animating the spotlight on Jack instead of using motion control.

A Crash Course in Management

Shot making was going great on our little oasis, but my primary responsibilities were getting neglected. Kathleen summoned me to her office. "You have to stop working on shots."

I saw it coming.

"That's not your job anymore," she continued. "You have to be available to your crew."

I hated to hear it, but I knew she was right. I immediately hired cameraman Rich Lehmann (from Colossal Pictures) and set him up with Sel to carry on shooting "Town Meeting."

Kathleen had thought of everything and gave me a short list of books to study: management stuff, of course. I found more value in her assignment than expected. Running a crew was more than barking orders. One book stood out for its use of applied empathy and common sense: *Why Employees Don't Do What They're Supposed to Do and What to Do about It*. Pretty good, I had to admit.

Curiosity prompted me to add titles to Kathleen's list: something about dealing with difficult people, and *Dismissal*, a primer on how to fire someone. Dreary material, but it shed light on two frequent realities in the business.

Thinking back, I had worked for a number of different bosses, but I doubt any of them had taken Kathleen's crash course on running a crew. I doubt it's even a course in film schools, but it should be. Most of us just pick it up along the way. For instance, I was micromanaging on a new setup with Jim Aupperle. I prescribed the exact type of light, pointing from here to there, and specified the diffusion. Jim's smile was eroding as I yammered on. Finally, he broke in. "I can't work this way; I have to figure it out for myself. Just tell me what you want it to look like."

It was a reasonable request. I remembered the last days of *RoboCop 2* and the rush we all got when Phil put us on our own. Delegating is a skill easy enough to learn, but it can be painful if you're a control freak. In short, know when to clam up and trust your crew to take ownership. Reserve some flexibility for surprises. Check in to make sure they're making the same movie. Overall, it's a win-win.

It wasn't as though there was a printed job description to cling to; it was more like in-progress responsibilities. I had to get smarter, because the job would certainly go on changing for the duration. So, improvise!

Lots of Candles

It was great fun seeing Joe Ranft and his guys pitching their work. One artist would tell the story while pointing to sketches on a corkboard. Joe had the gentle voice of a children's librarian and drew us into the story like little kids. All of them really got into it, using different voices for each character and even vocalizing sound effects.

Jorgen Klubien acted out this particular pitch, and I was enjoying it until he got into describing a room "full of candles, lots of candles burning!" That was a great idea!

I kept smiling, but afterward, I assigned myself a new duty: offering reality checks on what we could deliver. "We can do the candle trick a few times, but no overlapping them with the puppets."

It seemed part of my domain, so I started figuring out how we'd go about the effects. Our $1.98 budget pointed to the cheapest solution. That would be in-camera effects. In this case, we made a double exposure: Film burning candles in the darkened set; douse the flames, rewind the film; hand over the stage to the animator.

On Call

There were plenty of calls from the stages, which was fine by me. One call might be for a pre-Henry check in the viewfinder for composition. Another call might be about lighting or a camera move.

As purveyor of fine motion-control rigs, I got calls when something wasn't moving. Typically, people went to the software for a solution, but no amount of banging on keyboards would help—not until that loose cable was plugged in. For calls like that, I preferred to be addressed as the "motion-control janitor."

There was a more serious call: "It's busted," referring to a burned-out driver module. Inevitably, a thin wire in the cable had been yanked out. Zap! I nailed the pricey silicon corpses around my office, sort of an Appian Way for moco-drive modules.

Much more rarely, I'd find Bo Henry, the set construction boss, on set, holding a badass reciprocating saw and wearing a frown. Somebody wanted the set cut, usually to make room for the animator's access or for the camera. This was never taken with a smile, considering the damage it would cause.

I was supposed to break the tie: to cut or not to cut? My guys wouldn't ask for a cut unless they really needed it, and I usually went with them. The actual cutting was made as dramatic as possible. You could hear the saw anywhere in the shooting stages, indiscriminately plowing through everything in the way. If Bo was really provoked, he'd cut right through the beefy framing nails. Only a jackhammer operator could appreciate such sweet music.

Pete on *Nightmare*.

CHAPTER 30

Real Life
Crashes the Party

Tom, one of my half brothers, called from Michigan with some bad news.

"Dad's got brain cancer."

Christmas was coming up, and I should get there quick if I wanted some holiday time with my father.

Neither Tom nor I volunteered any emotions. After barely seeing each other for decades, medical shoptalk felt safer. The culprit was glioblastoma, an ugly name that fits the vile disease. As Dad was a doctor himself, he knew his future only too well.

I'd been briefed to expect some dysfunctional family activity, but when I showed up, it was all about hugs. Dad was visibly shaky in his armchair, steadied by one of his sons. We talked about anything but cancer.

"Shoulda worn something warmer."

"How long since ya seen snow?"

"What shows are you workin' on?"

I pulled out a VHS copy of Jack discovering Christmas Town. Pity this was all Dad would ever see of the movie. I don't know what he took in, but the rest of the family liked the Fred Astaire dance moves.

"What's the movie called?"

Giving the correct answer would have been a cruel joke. I thought my little white lie would last long enough.

"The movie is called *What's This?*"

Lying in the dark that night, I conjured up the Dad I remembered, a struggling medical student who sold his blood to buy me a kiddie car. He'd delivered 30 years' worth of children in his small town, and he loved it when people on the street called out, "Hiya, Doc!" He had more than his share of demons but managed to be a good person most of the time.

The next morning, I thanked his wife and handed her a check that cleaned out my account.

"This is for one of those in-home nurses."

I just couldn't see her changing Dad's diapers. It reduced my guilt. I already knew I wasn't coming back.

Dad and I had some time together in his hospital room. It wasn't full of important business; it was mostly anecdotes and ancient family history. And there was a smattering of from-the-heart stuff.

I had a question: After all the horror he saw liberating Dachau, how could he be such a reactionary jackass?

"I was 19 in the war, too young to grasp it all. Probably I couldn't have stood it if I was older."

That's about how touchy-feely we got.

We talked a little more, but Dad soon indicated he was tired. After a teary hug, I walked to the door. I turned back to him and saluted. At that, his eyes brightened, and he gave a subdued smile.

There was plenty of time to reflect on my return flight. It sure would be great to get back to the crew. We'd already been shooting for six months, long enough to develop into an extended family.

The next day, the company was gracious, as expected. First thing in dailies, Henry and Kathleen welcomed me back, followed by the rest of the crowd in the screening room. It was great to be home.

Everyone was so mannerly that morning. At one point, a certain production manager blurted out his opinion of a prop in a new shot: "It looks like a tumor."

You could hear the faint sound of the projector clacking along right through its soundproof window. He buried his face in his hands and inhaled with a muted groan.

Maybe I should've spoken some palliative words to him, but I felt uncontrollable laughter welling up already. His New Yawk accent made "tumor" sound funny. If I tried to help him, I'd just break out laughing in guilt.

26:16

Jack's Obsession

Those of us who like in-camera tricks reveled in several scenes with Jack, projecting in strange vapors bubbling and glowing over a Bunsen burner, peering in microscopes, and cutting origami and dropping the pieces while Zero gently places a painting in Jack's hands.

Bullet hits from *RoboCop 2* gave another performance in *Nightmare*, only, this time, they were recast as electric sparks and popping Christmas bulbs. The beat-up roll of film had spent the interim in my toolbox as a forgotten souvenir. What an encore!

Meanwhile, Sally is making her own potion, wafting out butterfly-shaped vapors. Our tricks were relatively simple, accomplished with ancient tools, such as a single-frame projector and see-through mirrors, and one Koz-Mo shot. And there was very little risk they'd detonate the shot.

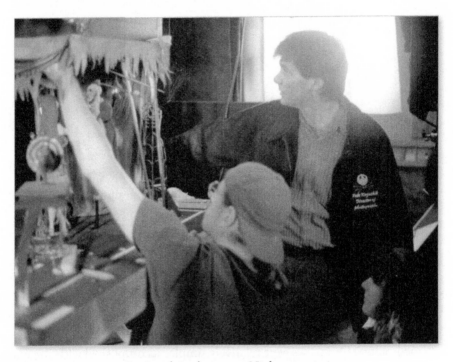

Pete and Anthony on *Nightmare* set.

CHAPTER 31

A Better Mousetrap

How do you know how far to move the puppet? An answer to that question can meander all over the map, depending on the animator you're asking. They may begin with a "right brain" understanding of the director's intended performance. From there, they get increasingly "left brain," acting out, over and over, maybe timing themselves with a stopwatch.

I'm certain that the maestros I've worked with have developed intuitive resources. Maybe it's part muscle memory, remembering the feel of pushing and pulling into the preceding pose. Phil Tippett once described his visual process, holding his thumb and forefinger 2 inches apart: "This means something to me, and so does this," shortening the gap by a half inch. He then closed the gap in diminishing steps. "So does this, and this, and this." Make sense? A skill like that would come from lots of hands-on experience and observing people in motion.

There are similar questions that require more utilitarian answers. In this case, the animator queries himself: "How far did I just move it?" "Did I already move that arm?" "Which way was it going?" It's not esoteric at all but screaming for answers. From the primordial beginnings of stop-mo, the surface gauge (a.k.a. scriber block) has been adapted to aid in measuring "how far I moved it."

You've probably seen photos of them: a hefty base and an adjustable pointer that can hold its position in space. Carefully adjust the pointer to the back of your puppet's head. When you move your puppet, the pointer stays put; you can see how far you're moving it (at least its head). There's no law against using several gauges for all those other limbs, but every gauge in use slows the process more.

Some prefer working more quickly, relying on memory and a consistent rhythm. That remained true from 1925 to the mid-1980s.

On Henry's Doughboy commercials, I found the animators using another kind of memory. The CEI frame store was an early digital device for use in a TV control room—nothing to do with stop-mo, but it had a function that could be quite useful. At the punch of a button, it would instantly digitize a freeze frame off a live video feed. A grand total of two frozen frames could fit in the memory. (Times change!) By toggling a switch, you could choose to see the live video or either of the frozen frames.

Flip-flip-flip, back and forth. Okay, *that's* how far I moved the head. And yes, I *did* move the arm twice, so I'll just set it back a little.

That new capability was about to eliminate the angst for every animator who had ever melted down while trying to keep all those arms and legs in control. (What about those shots with two or three characters to animate?)

Yes, *Nightmare* had some of those game changers. Of course, the film cameras couldn't hook up to a frame grabber; we needed a separate video camera placed beside the film camera—the closer the better.

We could afford these miracles in limited numbers. A complete grabber setup cost a few thousand dollars. Was it worth it? Ask the animator who was just saved from a reshoot. Most animators could access a grabber on a given day, but sometimes it came down to a triage.

Flipping through consecutive grabs and the current live pose, animators got a glimpse of the action's smoothness, a lot like a cartoon animator flipping drawings. These snippets were useful, but nobody really knew how the entire shot would play out until there was real film running in dailies.

The process quickly made everyone's work smoother. A few animators had always stood out in fluidity, guys like Dave Allen, Eric Leighton, and especially Jim Danforth. (Look at *When Dinosaurs Ruled the Earth*, my vote for all-time realism without a net.) Now, most animators could guarantee smoothness, given the time.

It was a valuable tool, but the technical widget couldn't deliver a dynamic, dramatic performance. That job remains the animator's, and it's much more complex and important.

For animators who wanted more than three frames, they just marked on the monitor with a black wax pen, as needed. It was good to see the increments finished, but animators could also mark a course for frames to come! Meanwhile, the camera team looked on with hungry eyes. We had similar burning questions: "Did that light burn out while we were at lunch?" "Did the set warp overnight?" (That happens a lot when temperature or humidity changes.) The grabbers could easily handle queries like those.

The grabbers resolved one common lighting problem: how to establish lighting continuity from frame to frame when you have to replace a dead bulb. This would almost guarantee a bad match, but with the grabber, we could search for the dead bulb's last grab and determine the correct dimmer setting for the new bulb.

Heating Up

By early 1992, our acutely extended family was showing rough edges, just like a "real" family. A poster hung high in the set shop: "Bring our tools back, you fucks."

We in the camera department were prime suspects, because we were already known to borrow drills without asking. Certain animators were also persons of interest.

Production runner Dave Teller accidentally imported some scorpions from Arizona—big ones!—and offered them as gifts. They brought joy to Jim (the stage manager) and me in our shared office, scuttling around their sandy terrarium, eating mealworms. Jim and Phil, good men both, were frequently at odds, and after one session of drama, it got personal. Jim made a cross out of Popsicle sticks, wrote Phil's name on it, and planted it in the scorpion cage.

We were close to full crew, and the pressure was on to not relent until the shoot was over. We kept getting bigger and taking on more people. Twelve stages wouldn't do, so we evacuated the parking garage and carved it into eight more stages.

People had to blow off steam, and this was mostly good-natured, especially if they were equal in rank. Matt yelled at Justin, "You're not the only animator I service. Picture yourself working on *three* shots, not just one!" Good thing Justin was the calmer; he had a black belt.

Supervisors had to be more civil, considering the bigger sticks we wielded. On one occasion, Trey had been animating on a shot for several days when Sel and his assistant, Cameron, accidentally bumped Trey's moco track. I called it a "train wreck," but Sel reminded me that we could fix these things later at ILM. I snapped back, "That's an insult, as if we could afford that!"

I was overdoing it while Sel was sucking it in, just trying to help. I'm still not proud of it.

As it happened, we could restore the track's position by looking carefully at the dust on the floor; there were clean spots where the track supports had been. When bumped from the other side, it slid right back in place.

The vibe was becoming cranky in dailies, and I wondered if this was like the original "sweatbox" in the early years at Disney. I tried to slip into some laughs, and speaking over a lot of people in dailies gave me a buzz—enough to make mirth and nonsense. It was fun, and for sure, the crew liked the frippery, but the vibe could still be harsh.

Regardless, Henry and I were respectful. Got an issue? We went out to his parking space for a little privacy to discuss it. After a man-to-man chat, we never brought it up again.

Amid all this, Kathleen was doing a superb job of keeping production on track, making the most of her close ties with the Disney suits. She sent our weekly footage for their approval and called in advance to alert them to shots that absolutely had to be accepted. (Those were the shots that would cripple production if we had to reshoot them.) She worked much the same way with Henry when he asked for a reshoot. Easy shots had the best chance of a reshoot. The more complex the shot, the more likely Kathleen and Henry would be at odds.

Despite the crunch, we still had room for being nice to each other. New friendships continued to spring up, and romances sometimes followed. DNA exchanges were plentiful, some spawning future animators. Kathleen gifted us with a Ping-Pong table, and we ended each week at "beer-thirty." Nonetheless, we were getting stale. More than once I heard, "It's time for this to end." Would that be so bad?

A clean sweep was coming, and it would save us from what ongoing companies often contend with: entrenchment, fiefdoms, power grabs, entitlement, drama as a sport, and—most crippling—a dulling of enthusiasm and creative juices.

Phil Tippett once referred to the phenomenon with a single word: "Lifers." My prescription was to turn on the fire hoses after the project. Everybody out! If the planets aligned the right way, we'd meet again and start fresh, brimming with the milk of human kindness.

CHAPTER 32

Fix It in Post

The signs were clear that we were close to wrap. No more sets were being built, most sequences had finished, and interview crews began routing us stop-mo types out of our dark and quiet havens.

I thought it would be easy, talking to the camera, but I flunked my first go at it. Henry told me to have a glass of wine next time. That led me to treat my crew to a long, liquid lunch at the Caribbean Zone. All those Mai Tais brought several cameramen to their knees. Upon returning, they opened the door and fell on their faces, right in front of a network video crew.

Now that we were on the map, visitors started showing up. One honored guest was Chuck Jones, creator of Bugs Bunny and many other classic Warner Bros. characters. I was in awe.

Jones's tour guide seemed nervous. Jones asked him, "Are you a producer?"

"No."

"Well, you sweat like one."

Seventy-six weeks—that's how long it took to shoot *Nightmare*, at least in my book. February 21, 1993, was wrap day, the last frame shot. Not everyone left the building that day, not for good. Who was gonna clean up that mess?

I rounded up my robot-babies for a photo with them. This might be the only time to do it.

I was getting ready to move into a hotel in Burbank, close to the Disney lot. That's where I'd be doing postproduction, which includes supervising the visual effects and, later, the color timing of the picture.

The movie had been recently sent to Disney. Prior to that, the original camera negative was kept in San Francisco. How to get it safely to LA? Throw it in the mail? No. Buy two plane tickets, one for the negative and one for the lucky production assistant who is told never to let it out of his or her trembling hands.

We got a little head start on opticals with locals Harry Walton and Michael Hinton, two separate one-man bands who each had an optical printer. The guys could take on a limited workload, mostly Zero, the ghost dog, and Sally's magic fog juice. It sounds cut-and-dried, but details like how to get a ghost dog without pink, yellow, or green tint were elusive. Chasing one's tail had always been part of optical printing. At that point, I considered it the state of the art, but a surprise was coming.

Disney's in-house effects company, Buena Vista Visual Effects (BVVE), was at our service. The same physics, optics, and film chemistry and the limits of precision machinery were there, waiting to go astray. Nonetheless, BVVE did some great work. That opening shot, the one with the cartoon ghost shadows? It had more complexity than shadows; we had shot several mist elements, flying ghosts, flying pumpkins, and mattes here and there, even rotoscope work on those flying ghosts grabbing fence posts. It went together painlessly.

BVVE also fixed a near disaster, a horrific scratch on the negative that ran the length of one shot. The process was fascinating; soak the negative in some smelly stuff, perchloroethylene, so the emulsion would expand. If it expanded just enough, the scratch would be healed. But if it dried, the scratch would come back, so they had to rephotograph it frame by frame while it was submerged in a wet gate, an attachment for the optical printer. Picture a film shuttle with glass windows, like a tiny aquarium.

BVVE did yet another job, the titles and credits rollup. At the time, credits were shot just like they look: a simple electric motor smoothly pulling a long roll of credits under a downshooter. To get the best contrast, they didn't use paper; they used sheets of high-contrast lithography film taped together and lit from below.

The opening titles and credits were originally spelled out in Halloween candy corn, forming letters on a black background. Toward the end of principal photography, two animators were working over a large black table for six weeks. The animation was flawless and fun to watch, but it was rejected; we'd left Tim's name out of the main title, which was supposed to be "Tim Burton's *The Nightmare Before Christmas.*" Because of time and money, we resorted to the simpler flat-art titles.

Kathleen's job was trickier. She had to make decisions on what the credits should *say.* She called me to verify my crew's credits; she had ranked my operators by how many shots they'd made, something I'd never thought of doing.

Initially, Disney questioned calling me a director of photography, because they'd never used that term in animation. It was a holdover from decades of flat art under a downshooter and the same four lights.

Kathleen had one other question. "By the way, who should we call the visual-effects supervisor?"

I had to think for a moment, and then, somewhat embarrassed, I said, "If that's figuring out how to shoot the effects, that's what I'm doing now, so I guess it's me."

CAPS Lock

BVVE was working toward becoming a digital-effects company, but it wasn't quite ready. *The Lion King* was finishing up, leaving us the run of Disney Animation's Computer Animation Production System, or CAPS. It was an all-digital system designed for 2D cartoon work, from scanning drawings and subsequent digital ink and paint to creating virtual camera moves. They had some color and density tools and could record digital shots back onto film.

My native guide to the world of digital compositing was Ariel Shaw. He knew CAPS very well, while I had never even tickled the keys in Photoshop. My first question was, "How's a cartoon program gonna handle pictures of real objects?" Ariel was confident. By any other name, that lineup of cartoon capabilities had a lot in common with digital compositing.

We were on a tour, and I was looking for anything familiar, some digital tech that corresponded with photo-optical tech. It didn't take long. Ariel opened a door and said in a slightly hushed voice, "This is the scanner."

There, in the semi-dark, was an ancient downshooter, minus the

50-pound Acme camera. In the Acme's place was a ridiculously small electronic camera, featureless except for a lens, a cable, and a pair of liquid cooling hoses. Below was a film shuttle, and it was advancing frames at a rate so slow I wondered if we'd miss our October delivery date.

The next stop was one of the ubiquitous computer screens. Ariel put up several shots. "We took out the bumps on these shots before working with you on the effects." I hadn't seen any bumps back in San Francisco dailies. "Yeah," said Ariel. "They're hard to see unless you zoom way in." I wasn't sure this was necessary, but it came with the dinner.

There were plenty of visible bumps in that three-animator circus shot of Jack and the crowd. Ariel had to slightly crop the shot to make room for bump removal. Already, I was seeing tricks that we couldn't ask for in traditional optical.

"How does the density look? And the contrast?"

Ariel showed me how to adjust that by typing in numbers. It was like ordering printer lights to the lab, but it didn't take overnight. Type your numbers, and in a few seconds, a still frame popped up showing the result.

"What about the color? Is that working?"

More numbers to tweak: red, green, and blue. They all worked together, just like those color-correction gels we put in background projectors. Is the shot too cold? Add a little red and take away a little blue. Being able to see the results in seconds was empowering.

Anyone who uses modern image editors will think what I'm discussing is way out of date, and it is, but at the time, it sped up the process by two orders of magnitude.

I noticed the greens were too green. The only thing to do was darken the greens. Hmm, come to think of it, the reds looked too red also. Darken that, too. Now the blues were too colorful. Darkening everything got us the same overly colorful shot, but darker. I asked Ariel if he had a button that sucks out some of the overall "colorfulness."

He paused. "Knock down the color? We never had a call for that."

Of course. They made cartoons there. But I needed a solution. What if we made a black-and-white version of the shot and blended it with the overly colorful version? That turned out to be easy, a matter of arithmetic. A mix of 18 percent black and white and 82 percent color was the ticket; it looked like the original film. This kind of noodling was fun.

One of the ongoing challenges in visual effects was getting a flawless optical blue-screen shot. We've all seen those wiggling blue edges around our favorite actor; you're looking at several strips of film, various copies of the same shot, trying to align in microscopic precision. Could a digital blue screen do better?

Pat Sweeney had shot one of our few blue screens, Jack and his skeleton reindeer flying away toward the moon. With a few tweaks, the matte absolutely fit. There would be no wiggling edges of any color, no fretting about whether the matte would fit.

While we were still on that scene, I asked if we could tone down Jack's cracking of the whip. In our first look in dailies, Henry was displeased that Jack was "beating the shit out of those reindeer."

Ariel couldn't stop laughing.

It was CAPS to the rescue, specifically the layout tools. It was easy to stretch Jack's travel into the distance and obscure any cruelty to skeletons.

Someone said I had a call. "This is Kathleen. I have a message for you. From now on, you will accept every shot they show you."

Did she think I was just polishing my Oscar all this time?

"Loud and clear, Kathleen!"

Her message was something of a relief. Balancing creativity and commerce can be difficult if you don't know the boundaries.

As we got into more complex and longer shots, Ariel noted another boundary—not time, but megabytes. So far, CAPS had only worked on cartoon images, and those used a lot less memory. An area enclosed by an ink line contains only one color, which means thousands of pixels could be described by the same data. But in our images, each pixel was slightly different from its neighbors. Think of film grain: It's messy and random. It took a lot more data to describe each pixel as an individual.

Ariel wore a serious expression while telling me how many "megs" and "gigs" were taking over the system. It all sounded mega-prodigal compared to the 640 kB of RAM in one of my motion-control rigs. I figured it would take 26 of those moco machines to hold one movie frame.

Our last tasks were to add sparkles blowing out of Santa's nose and several shots of snowflakes. Both used a particle system, animating a lot of objects not one by one, but by setting up conditions: wind, direction, gravity, turbulence, quantity of objects, and so on. Artwork like snowflakes is attached to the invisible particles, and then you let the program loose. Don't like it? Change something and try again. Pretty neat!

As we shot the sequence on stage, I had kept a color reference frame from each shot, starting warm and going cooler as the snow got denser. We did pretty well, but there were some discrepancies, and there were also a few other shots I wanted to treat differently.

The clock was running out, and I asked Ariel if we could possibly squeeze in some color timing on the 18 shots. Although he was feeling squeezed himself, he jumped in. Much appreciated, Ariel!

Pete and his robot-babies (moco rigs).

CHAPTER 33

Finishing Touches

Inevitably, movies aren't made of perfectly matched shots. Too many variables see to that, including lighting, exposure, and changes in the weather. We didn't have weather issues, but 20-odd setups clicking away at the same time ensured we'd have some unwanted variance. That's where the colorist and the film lab come in, and on *Nightmare*, I was lucky to work with Dale Grahn of Technicolor, a favorite at Disney.

Sara Duran, the Disney postproduction supervisor, told me that I had three strikes to get the movie right, so I came as prepped as possible. That included a log book and reference frames, with suggested color-correction gels to be used on individual shots. Dale listened to my prattle for a while and then patiently let me know that's not the way it was done.

"Let's watch the movie, and talk to me."

It was good to see the movie on a big screen. With only two or three of us in the seats, our medium-size theater seemed cavernous. As Dale asked questions about story, mood, and character, it dawned on me that this guy was a creative artist seeking to understand the soul of the film.

Listen to him, I told myself. *He's our ally.*

When Dale wrote notes, he glanced at a footage counter clicking along beside the screen. The film never stopped, probably to avoid overthinking (and overspending).

"These three shots really need to be balanced to this one."

"Got it."

"Sally's in love. The moonlight should be brighter, but it's still nighttime."

"Got it."

Those details needed less discussion as Dale grew familiar with the story. By the end of the session, we had a workable shorthand. The lights came up, and Dale said he'd have an answer print for me in two days. We'd see how he'd interpreted our conversation. This wasn't too tricky, but I did feel wrung out.

The next time we met, I was primed for a concentration marathon.

Sara sat down behind me. "Don't worry about the theater release; it's just the nose cone."

I interpreted that as *Don't go overboard on details here. We'll catch 'em in the home-video version, where we make most of the money.*

Henry joined us, and soon, we were rolling. I worried that the real-time pace would frustrate Henry. It sure had tweaked me in the first reel.

Dale's first answer print was looking good. I injected a few corrections as the band played on. Ten minutes into the show, Henry got up and said it looked good, but he couldn't stay.

He had one parting order: "Pete, just make sure we can see everything. Don't go too dark."

I took that as a vote of confidence. It felt good.

After this viewing, we moved on to concentrate on one half of the movie at a time: part 1 on Wednesday, and part 2 on Thursday. Every day had a new answer print. We'd covered the whole show twice, but I didn't get my third swing at bat. As it happened, the studio liked our second try.

Suddenly, after two and a half years, I was done.

Cover Story

Before leaving town, I wanted to see if *American Cinematographer* magazine would be interested in a piece on *Nightmare*. My availability for a meeting was today or nothing, which didn't faze Stephen Pizzello, the associate editor at the time. He hadn't heard about our film just yet, so I showed him some frame clips. It wasn't the kind of project *AC* usually covered.

"We've got a visual-effects issue planned for December," Pizzello said. "You might fit there."

There was no guarantee; there were plenty of effects-heavy shows and only so many pages in the magazine.

"If you want to go for it, here's what you're up against."

Pizzello handed me a list of film titles, most of which were unfamiliar. One stood out: *Jurassic Park*. Dennis Muren had written "JP looks great!" on a Christmas card to me. It was now late April, and that's all I knew about *Jurassic*, but it was enough to be sure that dinosaurs would have a place in the issue.

"I'll keep my hat in the ring," I told Pizzello. Why not? Just maybe our show could be sharing column inches with the heavy hitters!

Months went by without contact from *AC*, and I presumed *Nightmare* hadn't made the short list. It had always been a long shot. Then came a call from David Heuring, the magazine's editor. "We'd like to run a story on *Nightmare*, but we're running out of time. Do you have anything already written?"

As a matter of fact, I did. I didn't tell Heuring I was about to offer it to the camera union's publication.

"How fast can you get it to us?"

"Two days. I'll mail you a floppy disk. It's written in WordPerfect 5.1." That was up-to-the-minute technology at the time.

I spent a long night tweaking the article for *AC*, and then off to the post office it went, with photos to follow.

Years later, I heard the backstory about that last-minute phone call, thanks to Ron Magid, *AC*'s longtime visual-effects editor. Magid said up until the day Heuring called me, *Nightmare* wasn't going to be in *AC* at all. But Ron came by and urged Pizzello, his friend, to consider it, saying, "There's something you really gotta see!"

After seeing our quirky puppet film, Pizzello said, "This is going to be our cover story."

Going for the Gold

Encouraged by the *American Cinematographer* experience, I adopted a "give it a go" attitude toward pursuing an Academy Award for my work on *Nightmare*. Asking around for advice, I met with tepid responses. Everyone was either too busy or pessimistic. Then I got a call from Harrison

Ellenshaw. The renowned matte artist and effects supervisor was working at BVVE and had some tips. More than that, he was about to mentor me in how to get the visual-effects award.

The first step had already been taken: A committee made up of VFX practitioners had chosen seven films as preliminary contenders. Did anyone want to nominate *Nightmare Before Christmas*? A healthy number of eager voices called out, stepping over each other.

"I wanna nominate that!"

"Me too!"

"They did effects *in-camera*!"

"Rear projection!"

"Real stuff!"

One of those voices belonged to Hoyt Yeatman, the heart and soul of Dream Quest.

So, *Nightmare* made the first hurdle.

The second challenge was the VFX "bakeoff," a ritual whereby the seven would be winnowed down to three based on our pitches and effects reels. The reel had to be 15 minutes of our best trick-photography shots. Only the 200 Academy members who actually *did* visual effects could vote on the work. Days later, everyone in the Academy could vote on the last three standing.

Ellenshaw counseled me on the bakeoff. "You need to cut your reel for this particular audience. They already know how you did it. Most of the crowd comes to socialize and be entertained."

How would I entertain them?

"A lot of reels are hard to watch, crammed with every effects shot in the movie without room for how they fit in. The audience loses interest. Instead, let them enjoy several uncut sequences; they'll appreciate that."

Disney shipped me a used film print of *Nightmare*, and I cut it for an abridged version, ending up with five or so intact scenes. My mentor was right; it was easy and fun to watch.

The first hour of the bakeoff turned out to be a reunion party. Everywhere I looked, there was someone I'd once worked with. Several well-wishers had the same message: "Too bad! Any other year, but *Jurassic Park* . . . "

The reel entertained as hoped and finished on a sweet note: Sally and Jack on the snow hill. Applause, then time to stand up and take questions—and don't forget to make it fun!

Ariel clutched the microphone as he answered a litany of questions about CAPS. This was new stuff for a lot of people. I didn't get many questions about effects. Our methods were obviously old school. Their interest seemed much more about what it was like to work on the show. I was loopy and excited, feeling the adrenaline.

Laine Liska, bless him, asked in his cracked voice, "How many animators died on the show?"

I just gave him the truth: "Nobody died, but one week I saw five people crying, and they weren't all women." That drew some chuckles.

Someone wanted to know how animators rehearse. I answered, "Some act it out like actors for the director, but the shy ones just block shots with their puppets." That drew laughs, far more than merited, but fine by me.

Someone asked how many shots were in the movie. I repeated the question and moved closer to the mic. "Seven . . . hundred."

No laughs this time, but one guy swore. Then a buzz wafted through the room. Seven hundred trick-photography shots were a lot in 1993.

Phil Tippett wanted to know how we got the animation so consistently smooth. I got as far as, "It was really hard . . ." and the audience didn't wait for the rest, but bloomed into immoderate guffaws, the most spirited of the evening.

Phil persisted. "No, seriously, how did you do that?"

I described the frame grabbers.

On it went until time was up, and we made our way to our seats, where Sara Duran planted sloppy kisses on our grinning faces.

Weeks later, I was wearing a tuxedo, walking in a line of nominees outside the Dorothy Chandler Pavilion. Autograph collectors lined the ropes along the red carpet, hunting trophies.

"Hey, are you someone?"

Not sure how to respond, I yelled back, "For the moment, maybe!"

"What did you do?"

"Visual effects, *Nightmare Before Christmas.*"

"Nah, I got enough of that stuff already."

Look, there's Gene Siskel holding a mic! He and Roger Ebert had given *Nightmare* two thumbs up on their TV show. I broke out of the line and extended my hand. "Mr. Siskel, viz effects, *Nightmare Before Christmas.* Thanks for the review . . . ."

He turned his gaze elsewhere, intently scanning for glamour, not geeks.

Inside, sitting among the recognizable nominees was surreal. We all had to be close to the stage in case we were called to the podium.

I stared at the podium like it was a gallows. Just in case, I had written down some remarks. Was it good enough to spew in front of a billion people? Nobody had seen what I wrote. Shouldn't it be checked by a functioning adult? Although I knew there was miniscule probability of 5,000 Academy voters spurning *Jurassic Park* in favor of our puppet show, I had butterflies in my stomach—big, fat monarchs and dozens of squirming caterpillars.

Eventually, a papier-mâché dinosaur head delivered the envelope, and up went the winners behind us. I tried shaking my friends' hands, but they were doggedly focused on the podium looming before them.

Later, during a commercial break, I ducked out and into a brief brush with greatness. The only other guy in the men's room was Academy president Arthur Hiller. We had a pleasant chat about how the broadcast was going. I was thinking, "I'm talking shop with a famous director at the urinals at the Oscars!"

For me, the high point of the season was the bakeoff, where my VFX homies showed their enthusiasm for *Nightmare*. I took their esteem to be a last hurrah for a beloved craft. As I wrote to the *Nightmare* crew, "Winning the hearts of our fellow stop-mo aficionados was a big win, one to make us proud!"

Skellington Productions Inc.

February 10, 1994

Dear **Nightmare** brothers and sisters;

The academy nomination for visual effects was a nod of recognition from our industry peers in which we can all take pride. I've always maintained that visual effects is one of the most collaborative aspects of the film business, and in the case of **Nightmare** it is fair to say that everyone on the show contributed to its effects.

This was very clear at the screening of excerpts last Thursday, where we stood out as a continuous string of 800 effects shots that added up to an entire feature. Every production, design, and craftsperson on the project has their blood up there on the screen, and should feel proud of their efforts.

Nightmare's nomination is especially significant in the year of the dinosaur. Bear in mind that we were chosen over some cutting edge computer graphics, and excellent efforts in realistic effects using large scale miniatures. The 200 experts who nominated us must have found something more important to them than high tech or photorealism.

My impression was that our work touched their hearts in a way none of the other entries did; the audience reaction was incredibly enthusiastic. They had many questions, and several people gushed about how much they liked the show, how their kids had seen it 50 times, and how thankful they were to us for having made the film. Members of the **Jurassic** team called our film "beautiful", and stated that they were very glad to see our alternative style hit the screen this year in particular, providing a welcome balance.

The golden idol will almost certainly go to the dinosaurs, but we have won the gratitude and good wishes of many fellow practitioners for validating stop motion as a medium for everyone's future.

Good feeling all around!

Pete Kozachik

Henry Selick

Pete's Academy letter.

Tim Burton's The Nightmare Before Christmas

Visual Effects Synopsis for the Academy

Introduction

On **Nightmare** I had two overlapping jobs; as Director of Photography I was responsible for setting and maintaining the cinematographic style, interpreting Director Henry Selick's needs in support of story and mood.

As Visual Effects Supervisor I devised the means to create that style in our stop-motion environment for about 800 shots. Classic and contemporary effects techniques were combined and expanded upon to provide our basic production tools.

Similarly I determined methods to add atmospheric and other visual effects, with input on style from Henry and animation needs from Eric Leighton. This included about 270 in-camera visual effects and 100 opticals.

Working with three optical houses and Ariel Shaw at the CAPS digital facility I advised on methods, picked wedges, and gave final approval on shots.

In pre-production I built or supervised building of several major motion control rigs to accommodate the special needs of the show. Two were unique to the film industry.

I also wrote special motion control software to automate repetitive processes during animation, enabling the majority of effects to be produced in-camera. This is detailed in a later section.

Description of Methods and Highlights;

Process projection and multiple exposure

Primary means of adding atmosphere and specific effects was by dx'ing various sources in-camera. Sources were prefilmed live action and FX animation, airbrush art cards, moire and slot gags, and miscellaneous light and filter effects.

Several process projectors, including one built during the show were used to burn in live elements during or after animation.

Examples; fireplaces, torch flames, splashes, steam, smoke, boiling water, character shadows, snowstorm globe, sparks, match flame, saw dust, images in cauldron, burning sleigh, etc.

Pete's synopsis for the Academy.

Projector pan and tilt were sometimes animated by hand or motion control to make effects stick to moving objects. Some full frame rear projection compositing was also done.

Similarly dx'd art and light fx were used to create such effects as mist, sunlight shards, glints, glowing stew, fog moire, search lights, cannon fire, explosions, night vision display, boiling stew, candles, and pre-flashed color on the negative. Jack's ghost dog Zero was often dx'd in a separate pass.

Special Motion Control Software;

Scripting Process Automation

The original budget allowed for 70 opticals, amended to 100 including fixes. This necessitated a predominantly in-camera approach to visual effects.

To perform hundreds of effects reliably I felt some form of automation was necessary. This is because the non-repeatable nature of puppets often required that each pass be performed on a single frame before animating the next pose. Such an approach would be prohibitively error prone if done by hand.

My solution was to write a companion program to the Tondreau rp4 system software which enabled operators to rapidly script automated shooting processes.

The same hardware and software that was performing camera moves was at the same time sequencing light relays, running filter wheels, inserting art cards and light gags, performing fades, dissolves, and multiple exposures, and generally doing in-camera effects on a per frame basis during animation.

Some interesting applications;

- Selective diffusion and focus within a shot.
- Partial density Zero over moon, alongside full density Jack.
- DX'd flame on torch waved by character.
- Layers of mist moving between forground and background characters.
- Jack in rising fog, gradually more diffused and obscured.
- Dazed Santa's rotating double vision of other characters.
- Saving practicals between exposures to avoid melting props.
- Camera moves out of way of animator between exposures.
- Dissolve from normal lighting to flourescent UV tubes.
- Sequencing practicals, dimmer automation.
- Velvet window shade keeps frontlight off rear process screen.
- Alternate frame front/back light and normal/UV light mattes for optical.

This capability gave us the freedom to add new effects as needs arose with low impact on budget. More than 270 in-camera effects were ultimately produced, many with this program.

Pete's synopsis for the Academy continued.

Beam Splitter

When very tight interaction between puppets and a dx effect was necessary, the effect was added in the same pass with a beam splitter. Jack and other characters interacting with snow, cutting out a paper snowflake, and Zero interacting with solid characters and props are typical examples.

Perspective Tricks

The classic Darby O'Gill perspective cheat was used to alter some character and set size relationships. In the shot of Mr. Hyde stacking Russian dolls with his smaller twins, a camera move required compensating motion control movement of part of the set.

Special Motion Control Devices

Motion control was heavily used, with 14 mc systems running concurrently. Aside from use in camera movement, motion control rigs were designed to produce effects and move characters and props.

Examples include mist movers, Jack's sleigh, lighting fx dimmers, filter wheels, Zero flying, rising sun keylight, Oogie's roulette wheel, Sally's Xmas tree, gross puppet movement, dangling ropes, treehouse elevator, cloud and sky movers, and flying Santa. A laser was motion controlled to create a roto guide for Jack emerging from the fountain.

I designed and partly built seven motion control camera rigs. Most were track, boom and camera head units, intended to simulate the look of live crane and dolly work.

Two experimental devices were made to create more dynamic effects. One, named Luxo Sr., resembles a giant double jointed desk lamp. It was made to enable camera movement through sets unencumbered.

The other unusual rig is called the Screamer, and is based on a custom made pin registered camera about the size of a Bolex. Its lightweight magnesium body can pan, tilt and roll 360 degrees, and fly into tight spaces on a compact boom arm.

Unique effects were produced using the special capabilities of these devices. They were both designed and built by me before production began, with fabrication of large Luxo parts farmed out.

Pete's synopsis for the Academy continued.

In a few experimental shots gross puppet movement was pre-animated using a smalll motion control rig slaved to a hand held position encoder. Before production I had built single and double axis encoding devices, and written motion control software to use them in a"high touch" programming scenario, the single frame equivalent of live action move recording.

Post Production Effects and Compositing

Digital Optical Supervisor is covering this in detail. My involvement began with designing methods for shooting stage elements. Subsequently I worked with the four optical houses specifying effects, brainstorming on methods, selecting wedges, and approving shots.

My thanks to the members of the Academy for their consideration of our work for nomination.

Respectfully submitted,

Pete Kozachik
Director of Photography / Visual Effects Supervisor
Tim Burton's The Nightmare Before Christmas

Pete's synopsis for the Academy continued.

Sally Has a Vision

Tim Hittle was going to animate that Christmas tree that grew in seconds and burst into flames. He had just one chance to get the shot because he was working backward, snipping away twigs during the shot that were never to be restored.

I visited him to see how it was going, and we started gabbing about how awkward it was to describe our jobs to our families back East. Tim painted a visual of him and his dad sitting on the front porch, mostly silent. Finally, Dad Hittle broke the ice Midwest-style: "How's yer car runnin'?"

Henry wanted a time-lapse effect; right after the burning bush dies out, morning sunlight chases the vampires into the shadows. To do it right, we'd require one 2K light traveling in a semicircle over the set. The Butt Saver became a moving light stand. Surprisingly, it took every axis on the rig, even pan and tilt, just to fly the light where it had to go. Cameraman Dave Hanks put branches in the light, just what we needed to emphasize the shadow movement. It looked just like a time-lapse shot, very cool!

It seemed so prodigal at the time, when other setups needed real camera moves. Once again, it was evident we'd need another big rig. Phil took it as inevitable.

With the last three moco crane designs as trial-and-error exercises, I had a better idea for rig #4. It was a traditional full-size track, swing, and boom. It was tighter, more precise, lighter, and stronger. Eric Swenson did a lot of drill and tapping on his downtime. That gave Eric the honor of naming the rig whenever his muse got back to him.

When it was assembled, I asked Eric to see if the rig could lift me off the ground. There was no rational reason to do that; chalk it up to euphoria from bringing the monster to life. Indeed, it picked me up with ease, and that gave Eric the name: Mister Lifto. Wouldn't be my first choice, but it stuck.

Eric Swenson setting up a shot on *Nightmare*.

CHAPTER 34

Just Peachy

Toward the end of our two-year employment, we all started thinking about finding new jobs. *Nightmare* was a one-off; we shouldn't expect another fluke like it anytime soon, if ever. However, well before *Nightmare* was finished, Henry and Tim were working at getting a green light for another show that would be shot at the same studio. Smart move, because the Skellington Prods studio was a pricey asset to build and would soon be dormant.

When we wrapped, the whole studio was available to those who wanted to make their own short films, and several animators took advantage of that. Nice perk!

Getting that next feature green-lit wasn't a slam dunk. Roald Dahl's book *James and the Giant Peach* didn't seem to impress the Disney suits—at least, not enough to be Henry's encore. One suit's comment encapsulated the skepticism: "We've got a boy, some talking bugs, and a big peach. What do we do with that?" Later came a suggestion: "Maybe James has a girlfriend. . . ."

Everybody noted the original story was stuck on the giant peach, where the characters mostly talked and sang. Henry and his story guys would fix that with more action; they'd get those characters off the peach for a while.

Henry got his green light but remained under merciless scrutiny from the mothership in Burbank. As I saw it, the communiqués from the studio during *Nightmare* hadn't fostered a lot of goodwill. And this time, we didn't have Kathleen; she and Phil Lofaro had opted out on this one.

Shortly, we had a new producer, and I was summoned to meet him.

He greeted me by looking up from his desk and declaring, "You make too much money."

It was time to establish our relationship: "No, I don't make too much. I've been looking for a DP for the live-action segments, and those guys make way the hell more than me."

Our wannabe Harry Cohn's eyes opened wider, and I kept raving in a staccato tempo. "I'm the only guy who's ever done the job, and I'm the effects guy, too."

He waved his hand and smiled. "Okay, I'll see what we can do."

Nobody lost face, but it didn't mean I trusted him.

Soon, Henry told him that they weren't a good match, and we were out one producer.

Our next candidate charmed everyone: Brian Rosen from Australia. Like Kathleen, he was a straight shooter, no mind games. I could just walk into his office, and invariably, we'd make short work of the issue at hand. One day, Brian called me a "man of reason," a compliment that's still on my résumé.

Back to that live-action director of photography: The bulk of the film would be in stop-motion, but Henry wanted to bookend that with live actors. I'd be busy shooting the animation while a live-action crew would be shooting elsewhere in San Francisco. Henry asked me to find my alter ego. I gave several LA shooters due diligence, but the obvious choice was Hiro Narita, ASC. He was seasoned in VFX-heavy films, including *Honey, I Shrunk the Kids*, and he lived in the Bay area. To top it off, he was known as a good guy to work with.

This was a good time to check in with my crew. Who was game for another stop-mo feature? Most of 'em, those stalwarts! But there were a lot of jobs to fill because of opt outs and because we decided to add another assistant to each crew.

Henry had some more preproduction assignments for me, and I had some in mind, too. They'd all be more interesting than headhunting.

VFX Experiments

Could we somehow make a stop-mo ocean surface for the giant peach to bobble on? We wanted something stylistic, mechanistic—something more than those painted flats you see in school plays.

Henry had an idea for me to mock up: a stretchable cloth resting on rotating spiral cylinders. I gave it a reasonable go. My crude mock-up *did* suggest mechanical water but also revealed its shortcomings. The storyboards showed a submarine cruising, turning, and diving, seen from all angles. Both Henry and I saw the need for a solution that was much more flexible and animator friendly. Rubber sheets would never work.

After every mechanical idea fell short, I went to a freelance CG animator. All I wanted to see was a surface made with sine waves moving at right angles. That was too easy, so he threw in some shading. The image on his borrowed Silicon Graphics computer was encouraging: Mathematically smooth peaks and troughs were bobbing like cold molasses. My first look at the process had me encouraged. With just a little adjusting, we'd have our controllable ocean, right?

Not so fast! Revealing the devil in the details required more than a lone animator could create in his garage. Henry wanted foam on the waves (like that famous Japanese woodblock print, *The Great Wave*) moving in three dimensions! There were more details, like the interaction between the water and the peach.

Coincidently, we'd hired a VFX producer, Nancy St. John. She introduced me to Scott Anderson, a VFX supervisor from Sony Image Works. Scott had access to the talent and support that could deliver what Henry wanted. Henry and I looked forward to Scott's weekly visit, reel in hand. Usually, his shots were composites of our puppets and Sony's digital ocean.

That pesky submarine had been planned as a practical puppet, but it turned out Scott would have far fewer headaches using a digital model submarine and digital water.

Dahl's book describes "cloud men," giants made of cloud stuff who menace the peachonauts. Figuring out how to do that effect was another of my preproduction assignments. I turned away from a stop-mo solution after a minute or so. An armature covered with cotton wasn't going to cut it. Clouds have a measure of grace; they never jerk and pop, which was what we'd get by repetitive handling.

What if that puppet were loosened to be a rod marionette and then submerged in a fish tank? I threw together just such a puppet and almost had it—barely move the arms, and the effigy rippled gracefully, like a cloud. But it couldn't act. It could flail, but it was no good at throwing thunder-bolts or cloud spears.

All this was going on while I was working with the freelance CG anima-tor, so one day I showed him the soggy puppet. Eyes wide open, he said, "I couldn't do what you've already got here."

I turned to three CG companies in San Francisco and asked for a sample image: best cloud man wins the job. None came up with a usable sample, so I asked them to give it another go. That wasn't popular among the con-tenders, and I got a call from Disney's feature-animation president, Tom Schumacher, another straight shooter.

"Pete, you can stop worrying about choosing the right CG cloud com-pany. You're going with the cheapest."

Ah, freedom! That order was about as welcome as Kathleen telling me to "accept everything they show you," but this time, I feared we could end up with unusable material.

Henry could sidestep this conundrum by making a major design change: "Forget the cloud men, and make it a big cloud rhinoceros like your underwater puppets."

Excellent! All this critter had to do was roar, gallop, and maybe snort clouds! We'd require more than a fish tank. I immediately called Gary Platek, who'd bought ILM's gigantic glass water tank. Yes, he was open for business, and his 6-foot-by-6-foot, 4-foot-deep water space was ready to go. Gary and company would also build an underwater mechanical rhino about 18 inches long. One motor and lots of linkage. The beast could gallop and nothing else.

The tests with fluffy fur on the rhino looked like a cuddly rabbit, not a menacing rhino. Henry saved us again, calling for no fluffy stuff, just tight black spandex. It looked great, even better when Gary added tubes injecting white paint and black ink to seep right out of the critter's skin and swirl into the water.

Since it took half a day to flush and refill (from Gary's industrial fil-ters), both takes were precious, and they always depended on skill and luck. Some anomalies could add to the effect, but losing focus wasn't one of them.

Gary's assistant pulled focus as the beast raced toward camera, and he struggled day after day. I had to steal his fun and bring in the live-action moco. Once we rigged an encoder to the hand-driven track, the moco always knew where the rhino's snout was and nailed focus on every take.

We kept Gary busy creating plenty of material for the big storm the rhino lives in. How did he do it? Visualize milk dripped into a cup of water. That's the initial effect, but then it's much refined; you start by depositing a blob of white paint (not milk) in the water, then gently controlling water motion (like coaxing cats to perform) with various water jets, paddles, and saline boundaries. It's part tinkering, previsualizing, art, and physics.

Gary is a master, the best in the world, and will likely always hold that title. How do I know that? Some years later, Gary sent me a photo of his beloved cloud tank rolling off a truck and into a landfill. CG clouds have come a long way since 1994, and they're plenty good enough to do the job, especially if you're looking for the cheapest.

Would This Be *Pinocchio?*

Giant Peach couldn't look like *Nightmare*. We were playing a different tone to a younger crowd; *Nightmare's* prickly look wasn't going to fit. However, getting too cutesy would land us in the dreaded world of *Pinocchio*. Henry found what we needed in Lane Smith's unique illustrations in children's books. I'd describe the look as "quirky but smoother."

In translating Lane's paintings to puppets and sets, we retained much of their character. It's difficult to translate from one medium to such a different one, but the puppet makers really nailed it, setting an example for the rest of us.

We in the lighting and camera department could start making it "quirky but smoother" by reining in the extreme contrast while embracing theatrical lighting. That mantra defined our look as we waded into real sets populated with real puppets.

That's not to say we had a lot of puppets and sets to shoot—not in the early days, anyway. Our first shots were simple model shots of the peach rolling down to the ocean while camera prep carried on. Some of that prep was quite interesting.

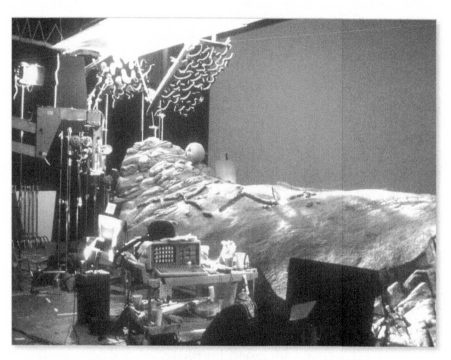

James and the Giant Peach set.

CHAPTER 35

New Toys

We were lucky to have the gear on-site from *Nightmare* because I could improve on all of it. One critical need belonged to the animators: Most of the time, they couldn't see their work in progress. There sat all those rackover Mitchell cameras, just waiting to be modified with a video tap. Wouldn't that be nice for the animators?

Richard Bennett of Cinema Engineering was ready to take on the job, and we met for a sketch session. What I needed was easy to describe but a challenge to deliver: Embed video cameras within our Mitchells, right in the viewfinder, such that we could see clear and accurate video. Also, eliminate the need to ever touch that bumpy rackover.

To get such a clear video image, I needed as much light as possible to fall on the sensor, because we were usually shooting under small lamps with the lens stopped way down. I nixed using a pellicle, a small, two-way mirror that divides the light between film and video. It's easy to install but eats up a lot of light. I needed *all* the light on both film and video. Modern movie cameras had mirrors spinning at 24 fps, one at a time, but those were far too costly.

Richard devised an animation-only version that we could afford. A mirror sits there, bouncing image to video, and then we push the shoot button, and a motor slides the mirror out of the way to expose the film. Then the mirror settles back to video position. The animators never had to touch the camera and could always see what they were doing. Excellent!

The Peach Cams were never said to be beautiful, but they did the job reliably, and we could afford enough of them to use in half the studio. I bow to Richard's skill and talent.

As for where those video feeds would go, it wouldn't be any more CEI frame stores. A better and cheaper device was now available to anyone with a checkbook. It was called LunchBox, as the electronics were housed in a genuine lunch pail, and it was designed just for animators. Cute. Lots of frames to store, not just two. Some animators wanted their own, and it didn't take long before they started asking for Henry on set to approve their work *in progress*!

With a name like *Giant Peach*, we would also need something to move 6-foot-wide peaches. We achieved this on-site, and it was made by machinist Chris Rand. Mostly half or quarter peach slices would have to pitch, roll, and yaw, plus move a couple of feet up and down. Lots of puppets would be animated on these platforms, programmed to float gently or struggle against hurricane-force winds.

I was intrigued by those six-point platforms used in simulator rides, but our Kuper systems didn't have the particular software for that stuff. It wasn't that Tondreau couldn't write it; it's just that our time and money required dumber and cheaper. It was easy to leave out three of the six linear actuators just by using the less exotic, more practical Kuper software. Chris did a super job on the rigs—four of 'em—and they looked cool!

Bookends

As we carried on camera prep and shooting runaway peaches, the live-action crew was shooting the opening bookend on Treasure Island, the hill midway across the Bay Bridge. Another defunct military building on Mare Island was the location for the closing bookend.

Luckily, Brian Van't Hul was available to supervise the live-action VFX. He'd been on *Nightmare* and had experience at ILM in the digital world. With just the skills we needed, he could make calls on how live-action plates should be set up. There wasn't time or money for moco in the live shoot, but Brian could at least get his hands on a Kuper system and a few encoders. He attached encoders to joints on the live-action camera crane. For Brian, the raw encoder data he'd collected would be useful when sticking our stop-mo characters to the live-action plates.

I got a few visits to the live-action shoot and got to know Hiro Narita and his crew. Hiro had an understated presence but was quite effective. Once, I asked for a less bumpy crane performance, and Henry cautioned me, "Pete, you gotta give him a break. When Hiro says that's as good as it can get, that's *it*." I wondered if that would fly in the animation studio. Later, in dailies, Henry pointed out a shot as too dark. Hiro was silent for a moment, then respectfully responded, "It will look better when the music is cut in." It wasn't a joke; it was true!

Live action had some interesting differences, like multiple takes and actors giving their all in a few seconds, in real time and real scale. The only way to transport the full-scale giant peach was by sea. It was quite a sight, a truly gigantic peach on a barge, chugging along in San Francisco Bay.

Hiro's crew had rigged all the lights to a dimmer board so he could quickly adjust a light here and there. Because a lot of the lights were way up in the ceiling, this really made a difference in efficiency. New to me, this process was gaining in the live-action world. I would've liked to have such a marvel on each animation set!

Big Sky

Shakedown time! We had a whole lot of shots coming with puppets performing on the peach against a background of moving skies. With budget in mind, I'd sold my bosses on motion-controlling painted scenic flats as the way to go. It worked okay on a daytime setup; the 10 x 12–foot canvas painting fit right into the puppet world, gently bobbing along.

Now we were ready to try a night. Good. It was a simple camera move, so bathing the scene in moonlight was not a concern. I was more interested in the night sky drifting by. Henry would want serious magic in some scenes. Sure, we could do it with backlight tricks and see-through mirrors. Practical background effects would deliver at a fraction of the cost of a comped-in sky.

In dailies, my test got a solid no-go from Henry. It was too restricting. I had underestimated the magic yet to show up in storyboards. What Henry really needed was the freedom to hang a blue screen behind those peaches. Later, he could finesse his stellar backgrounds and insert them into our shots.

There was just one obstacle: "This is what we budgeted for," I noted. The cost difference was enough to warrant a meeting in Brian's office with the big kahuna, Tom Schumacher. He quickly saw that what we needed was, essentially, to have a VFX company on call.

And Schumacher essentially had one. He also had us and the clout to mix and match as needed.

He asked, "You can save stage time if you don't have to set up backgrounds for every shot, right?"

That was a certainty.

"Then you can spend those savings making elaborate backgrounds at Disney's facility." Tom grinned at me. "That'd work, wouldn't it?"

Yes, in the flexible-reality universe that only top dogs live in, it would work very well. Schumacher worked fluidly, moving budget items around for the good of the film. I admired that and decided to adopt his big-picture view.

No, we didn't suddenly gorge on blue screens. Most daytime shots were in-camera. Up went a large sky painting on a pair of moco hoists, and my guys programmed the background.

The scenic artists had a lot of paintings to make. Henry asked art director Harley Jessup to make a cloud map to indicate what we should be seeing in the sky based on the camera's compass direction. The idea was to help viewers follow the action on the ocean without landmarks.

As more storyboards appeared, Buena Vista Visual Effects' (BVVE) presence would be more crucial in opening up the scenery. I can recall only three blue-screen shots in *Nightmare*, whereas we used traveling mattes all through *Giant Peach*.

My go-to guys from BVVE were Dorne Huebler, in Burbank, who made it all work, and Tim Alexander, who worked on-site with us in San Francisco. Tim would put together a "slop-comp" for something to slug in the cut, or he'd make a more finessed shot with me or Henry coaching him on the look.

With a single workstation, Tim's resources were slim, so the plan was that we'd send a sample shot to Dorne and his crew via a T-1 line so they could work on blocks of similar shots. But it really wasn't all that cut-and-dried. Shots were flying back and forth; Dorne worked on many sequences from the start while Tim was busy with his own load.

It didn't take long for the camera crew to begin calling Tim on set to advise on this or that detail; we wanted to ensure we'd give him what he needed to do his job efficiently.

The only downer with all those blue-screen comps was that it's boring, at least to the camera crew. I was reminded of Dave Allen saying it his way: "We expected to work on real sets, like they did on *Kong*, all the props right there in the environment. But there's only this screen, and we just light the characters and animate them in a void."

Here is a "real set," more fun to work on!

Building sets for shoot.

Painting a cloud map.

CHAPTER 36

No Cameraman is an Island

I t's no secret that animators prefer taking on a whole sequence rather than sharing shots with their colleagues. When possible, that's the way to go, because if it's "my sequence," I have more skin in the game, and it shows in the animation.

Big Stuff

When Ray Gilberti first saw scenic artists building a large Arctic Ocean set, he seriously wanted the assignment. Why?

"I like the big stuff!"

It *was* big. Moco rigs would move ice floes and icebergs in a frozen Sargasso Sea, where lost ships list and bob. The background was an expanse of Northern Lights, actually layers of bridal tulle. The set took 70 lamps, some on moco dimmers. That's a lot of lights in stop-motion.

The sensible way to shoot all this would've been as backgrounds and then comp it in behind the characters. The near certainty of lamps constantly burning out should have prompted us to proceed that way.

But no! We shot the scene mostly in-camera, beautiful and dearly won, excepting the necessary FX shots.

Determined to get as much as possible in-camera, Ray and I employed an old RP projector to add water splashes. The reason we chose the hard way is elusive. Yes, BVVE was swamped, but we also wanted to light and compose everything right in the viewfinder!

Once Brian Van't Hul had enough blue screens, he asked me for the underwater Arctic segment—all of it. In fact, he'd only take it in its entirety despite the daunting shot count. And they were all tricky shots.

Bill Boes made a pirate ship, sunken and haunted, for this underwater adventure. For Brian, this was a chance to make some spooky fun. For a watery look, Disney loaned us its legacy ripple glass. Some four decades before, the artfully ground and polished glass had hung on a downshooter to film *Pinocchio*. It was a pity the ripples were too strong. Brian made his own out of Plexiglas disks that were gently rippled with a thin coating of epoxy rotated in front of his lens.

Amping up the spook factor, he added moving gobos, projected in bubbles and ultraviolet light, revealing a host of glowing goons coming through the floor! Brian gave it his all, but when time ran out, he had to pass a setup to another crew. That's one of my favorite scenes.

Kendal Cronkhite cooked up the notion of teapot-shaped clouds for a scene featuring sweltering heat. The cotton-batting clouds would create a fun look, but we were anticipating making 38 background plates in the scene, and those cloudscapes would be big, 20 x 30 feet or more. How long would it take to make and shoot them? Nobody knew.

Sadly, Brian Rosen had to say no to cotton and yes to digital paint, the only surefire way to make our deadline. But a number of us pressed Rosen to endorse Kendal's cotton version. He offered a tough deal: He'd allow it, but only if Kendal and cameraman Eric Swenson could deliver all 38 teapot-cloud backgrounds in 38 days.

They immediately took ownership, creating a beautiful scene and finishing on time!

Everyone's Skin in the Game

Remember the concern about *Giant Peach* being too boring because of characters spending most of their time on one set? Henry, his story guys, and the design artists went to work with a vengeance. They really punched it up, staying true to the story while devising more of my favorite scenes.

Model makers, carpenters, and scenic artists gave us flyboys an interior peach-pit set, something to light and a relief from endless skies. The cave-like set could be lit and relit for any occasion and would always look good.

For example: "That's the Life," a song and dance in the pit featuring Dave Hanks's theatrical light changes as each bug gets its own solo. The scene was topped with a glowing translucent floor.

A very big pit shot, too big for a regular set, was pieced together by filming four segments on separate sets with separate crews. We start with an up angle from outside, then move inside the pit, passing snoring bugs in a very sweet scene as Miss Spider puts James to bed.

There was a lot of moco passing on moves to the next crew, and it was all tied together at BVVE, creating a show-off shot with taste.

You can't beat the climactic storm scene, which starts pretty, looking down on a beautiful backlit model of New York City, before diving into the tempest. Gary Platek's water tank magic is blended with the work of all, and we pulled out every trick to make it look windy and wet: animating flapping costumes, creating lightning effects, nonstop camera motion, mixing projection and blue screen, and plenty of magic from BVVE, including animated lightning bolts from the monster rhinoceros.

Wrap It Up or Not?

One wish we couldn't grant Henry was a slow-dissolving rhino puppet. Carl Miller spent several futile days experimenting with dropping cotton-candy rhino stand-ins into various solvents. In dailies, I reported that no solvent worked slowly enough; cotton candy just disappeared in a trice. That didn't please the boss. Dorne at BVVE gave Gary's roborhino a beautiful digital demise.

Dorne had started saving our bacon very early on. We had five shots in the can when the James puppet's eyes were declared inadequate. Too much detail; somehow, he looked like a zombie. In the first digital paint-out I'd ever seen, Dorne swiped away the offending orbs and replaced them with Henry's preferred black dots. Magic!

I didn't spend a lot of time at BVVE thanks to Tim Alexander's T-1 line, which enabled me to view what Dorne was doing via the phone. Still, Dorne visited us on occasion and brought real film to show Henry. Those trips became popular among his crew when they discovered the cute girls working on-site.

The visits were also inefficient. Screening one shot by looping over and over just invites nitpicking until the film breaks. And since we didn't have Kathleen, we didn't have someone to advise us to approve everything we were shown. Close to the end of production, I happened to overhear Nancy, our VFX producer, on the phone. "Sure, I can get him on a plane in one hour." She winked at me. A long day in a long week was about to get longer.

Nancy chirped that our friends in Burbank had asked for my eyes on a long and complex shot right now, or there'd be no chance of a change. "Actually," she added, "they already don't have time to change. They just need a buy-off."

Soon, I was standing in a cubicle with an overworked digital artist, who asked, "Whaddaya think?" It was all there: Miss Spider singing like a chanteuse while blowing exotic smoke fingers at Mr. Centipede. Tough shot, and it worked on the first viewing.

I gave him my thumbs up. "Fine, perfect, great job! You like it?"

He looked nervous. Considering the cost of this single-purpose visit, I felt compelled to take a second look. Nothing was different. "Still perfect!"

As crews finished their last shots, I became last (camera)man off. The Butt Saver rig and I had the whole studio to shoot a period-look parade of newspapers, the last shot in the show. When it was cut in, Technicolor and Dale Grahn were ready for color timing.

Three or four timing sessions, one a day, and it was smooth sailing, even with a few shots made on a bad batch of film. Then, near the end, I got a call from Hiro Narita up north.

Oops! Dale and I had cruised through his live-action work, and I hadn't even thought to invite him to join us. Was that a bad thing? You bet it was! In filmland, the cinematographer has long been understood to be keeper of the image right through post. Timing another cameraman's work was like taking a paint box into an art gallery to "fix" the exhibits.

Hiro was a gentleman about the oversight but firm in asking for a session on his work. The next morning, he scrutinized what we'd done and quietly approved. A lesser being might've called for changes just to reaffirm ownership.

Upon returning to the studio, I noted several unfamiliar sets under construction. Did Henry get another show? Not so fast. He was wooing Miramax (owned by Disney at the time) to partner on several concept offerings. Those mysterious sets were to demonstrate how the stories would look in stop-mo.

Some of us were asked to sign up in case it came to fruition. Talking contracts with Bob and Harvey Weinstein? Surreal! But first, we all needed a rest: two shows, back-to-back, in five years. One wrung-out animator insisted he wouldn't sign on "without the right to bail out!"

I threw my hat in the ring by photographing the dioramas, which were populated with figurines. I knew there would be plenty of time to rejuvenate. I found a two-week scuba sojourn in Mexico, but I wanted a lot more.

Then the phone rang: Alex Funke, calling from LA!

Eric Swenson, cameraman setting up a shot.

35:40

Glory Shot

S ome establishing shots become glory shots, like this one. The Halloween tricksters are running to their clubhouse while we see it close up. Behind is a chasm with a rickety bridge, and in the deep background are hills and a cloudy sky.

The whole set took to backlight beautifully, softened with sky fill. I had to add fog in the chasm by double exposing with airbrush wisps on black card. In the background, we layered on mist with a theater scrim to make the hills look farther away.

While Rich Lehmann was doing this, I was pinch-hitting for the interior, where the kids arrive in their rickety elevator. It was a quickie setup, and we got the shot.

Could I tear down the set? Sure, we'd never use it again. A month later, I needed to bring it back to life for new storyboards.

CHAPTER 37

The Last Spaceship

"**Y**ou've gotta get down here, Pete! We're getting ready to shoot the *last real model spaceships ever*!"

Alex's lure was tempting. Paul Verhoeven was directing Robert Heinlein's *Starship Troopers*—a future fascist state waging war on an alien species. No doubt, the satirical talents Verhoeven had used on *RoboCop* would be aimed at Nazism. That would be considerably meatier than *James and the Giant Peach*. And the spaceships were going to be totally big and bitchin'! It was certainly worth a look-see.

Alex ushered me around Sony Studios. In a big stage, first unit was filming space pilots at the helm as they dodged incoming enemy plasma (movie lights on moving ropes that would later be replaced by animation).

Atop the parking garage was Phil Tippett's green-screen unit, where an actress was pretending to be impaled on giant alien bug claws, emoting appropriately. Phil had stuck his neck out to create all the CG bug animation. It made sense; without top-notch bugs, there'd be no movie. He paused to introduce me, adding, "Pete's my *friend*."

We moved on to meet producer Jon Davison (also producer of *RoboCop*). Then VFX producer Ernie Farino appeared out of the past, pointed at me, and boomed, "This man once killed a hacksaw, that I would live!" in a tone right out of *The Ten Commandments*.

Whether intended or not, all the good vibes made it easy to join Verhoeven's Terran Federation. Let's see . . . it was summer 1996. I'd be home for Christmas for sure.

Finding an LA crew wouldn't be easy—*Troopers* and *Titanic* were shooting at the same time, so model-photography people were in short supply. And even if I'd had a little black book, it would have been way out of date. But Alex had managed to rustle up a crew, and I was eager to meet them.

Lock and Load

Actually, there would be three crews in our off-lot warehouse. Each crew had a director of photography, a moco cameraman, an assistant cameraman, a gaffer, an electrician, a key grip, and so on. I'd spend most of my time running my unit, looking in on the other two as needed.

The guys assigned to my crew already knew each other, which facilitated smooth coordination. I was the outsider boss. Some had questions, mostly about expectations; the answers were about responsibility. Then came handshakes. Ice breaking would begin as we tackled our first shot.

I used some of my prep time to settle on a look for lighting the ships in space. The work of three crews had to tie together visually. Specific keys and fills, plus glow from a planet below, were the main concerns.

It was best to shoot single frames, adjusting lights every which way. Pick the frame that fits our intent: danger, combat, and massive. It must also fit in the environment, and we must be able to see plot points. I made a pick and then asked for a moment with Verhoeven.

His entourage took up most of the space in the room. Someone introduced me. Paul beamed, "Ah, you are *he*!"

I gave him the viewing loupe. The room was silent while he pored over film clips, and he quickly made a selection. Holy shit, he pointed to my favorite! This was going quite well.

I joked, "You have good taste."

He looked at me quizzically.

"You picked the same clip I did!"

His expression changed.

Silence. The entourage looked at each other. Was I too cocky? There was a beat, then Paul laughed. All clear, and everyone chuckled nervously.

Don MacBain, the production supervisor, had told me about our shot list: long and complex. I intended to set a standard of efficiency right out of the gate, and we had the perfect prototype: Shoot one battleship in six different positions to create an armada cruising in formation that would overtake the camera.

My strategy was to mount the model in one static position and let the moco crane do all the repositioning. Then we'd program all six moco moves before we started shooting. Next, we'd balance movie lights, green screen, and interior model lights so we wouldn't have to shoot separate passes. That gave the compositors six pieces of film to work with rather than 18 or 24. The crew got right into it, and we went home feeling good about getting it all in a day.

Oops! Turned out the compositors wanted everything separate so they could tweak things—change a practical light, for instance. That'll cost ya!

Alex wanted us to test an arc lamp as a better key light. Take out the Fresnel lens, leaving a naked globe. Such a source should cast much sharper shadows on our ships, which would make the models look bigger. Clever! None of us wanted to spend six months under a glaring ultraviolet arc, but we honored the request. The results showed little difference in sharpness, and without a lens, it would be very dim. Better to stick with incandescent lights. Alex took it like a gentleman.

"What stop do you want?" That was gaffer talk from Mike Curtis, asking how bright I wanted the key light to be.

My answer was easy. "Enough candle power for really deep focus shots, like a 2K!"

Yes, in the stop-mo world, a 2,000-watt lamp was extreme overkill, but it would be wimpy in our 40 x 80–foot stage. I had to adapt.

Mike had a better idea. "Let me show you a 20K."

Big and 10 times brighter than a 2K, it was just what we needed for speeding up exposures. We were moving in the right direction, so it was time to visit the other crews.

Trooper~Size It!

Scott Campbell (the apple thrower I'd last seen on *The Abyss*) had a similar stage and crew but a different vessel: a boxy, bulky, large rescue ship. My 6-foot beauty mimicked a World War II battleship, easy enough to manage, but Scott's model evoked a washing machine in design, size, and probably weight.

Going big was Ken Ralston's idea. "Small models, we've all seen them. If we're going to do models again, we have to make them better." (By the way, Ken was now running the whole effects company.)

Campbell had a matching model mover inspired by the time-honored Worrall geared head, tough enough to hold the heavy cameras of yester-years. We model shooters use them to make pitch-roll-yaw moco mounts. Campbell's rig was nearly as big as a sedan. Once some weight and balance issues were addressed, the rescue ship could perform. There was an interesting solution for stepper motors stalling under considerable load: Pneumatic cylinders could be programmed to give the rig a boost.

Josh Cushner's assignment was to shoot all the background ships. Several 2-foot battleships were usually on grip stands as Josh and his crew composed, programmed, and filmed group after group.

Our next assignment had us passing the 6-foot ships to Campbell. We took on a bigger version, a 13-foot battleship. It was built for close-ups, but there was a rumor that Verhoeven wanted it for his front yard. I doubt it; it wouldn't have survived aviating on a moco rig.

Nonetheless, several shots would feature Big Boy pitching and rolling while cruising by the camera. With only an immovable model stand, the moco cameraman would have to simulate that motion with his camera rig. The illusion worked thanks to moco master Eric Pascarelli's brain-twisting programming. If our crew had been a French Résistance cell, he would've been the cipher brainiac.

CHAPTER 38

The End of an Era

In the middle of *Starship Troopers*, word came that Miramax wasn't interested in Henry's story offerings. Moving out commenced, and the studio's contents were scattered around San Fran, mostly sold to other businesses. I was lucky to find a home for my bulky rigs in the Colossal Pictures building, which was now a studio for hire.

Too many set and prop treasures ended up in dumpsters, and Disney sequestered the Peach Cams somewhere in Kansas. Perhaps the unkindest cut was that the building that housed Skellington Prods became a warehouse for toilet paper.

I may never again enjoy a diverse semi-family like Skellington.

My *Troopers* crew was a bunch of rowdy guys. The grips built makeshift exercise machines and hid them behind a huge green screen. Most of us were into pumping up in hopes of charming the ladies. Lacking any on set, language took a dive, and some altercations were resolved by yelling, throwing, and getting physical. The clipboard girl checked in every other day, and we snapped to while she basked in our suddenly intact manners.

Waiting for a long shot to finish fostered a campfire feel: dark around the perimeter, eyes on the lights, insect sounds from the moco. It was bonding time. We shared our life experiences, including what it's like to work on pornos or to be thrown in jail for calling a traffic cop "Officer Little Mouth." We were having fun and delivering great shots.

Producer George Merkert asked me, "How do you get so many shots done without coffee?" It was a nice compliment, and I credited the crew.

My contract was about to run out, and Merkert wanted me to re-up. It was beginning to look a lot like Christmas, and the show was running late. Tension was in the air. Phil Tippett asked someone, "When are you guys going to tell Pete that he's never gonna get outta here?" I told Merkert I'd never bail on him, but I didn't want to sign anything.

"Death from Above!"

If you've seen photos of WWII landing craft on Omaha Beach, the *Troopers* vessels will look familiar to you. We had a massive sequence ahead: Dozens of troop ships would detach from battleships, drop to the embattled planet, and disgorge live-action troops.

At the top, one docking bay and one landing craft stood in for six, similar to the way we'd approached our first shot. There was something new, though: "Red screen" replaced green screen due to a space shortage. We could hang red screen very close to the models by lighting it with ultraviolet tubes. There was also something old: shooting in smoke for ships buffeting in atmosphere. Drifting smoke looks dangerous when filming at 2 fps.

Once the ships land, we had a trick I thought would bring us to our knees. The idea was to pull a last-minute switcheroo: At touchdown, the model door would morph into a live-action door, letting actors stampede out.

How closely could we match the lighting on the live-action door? After three valiant tries at it, we handed off a work in progress to the digital artists. When I saw the resultant comp much later, I was amazed. I asked how they did it.

"Well, we did a lotta things. . . ."

We were still dropping landing craft when I was asked to step away and take on a more urgent job. Uh-oh. It seemed Verhoeven was hearing too many voices, so to speak. "We need one person talking with Paul about the model shoot."

I'd had a little taste of that at Skellington, but Paul's load must've been astronomical by comparison. I can't deny that the prospect of hangin' with *RoboCop*'s daddy was tempting. But I scanned the stage and my crew and decided this was my natural habitat.

"Sorry, but I have a lot to do right here."

I referred Scott Anderson for the job. When I told Scott a few weeks later, his eyes opened wide: "So you're the guy I should kill for getting me into this!"

John Henry Meets the Model Hammer

One bottleneck we had was getting the boss to approve the previsualized animations ("previs"). When Paul finally signed on a blocky digital cartoon, no one dared tweak it. But, sometimes, we had to. Typically, we'd refer to them as moving storyboards, making adjustments when our real models didn't match the cartoon. That was gonna stop.

In the interest of greater efficiency and directorial bliss, it was decided that data from a previs would be loaded into the moco, and the rig would ape the cartoon perfectly.

But wait! Vagaries of real-world messiness demanded the squeaky-clean data be modified. Otherwise, things wouldn't line up in the frame. Eric's solution was to simply blow away the data and jog motors to key frames that mimicked the cartoon. With care, he was successful.

Scott Campbell's moco guy, Joe Stevenson, had a longer schedule, and he eventually got closer to the upload and shoot dream. Precision was their teaser; their toughest shot had two ships in a grinding, scraping collision, and the ships' trajectory threatened to get intimate with the camera. How could they barely avoid the unwanted ménage à trois safely? Sony's brain-bugs created accurate digital models of everything: camera rig, model rigs, and the ships themselves. Then they programmed a move in Maya 3D animation software. It never achieved perfect perfection, but it prevented a disaster. Okay, then. Upload and shoot!

As we approached wrap, we were instructed to take stills of models as they were retired—not pretty pictures, but front to back, top to bottom, and various elevations in flat light. It looked like Alex was right about *Troopers* being the last big model shoot. Our stills could become skins to wrap around digital models.

A poster showed up on the common wall: "Models are still an option!"

An anonymous dialogue sprouted around it, accusing and consolatory. End of an era? A clue was waiting back home. I was discharged from the

Bug War in June 1997. Good to be home after eleven months. Then the phone rang. How do they know?!?

Interlude with an Ogre

It was John Garbett from Pacific Data Images/DreamWorks, known for *Antz*. He'd like to meet in Silicon Valley about a show.

Several people were in the meeting. The company's next project, *Shrek*, was to employ model sets in which the CG characters would live. My job would be running the model shoot. Shoot? It would be a whole movie! The concept art was inspiring—exteriors with scope.

We got down to methodology, and one guy was bent on the CG animation driving the moco—and perfectly. I had a déjà vu moment from *Troopers*. Want to drive the truck? Fine. Perfectly? The real world just isn't as squeaky clean as the pixel world. I was honest about mechanical linkages and repeatable slop. Like a trial lawyer who wasn't getting the answer he wanted, the guy modified his question and asked it again and again. We finally agreed that a teeny-tiny tweak in post could fix any anomalies we'd encounter.

Overall, I came away feeling optimistic. In fact, I was so fired up I bought a massive moco crane, the Boomasaurus, at the Boss Film auction. It was perfect for shooting large model sets. And it wasn't cheap. Nor was it cheap to ship it to mingle with my other babies. John Garbett would certainly be pleased.

He called. "Pete, I don't know how to tell you this except to just say it: I don't have a job for you after all. Jeffrey Katzenberg decided to make the show all CGI."

There was my clue: It *was* the end of an era. On that raw note, I decided to give my brain a saltwater rinse. There's a lagoon in the central Pacific Ocean where dozens of sunken Japanese warships rest in peace with downed Allied airplanes. Beautiful sea creatures live in those eerie ghost vessels. Just a few days of diving at the unique site made everything better.

My scuba gear was still wet when Henry Selick called. He had an interesting project in the works.

On the set of *Starship Troopers*.

CHAPTER 39

Monkey Kong

s I listened to Henry describe his new enterprise, it dawned on me that this would be another "last chance" to work on a disappearing genre. The film would have a stop-mo-animated ape that makes trouble for a cast of live actors. Was I interested? Sure! This was a pitch I couldn't turn down.

It sounded like a Harryhausen show, only this wouldn't take place on a mysterious island. Instead, the action would unfold in the hero's mind while he was in a coma. And the simian wouldn't be a giant ape, but a monkey.

There would be plenty of interaction between humans and Monkeybone. I salivated, thinking of the technical challenge ahead. And part of the job would be on the live-action shoot, working with the crew to make shots to blend with the animation. I'd practically never done it and had never seen it done. I was excited.

Henry had found the graphic novel *Dark Town* to his taste and enlisted a few talented friends to bend it into a property a Hollywood studio couldn't turn down either. Sam Hamm, who'd written the screenplay for *Batman*, was working on the considerably different script. In the original, the monkey is a red bag where the hero stashes his imagination. In the script, it's an orange monkey named Monkeybone, cartoonist Stu Miley's brainchild, who comes to life. That would be much more cinematic than a suitcase.

Another score was Mike Cachuela, the storyboard artist who'd worked on Henry's shows. His twisted character ideas, beginning with a cyclops with stunted trunk and dangling legs that walks on its hands, were a whimsical nightmare. Gnarly!

It was time to get to work.

How Much Is That Monkey in the Storyboard?

The picture was bound to be heavy on visual effects, and Henry wanted two VFX supervisors: me and Peter Crosman, who was more familiar with LA visual-effects companies. Crosman and I divided our tasks. I'd be there if we had a monkey in the shot and for live-action plates and animation. Crosman had a raft of work that would keep him on the entire live-action shoot.

Initially, a few of us moved into a San Francisco office to help obtain a green light. Sam Hamm and Henry had scoured Hollywood for an agreeable studio, and, finally, 20th Century Fox showed some interest. Of course, they required a budget that was both affordable and believable. I needed to show we could pull off the Monkeybone effects, which would represent a big chunk of the show, without breaking the bank.

When you have to put a dollar amount on VFX scenes, your best guide is the storyboard, because the script is usually open to interpretation. In order to estimate how many shots might be in a given scene, I made up some of my own boards while waiting for Mike's. After several script changes, I had some numbers I'd stand by.

A studio rep expressed "concern"; we had nothing for a rainy day. I learned that everyone adds a little padding, typically called "incidental," that often blends into invisibility. The studio rep wouldn't give us a thumbs-up until he could see 10 percent extra cash in the monkey stash.

The executive producer at the time—soon to be replaced—then pulled in most of the department heads for a script breakdown. Page by page, he quizzed us about specific props, sets, physical effects, costumes, and, of course, visual effects. The process gave us all a better view of the whole production. At the end, he told us how much the studio was willing to invest in the show.

"The magic number is 60. I could easily spend $60 million on a movie about two people talking in a room."

Then he asked us for our department budgets. We all scurried back to our Excel sheets, hoping to get a big enough piece of the pie. Was this making movies? That's why they call it "show business."

When I found out what our piece of the pie would be for monkey shots, I gave Mike a list suggesting how we could distribute the work. Example: "We can do 18 monkey shots in scene XYZ, and half of them allow climbing on Stu."

That exercise in knowing our boundaries may seem a bit cheeky, but there was precedent. On *Jurassic Park*, Spielberg had asked Dennis Muren why he wanted to tilt the camera up a little.

Muren: "If we see the dinosaur's feet on the ground, the comp will be more complicated."

Spielberg: "What would it cost if I tilt down and see his feet?"

Muren: "Another $10,000."

Spielberg (to his operator): "Tilt up."

Monkey Menu

Not every suit was sold on a stop-mo monkey for our titular character.

"We still got the time to try some options. Henry, you know Verne? You gotta see this guy!"

The next morning, I was stepping into the elevator and reaching for the button when I heard a kid's voice.

"Hi!"

I looked around, then down, and there was a man beaming at me.

He extended a hand. "I'm Verne!"

It was Verne Troyer, probably best known as Mini-Me in the *Austin Powers* comedies. That day, he impressed everyone with his hyperenergetic monkey act, even going so far as to climb on a couple of the suits.

Impressive, but Verne didn't get the job.

"What if he gets injured? There'd be no backup."

Any more options?

Someone had a bizarre comedy skit on tape that featured an actor rigged up with a shrunken body from the neck down. It was disturbingly funny, but a one-trick pony. (You can find it on YouTube: *Titanica Visits a Fan.*) Nonetheless, Henry wondered if it could be improved enough to carry the show.

Cameron Noble created a monkey suit to Henry's specs. This version would allow more range of motion in the arms, but the rest of the shrunken body remained. We shot a thorough test with a professional actor to see what we could get out of the contraption.

In dailies, Henry was not amused with Cameron's creative embellishment of the suit: a prominent male member. It kind of drew the eye. Cameron spent the night with his computer, erasing frame by frame.

The test showed the trick lacked the versatility necessary for the monkey's extensive job, but we decided it suited another character: Hypnos, who had stunted goat legs and would move around a lot less.

So, Monkeybone would be the stop-mo puppet he was always meant to be!

Casting Drama

There were other disagreements, each with its own drama. For some time, we'd pictured Nicolas Cage as Stu Miley. He seemed perfect to play a beleaguered and unsettled cartoonist. The studio producers didn't agree with the choice. Too old? What group spends the most on tickets? Teenagers, especially boys on dates.

How about Ben Stiller? He's younger, but he had ideas for his dialogue. "Stiller's out."

The final selection, Brendan Fraser, wasn't as bent, but the kids would like his physical comedy.

What about the vixen, Miss Kitty? Casting mouthy Sandra Bernhard assured a comic Kitty with an attitude. Later, they swapped in Rose McGowan, closer to the younger crowd. It was all to the better if you were a male teenager.

What Would Ray Do?

We'd won our stop-mo monkey, and now the animators would need help. The monkey had to not only perform on its own but also cavort on Brendan, who would be in constant motion himself, in live-action plates. Adding another layer of complexity was the mandate that the plates would be filmed with a moving camera.

In a nutshell, the camera crews and animators would have to align their work with Brendan's performance frame by frame. That was what Ray Harryhausen did from *Mighty Joe Young* (1949) to *Clash of the Titans* (1981), when he loosed the Kraken. The only difference was some 50 years of technology.

Ray had to squint through a grainy viewfinder and line his creature up with a dimly projected background. In 1998, there were a lot of new widgets we could combine into a system to help the animators get the job done. The dream was a big, bright, clear screen with two images mixed together: sequential frames of live-action plates and live video from the animation camera's video tap. No more squinting. The animator should be able to grab the monkey and push it into position with Brendan frame by frame.

Computer tech Derek Gatlin put together several workstations that could do mixing and sizing tricks, shuttling backgrounds while running a LunchBox application. In an especially nice touch, Derek added a video-style "fader bar" so the animators could see through the monkey to see the background.

Tackling the "bright and clear" objective on the camera side, I sought out ILM optical engineer Mike Bolles. I wanted to get rid of the grainy viewfinder's ground glass and swap in a lens, one so perfectly curved that the video tap would see the same picture, but as a crystal-clear aerial image. The physics would work, but there would be some spending on machining the camera's inner sanctum.

Oops! We had only one camera suitable for the modification: Henry's. It was a slicked-up Mitchell 35 that had already "had work done" to become a Fries pellicle reflex. Stage manager Kirk Scott and I trolled for workable Fries conversions. We found eight and paid around $9,000 each for them—a bit more than my camera budget. Sorry.

We got a clear image but still had to get brighter. A few of the newer instrument cameras were advertising long-exposure capability. There are our new video taps! They could make a muddy image bright. The brightness came at a little refresh jitter on longer exposures.

This wasn't going to be just any rear-projection setup. Bow down to the Monkey Cam!

Santa Gets Double Vision

What does Santa see when his eyes are rolling in opposite directions? We'd find out as soon as Eric Swenson filmed it. It'd be easy if Santa was looking at an immobile pile of rocks; we could shoot one camera move, then rewind and shoot another move. But Santa is looking at a lot of moving characters. Was there some way to shoot two moves on one camera at the same time? Eric's quandary set me up for a weekend of fun, fiddling with the scripting program.

"The new trick is mostly bookkeeping. Make two camera moves, one rotating clockwise and the other rotating counterclockwise."

I had fun introducing new stuff. "The new trick lets you alternate between the moves, shooting a frame from move A, then wind back and double expose a frame from move B."

It sounded easy, but it took a while for Eric to finesse it so an audience could follow the action and not vomit.

The trick was never used again, but I remember it as the elusive "perfect stop-mo experience" we seek; everything is working, and everyone's in the zone. At moments like that, I'd growl a line from *Patton*: "God help me, I do love it so!"

CHAPTER 40

Three Months among Live-Action

It was time to join first unit in Hollywood. They were almost finished shooting the real-world scenes and were moving to Down Town, where Monkeybone is. We'd be shooting in Desilu Cahuenga Studio, where the original *Star Trek* was filmed—holy ground for a lot of Trekkies.

The "Coma Bar" scene made an excellent introduction to the job, the people, and the protocol. I found Brendan Fraser in the makeup trailer. As polite as could be, I told him what to expect for our first monkey shot: "We'll be pushing your face around with these sticks so it'll look like the animated monkey is really in contact with you." It was okay by Brendan.

I continued, "The monkey also gives you an aggressive, yucky kiss."

"Like this?!" Brendan grabbed my face and smacked one on me, just like Bugs Bunny pestering Elmer Fudd.

Fraser grinned. "Sure, you effects guys can dish it out, but you can't take it!"

He aced that shot, as well as a lot more in the scene. It couldn't have been easy to perform with his invisible costar. First, Brendan would rehearse a shot with a dummy monkey in hand. Then we'd shoot a take, still with the dummy, for animation reference. Then, quick as he could, Brendan dropped the dummy and repeated his performance.

Before moving on, we shot a short burst of a mirror-surfaced ball positioned where the monkey would be. Reflections on the ball helped to analyze where the lights had been placed. Then I grabbed my camcorder and filmed reference for recreating the lighting and camera in the animation studio. There wasn't much time to collect info, so I pointed and talked: "We're on a 17-millimeter, the monkey is 5 feet away, and that's a 2K up there with a quarter-blue gel, and it's hitting the monkey with 24-foot candles." That routine would carry through my tour of Down Town.

Andrew Dunn, BSC, the director of photography on the show, seemed amused by my home moviemaking. That sparked a friendship, and he showed me a demo of the digital camera he was using to preview contrast and color on film.

Assistant director Mike Topoozian liked the time-saving camcorder, too. He was the guy keeping it all moving. A good AD has to be the hammer. Mike once let it be known that our burn rate with a full crew was $300 per minute, and he would invoke that number to speed things up.

"Hey, Pete, how long to rig your strings?"

I guessed that I needed four minutes.

Mike announced, "Pete wants another grand!"

Not everyone liked my little video cam. The electricians teased their new assistant, lying about what I was doing with it. He strode over to me.

"Are you filming my plumber's butt and uploading it to the internet? Are you? Because I just couldn't stand that!"

I assured him his chastity was intact, but he still glared at me for days.

We added tricks to our monkey routine as needed. With motion control, of course, whenever we had a rig or wire to digitally paint out, we shot a clean pass of the set using the exact same camera motion. As moco ate up minutes, Topoozian increasingly wanted to skip it. "Fix it in digital" was the new "kick it down the road," making first unit look sleeker.

The gag in which the lusty monkey dives into Miss Kitty's bosom proved we could get away without moco. Making room for Monkeybone's entry required parting Kitty's cleavage on cue. It was an easy rig: A talented puppeteer pulled a string from below, dragging an overstuffed sock. Rose McGowan did her part like a trouper, and then it was up to a digital artist to erase the sock and insert the monkey. If a lone digital artist could clean that up, there'd be no more live-action moco.

Instead, camera operator Mitch Dubin would shoot future clean passes, panning and tilting, relying on his muscle memory and the viewfinder. Mitch was a proficient operator; his freehand clean passes left little for digital cleanup.

One overtime night, I got a chance to perform as a monkey, furiously running and bouncing a dummy monkey on a stick to Henry's directions. Mitch, the actors, and some future animator needed something to follow as Monkeybone bounded through the Down Town set. As soon as we got the beat-up dummy on film, Mitch would reset and film the real shot with a host of actors and no dummy.

We had several similar shots to go and were losing steam. Feeding the crew, even at midnight, would be helpful. Despite the union rules declaring "pizza is not a meal," that particular food often shows up anyway. But we were pampered; we had tasty burgers at 2 a.m. Yum!

While shooting continued in the big Down Town amusement park, gaffer Pat Grosswendt had already leapfrogged to the next set to start lighting. I sneaked over to watch him and his crew at work. I immediately got hooked on the colored gel covering all the overhead lights—Congo Blue. It was a deep, purply blue and sucked light like a black hole. The effect was a perpetually dark sky not of this earth—in a good way! I spent 30 seconds worrying about how this would affect pulling blue-screen mattes. We'd make it work. At least the monkey was bright orange.

By the time we came to shoot the "Hypnos Pajama Party" scene, the monkey shots were getting simpler, and I was a more familiar face on set. Sometimes, the shoot felt like a real Halloween party, with the cast in beautifully deranged costumes. In that spirit, a transient twosome found cover behind the set wall for a quickie.

Only by contrast, my argument with Henry was as public as it could be. Invoking Spielberg's order to "tilt up," I argued against complicating a shot despite Mitch's suggestion that it would be more dynamic. Maybe I was being too protective, too shrill. Henry went for the simpler shot.

Andrew murmured in my ear, "You have an interesting relationship with that man."

The Brits have a mannerly way of communicating more than they say.

I smiled, in one singular eye.

I began working on my last set, "Death's Office," by gently mashing Whoopi Goldberg's hair.

"We'll press here and here so it looks like the monkey is jumping on you."

Whoopi's hairstylist looked horrified. Whoopi responded with her eyes and a nod, which I took to mean, "Calm down; he's a neophyte."

No drama. There are divas, and there are Divas. Whoopi must be one of the good ones. I know nothing about being a comic, but when I heard Whoopi allowed only two takes, I understood. A joke has a short shelf life; too many repeats, and it's circling the drain.

My load was pretty light on this scene, so I could enjoy the show. Whoopi, playing Death incarnate, and Tom Haden Church, playing Death's waggish assistant, made a good pair. They kept it fresh, changing every take. Henry voiced his concern about continuity. What if this medley wouldn't cut? I'd have to wait to find out. There were no more background plates, and my Tinseltown tour was over. The monkeys were waiting.

CHAPTER 41

Shanty Town

B ack in San Fran, the model and animation studio offered less glamour. It was in a dodgy neighborhood on the South Bay. Even with the dead body floating into our channel, it felt like home.

I'd hired my crew before going to LA, and some were already there, setting up the stage. Eric Swenson had a model shot in the making, a scary roller coaster that was Stu's way of getting into Down Town.

Henry hadn't liked the first test; he thought it was too slow, but mostly, he didn't like the design. It looked safe, sturdy, as though built in a real carnival. Henry wanted one that looked like something Dr. Seuss would draw. The new version was so spindly that it couldn't hold itself, and the camerawork was fast and queasy. Perfect!

There was another model, much grander, across the street. The model shop, M5 Industries, was owned by Jamie Hyneman and his buddies, better known for the TV show *MythBusters*.

Bill Boes, the production designer, had it that all of Down Town nestled in the palm of a huge mechanical hand that opened up for new arrivals. The model was big and complicated, just the way we liked it: 12 feet across, with carnival rides and the giant fingers all rigged for motion control. Don't forget the blinking carnival lights and the smoke beams!

While the giant hand was flexing in one stage, the bulk of the crew claimed space throughout the building. Kirk housed them in black curtains, creating a scattered community of large tents. Each had a blue screen, a Monkey Cam setup, and a monkey puppet. Most had some form of motion control, depending on what the shot needed.

Nick Blake made some custom rigs in the form of Brendan's torso and another of his head. Both were painted blue screen and able to mimic Brendan's movements, programmed by a cameraperson. With that, a monkey puppet could cavort on the robodummy any way the animator wanted while the dummy copied Brendan's movements.

If it all worked as planned, we'd have a monkey element that would line up with Brendan moving in the background. I'd expected some mechanical slop that would require digital cleanup, and we got it. But we also got what I wanted most: the monkey's changing perspective while climbing on Brendan. That trick spared animators the grunt work and, more important, helped get the show delivered on time.

In addition to head and shoulders, the crew moco'd Stu's wrist, backpack, and the handle basket on a flying bike so the monkey could clamber on all of them. The most brain teasing was Nick's moco treadmill, built to keep Monkeybone's feet in sync with the floor running under him as he runs by his well-wishers in Down Town. Why not just mock up the live-action floor and animate on it? Too easy? No, for space and lighting, the puppet had to run in place while the camera pulled back, making it look like Monkeybone was going forward, away from us. Marks on the treadmill indicated to Trey, the animator, where to put the monkey's feet.

At about this time, we got a visit from one of the producers. I showed him around, explaining the puppets and the improvised technology. With a pained look, he interrupted me. "Didja ever hear of computer graphics?"

As the giant hand was finishing, another big model was loading into a separate building. This model was a roundhouse, the rotating train track used to move a train car from one line to another. In the movie, the roundhouse was for sending souls on their particular destinies, so it had to be grand, kinda like a Gilded Age glass dome.

Back in LA, we'd had a look at a real roundhouse, and it wasn't at all grand. In fact, even I, with my liking of machinery, thought it was butt-ugly.

I was glad when we commissioned M5 to make the model. It was beautiful and a challenge to shoot. The lighting would be somewhat complex, but programming its motion was more like a moco Gordian knot. The shots came in slowly, which made production itchy. I stood by my crewman, but others thought we'd gone rogue. One coordinator tried a novel way to clear the bad juju, bringing in a Marin County swami to burn sage on the roundhouse stage.

Soon, they brought on Dave Dranitzke to coordinate the train set, and that introduction turned out to be a lucky break for me. Dave would later call me about another project.

Peter Crosman had been working with post companies in LA while I was in Shanty Town, and now it was time to join him in putting together all those elements.

Outsourcing in LA

Crosman; VFX producer Terry Clotiaux; VFX coordinators Laura Schultz, Tricia Mulgrew, and Jenny Spamer; and I formed a tight unit during the live-action shoot, and now we were juggling work at 10 independent facilities, massaging our film elements into shots ready to splice into the show.

There was no single facility like Disney's BVVE. Instead, Terry and Peter had allotted bundles of shots to each of the smaller companies based on each company's size and specialties. That wasn't new, even then. Even early Detroit automakers bought spark plugs, tires, and other parts made by others to put in their flivvers. That's outsourcing, and it's showbiz, too!

Here's a look at the companies we were working with:

- Captive Audience Productions
- Centropolis Effects
- Digiscope
- Giant Killer Robots
- Howard Granite Films
- Look Effects, Inc.
- Menace FX
- Pacific Title Digital
- PTM Imaging
- Riot

Generally, Crosman and I took on separate bundles of scenes, working with the digital artists much as I'd done with Disney's artists. My typical day included plenty of driving, ping-ponging from one post company to the next. A chunk of my duties was ensuring that colors remained consistent in shots done by different vendors and picking at matte lines. That stuff was easy, as they usually had it nailed on the first shot.

The best part of the job was getting down to the nitty-gritty of bringing the shot to life. We'd start by lining up the various film elements if they weren't already lined up. I was surprised when a digital artist said he would have preferred it if we'd skipped our moco trick, trying to make the monkey element imitate the live-action camera's trajectory. It would never be close to the perfection they needed. In fact, they'd have to do more work. They'd have to stabilize our work so there was no camera motion at all, and then the match-move artist would stick the monkey in the spot, frame by frame, perfectly. As for the monkey's acting, that is still the animator's performance.

I found that some artists had developed their eye reading warrior-babe comics, while others learned by looking at the real world. I didn't expect to have to explain why faraway things should look misty, but there it was.

Although I like flying, I found it irksome to fly up to San Francisco once or twice a week to screen dailies for Henry. Sometimes it was solo, and sometimes Crosman came with me. Too many times, we went back with tails between legs from all the thumbs-downs.

After one happy screening, I called Terry.

"It went well, and I'm about to get on the shuttle to the airport. See ya back in LA!"

Terry had a surprise. "No, don't. You're not coming back."

"Whaddaya mean?"

"We don't need you. Just a few shots to go, and Crosman's here. We'll have Jenny send your clothes and stuff."

"No way. You can't make her pick up my dirty underwear; I'm gonna do it."

"No, you're not."

"Yes, I am, goddammit!"

"Okay, come on down."

Twenty-four hours later, I stepped off the same shuttle with a full suitcase—and freedom.

Short Subjects

Freedom also meant a lull of unknown length without a job. I wasn't hurting after a good decade of work, but I was skeptical about the future. Stop-mo-driven features had peaked in popularity with *Nightmare*, and, although I didn't know it, *Monkeybone* was about to tank.

How many years would pass before a studio subsidized the genre again, if ever? Same with *Troopers*. By that time, more models were being made of pixels than plastic.

At the grocery checkout line, a toddler pulled a DVD off the rack. It was some treacly cartoon. I got fired up at the possibility of making low-buck shorts for kids. It had been a long time since I'd known what kids liked in stories, but there were plenty of examples in bookstores.

One popular story was so right for stop-mo I contacted the publisher in New York by phone, then mail, including a DVD of us making *Nightmare*. My contact suggested I meet her at a publishing convention in San Francisco. That was quite an eye-opener; there's a lot of books being printed every year. When we got to film rights, the 9/11 tragedy erupted, and that's the last I heard from her.

I found another promising book, and the author lived only two hours away. He was excited. I made a maquette of the main character to show how it might look. The illustrator liked the idea, too, but static from his rep soured me on the project. It was three months of wooing and too much for nothing. Forget that.

I could write my own story, and I did, along with a screenplay. Not to say it was great, but it was mine. While writing, I created an Excel doc and played "What you can get for the money," keeping myself honest.

I purged the living room of furniture, carpet, and anything on the wall. Then I installed shop tools and camera gear. Voilà—a studio! I started on the three characters and worked on into winter.

Then I got a call from ILM. They hadn't called me in 10 years. What was up?

CHAPTER 42

When the Moon Shines

John Knoll's invite came while I was feeling the tug of cabin fever. He was shooting some models for the *Star Wars* chapter *Attack of the Clones*—a big, beautiful battle arena. It looked like it had been carved out of a sandstone cavern. Soon, Pat Sweeney, Carl Miller, and I were pounding out shots on two models, with Carl working the night shift on both.

They'd compounded the three crews with the goal of getting all 300 (or so) shots in the scene done by end of the year. I recall being told that four shots a day were expected, but seven would be better.

Lucas was said to want lots of quick cuts rather than a few long masterpieces. While waiting for a thumbs-up to shoot, the word was, "If John isn't there in 15 minutes, move on!"

Almost every shot in the live-action green-screen battle had camera motion that had to be match-moved. The data was sent to our assistants to feed the hungry moco rigs.

ILM had made considerable progress. First and foremost were the cameras, which were electronic—no film. Sony's CineAlta HDW-F900 was the high-definition camera of the time. Like many doubters, I sniffed at certain specs while comparing it to film. How sharp could three dinky 2/3-inch imaging chips mounted on a red-green-blue prism block *really* be? All three had to line up within specs that would make you cry. Could cine lenses ever be sharp enough on such small chips? Film was way bigger! What about pixel count, everyone's favorite? It was a good number,

1920 x 1080 pixels, almost the standard 2K for filming out a digital feature—unless that number was divided among three colors, and, if so, wouldn't it really be a third of that number?

It was irrelevant. That's the camera we were going to use, so stop nit-picking, and use the Force. I glimpsed an image on the flat-panel monitor, and it looked beautiful, like a movie.

A greater beauty to us shooters was having a live image to quickly and accurately line up on moving backgrounds so we could check composition, lighting, and smoke density and compare with adjacent shots. The bottom line was that, without the digital camera and the rest of ILM's system speeding up our capability, the scene wouldn't have been doable.

Still, Christmas was a couple weeks away, and we weren't going to finish in time. I went to the company party in San Francisco, although a good rest was what I craved. Nobody else from the shoot showed up. No surprise. Mingling, I saw mostly digital artists I didn't know.

Wait, look over there. There's an angelic blonde with baby blues in a skin-tight, dark purple dress. Who's *that* lady?

Easy. She was talking with a buddy of mine.

"Hi, Alia! Who's your friend?"

Katy was visiting Alia from the Monterey area; they'd gone to high school together. Did Katy know there was a famous song with her name on it?

She received my clunker with grace. I quickly got better—or at least less lame. She seemed happy to talk with me. We chitchatted, slowly drifting from the group.

I learned that *Professor* Katy Moore was a painter and an art teacher. Smart was good. So was her Peace Corps stint; she'd taught African kids in French.

She must've known that asking my age would show she was interested, but I imagined she'd find the number too high. Be smooth; be vague.

"What's your age?"

Around my upper forties.

"Like 45?"

Nope.

"47?"

Negative.

"49?"

Heh, not exactly.

"You're 50!"

Well, it happens.

Katy found the big five-oh her magic number, chirping, "I'm 44!"

She radiated a playful smile when we danced. Fast or slow, it was a tactile pleasure; she was a runner, and I liked the feel of her girly firmness. When we were tired of dancing, we stayed together until she and Alia had to leave. We agreed to meet soon.

Just after Christmas, we were in a bar, chatting during the crooner's breaks. Chat became questions, big ones for a first date. We smiled when we found neither wanted kids. She had taught several *thousand* kids, from K to 12, plus college. I was still working on growing up myself. After that, the rest was easy. We congratulated each other on learning from our starter marriages.

On the way to the car, we walked through the neighborhood, stopping at the most overdecorated house. We looked up at the clear and cold night sky, and I told her I wanted to try something. I gently kissed her, and she pulled us closer together.

Our little scene took place on my turf, but next time, it would be somewhere in the Monterey area. I already had the directions. I had *always* had them:

K-k-k-Katy, beautiful Katy,

You're the only g-g-g-girl that I adore.

When the m-m-m-moon shines

Over the c-c-c-cowshed,

I'll be waiting at the k-k-k-kitchen door.[1]

Four-Way Matrix

The kid-vid project would now be one of two activities. Weekend visits with Katy became the preferred activity. As I got to know her, I was convinced that she was a keeper; my mental checklist came up all okay, and

---

1   Geoffrey O'Hara, "K-k-k-Katy," 1918

my gut acquiesced as well. We had three months of part-time familiarizing, not a lot, but I figured it was enough to make a decision. From what I knew about long-distance relationships, they tend to fizzle over time. Yeah, maybe it was the time to make a move. Three months later, we were in a Sonoma vineyard, with family and a jolly preacher man throwing petals over us.

In no time, I got a call from Dave Dranitzke, who was coordinating a "really big" model shoot for the *Matrix* sequels. Dave needed a big moco rig—namely, the Boomasaurus.

"Want a package deal, Dave? You get a camera, rig, and me to run it!"

"Yeah, that's what I was thinkin'."

The model was designed as a massive gate with surrounding wall and deck. It looked like a steampunk version of a medieval castle gate. Cool. For a model, it really *was* big, spanning 40 feet and rising to 20 feet.

The angles on the storyboard would be hard to get on film. It would have me flying the camera from 30 feet, up in the perms, down to the deck. No can do. The Boomasaurus reach envelope was much too small.

But we could build a moco crane more in the scale of good ol' Argentinosaurus, holding the camera in his mouth. There was a talented welder on-site, my hefty floor track was suitable, and studio space was plentiful; we were in a World War II aircraft assembly hangar.

I gave the welder a sketch with a track-swing-boom rig mostly made of triangle truss. Chris Andrews, a very smart guy, would handle the electronics and assemble the whole thing, stacking it up in pieces—*heavy* pieces. Just how to do it could've been a real conundrum. In a stroke of luck, the hangar's ancient gantry still worked; it had been hanging overhead for decades, hoisting heavy bomber engines. Solved! The project inspired a lot of unwanted advice. At the end of his patience, Chris painted on it, "The Amazing Cluster-Flex."

As it turned out, the rig was as clean and simple as could be for a rig with a 30-foot boom that parked level at 21 feet overhead. To make sure the rig was precisely on the start marks for each pass, Chris attached three lasers to the camera. Three beams shined down on targets taped to the floor. Those red dots landing on each bull's-eye was all the assurance we needed.

With all the counterweight up there, I had safety rules, starting with

"Never get under the rig." The contraption was top-heavy, likely to tip, so we had to avoid jerky starts and stops. I clung to my OCD routine: "Slow in and slow out."

The cinematography had been designed long before my crew and I came onto the show. A concept painting showed a badass vertical laser beam bouncing off the underground ceiling, much diffused. That's what they wanted. My gaffer, Jeff Gilliam, and his guys went hanging bounce goods high over the set and sneaked in a couple of small hard-light sources to rake up the door.

Much like *Clones*, the camera motion had been designed in CG. My slice of satisfaction was seeing the rig perfectly copy the CG and turn shots in on time on another squeezy schedule.

Toward wrap, I heard from Jo Carson, my assistant, that Tim Burton was going to do another stop-mo show, this time in England. Maybe it was something to look into.

But Katy had already been uprooted once this year. How would she take another move? Sure! She was all in. I was, too, assuming there was a job to be had.

It was easy to find out that Mike Johnson, a veteran animator from *Nightmare*, was going to do the heavy directing for Burton. I asked for some face time with Mike and was soon driving down to meet him and his producer in LA. It was good to see Mike again, and I met Jeff Auerbach, producer and rep for Will Vinton Studios up in Oregon. Jeff had put together a dynamic duo: Mike directing and David Bleiman as line producer. Both guys had solid stop-mo experience, had recently worked at Vinton, and were friends of mine.

All I knew was that Tim's show would be based on the Jewish/Russian tale *The Corpse Bride*, which I'd read. One passage had stuck in my head: A dead girl, scary but beautiful, climbs out of her grave and demands some rube marry her. Would that scene be in the show? Mike assured me it would. The scene was so vivid in my head; it must've been percolating since I was a snot-nose kid sneaking peeks at horror comics!

Yeah, I really wanted that scene, and I told him. Well, Mike had a bloke in mind who was already in London. Jeff told me I'd have to sell myself to Mike real hard . . . because I was "Henry's guy."

I tried to figure out how to calm any qualms about my allegiance. I would be a subordinate with some significant film experience behind me. Someone like that could be a trusted ally or a threat to one's authority.

Out came my new CV/résumé, and I emphasized that I was wingman to the director, knew how to take orders, was a great team worker. "My job is mind-melding with Mike's vision, putting it on film, and staying on budget."

Jeff had his turn. "Pretty pictures, but can you really stay on budget? This one isn't going to as big as you're used to." (It was just over $30 million, slim for the times.)

I told him I was a tightwad from the Midwest and explained how I'd saved on opticals with Koz-Mo and helped to get *Monkeybone*'s green light. He liked that "I usually do the VFX supervising, too." And, finally, I had been testing a new way to shoot stop-mo that would help the whole animation process save time. Would they like to know more?

One of the VFX guys on *Matrix 2* had told me about a digital camera that had a unique sensor design. The three color sensors were stacked, just like layers in a color film negative. I'd recently tested the Foveon camera at home. What can I say? It worked. Anyway, the pitch was that any suitable digital camera would be better than 35 mm film for stop-motion.

Mike and Jeff enjoyed hearing about my ultrapositive experience on *Clones*, but the *Corpse Bride* camera budget had already been spent on Mitchells, rented from Vinton. Could we send 'em back? That was a touchy subject, so I let it go.

It appeared that Jeff, and maybe Mike, wanted me to sign on, but no offer was forthcoming. At hand-shaking time, Jeff asked, "Are you still interested, knowing it's going to be on film?"

I was there for the picture, I said, not the toys. I'd been inspired by our chat and wanted to help the film achieve its potential.

They'd be in touch.

40 foot moco rig Pete built and was used to film
large gateway door in *Matrix II* named "ButtSaver".

Santa Slides Down the Tube

The first storyboard drawing came to me as a conundrum. We're close on Santa, face to lens, as we slide down through a very claustrophobic pipe. With a 2-foot-long, 2-inch-wide pipe for a set, we'd have some space issues. But we solved those puzzles.

Because the animator's hands couldn't get in there, he carefully slid the puppet out for each frame to adjust Santa. Because there was no conventional way to get light in there, we used a clear tube and wrapped it with dark blue gels, much like I'd done on *The Abyss*.

This shot was only a quick passage to Oogie Boogie's lair, where Santa gets roughed up by the gambling bag of bugs. Deane Taylor's "dungeon with casino décor" look was pretty good in his color sketches, vivid colored chalk on black card. We wanted the sets to have a lot more vivid colors, like the one-arm bandits, garish colored lights on the slot machines. We wanted a look you didn't see anywhere else in the film.

Tests got us part of the way, and we used lots of strings of tiny lights, but they had their limits. "Black light" was the key. Use the right paints and flood the set with ultraviolet radiation. The UV paint looks like a light source, and everything else is black. Of course, you have to paint under UV to see what you're doing. That's what Deane and his crew, Kelly Asbury and Kendal Cronkhite, did.

Animator Owen Klatte was getting scratchy eyes from the UV lights, even with anti-UV glasses on. The invisible light was all over his setup. A simple Koz-Mo script enabled him to animate in peace—no UV, just a pleasant work light. When he was ready to shoot a frame, he would duck out and hit the button. The work light turned off, the UV turned on, and the camera took the frame. Then the lights changed back, ready for Owen to animate another frame.

There was more than UV in Oogie's world. When Oogie is menacing Santa and Sally with his lava pool, we used movie lights. The key light became the bubbling, yellow magma. This was another use for methyl cellulose; we installed a large, clear tub in the set. It was filled with artificial snot, and a 1,000-watt light pointed up the pool. For that bubbling effect, we threw in some dry ice.

Of course, we had to shoot a "lava-only" take running at 24 fps or faster. Then it was Eric Leighton's turn, and he animated into the next day or more. We could've shot each take on different strips of film and married them in post, but that was too easy—or too smart.

Instead, we decided to shoot both takes on the same piece of film. Shoot the lava, wind back, and shoot the animation. We got away with it and saved an optical.

When the chase gets really hot, we fogged the atmosphere with yellow and orange light. In the same way, we doubled-exposed in airbrush art.

The last shot (50:58) called for a long dissolve: Santa and Oogie slowly transform from unhinged UV to normal movie lighting. The dissolve could have been done with dimmers: one light setup cooling down while the other lights get brighter. The only snag was that UV tubes weren't dimmable. But with a tweak of the Koz-Mo script, we could get both lighting setups in full brightness and on separate frames. The checkerboard strip of film would be easy to unravel, and we could finish the dissolve in post. Cool!

Nightmare Oogie Boogie set

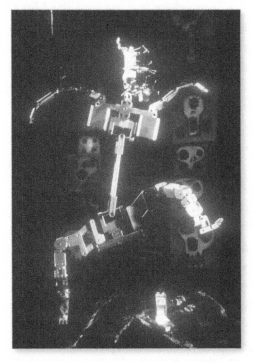

Oogie Boogie's armature on *Nightmare*.

CHAPTER 43

In Old Blighty

I n time—not much time—Jeff called. The boys had agreed to hire me as DP. How did I feel about that? In the King's English, I'd call it "brilliant!"

A few months stood before takeoff; it was time to visit Will Vinton's. Jeff wanted me to fly up there and approve the Mitchells. They looked good, recently used on a TV series. We got about 25 cameras in the deal.

More stuff was in the deal. It turns out that Vinton had been developing a frame grabber of its own. It was more advanced than anything else at the time. It was clear that input from animators and camera crew drove the design. I was glad to have 'em.

The package included a raft of Inkies, compact 200-watt lights. We'd have to find a bulb type for the United Kingdom's power, twice the voltage of the States'. A couple of small moco rigs, and maybe some Kuper controllers, topped up the deal.

I couldn't march into production without a way to let animators see what the camera sees on the grabbers. Somehow, we got permission to hire a camera machinist to do a low-budget version of the Peach Cams. Instead of pricey servo motors sliding the mirrors, it was to be done with solenoid magnets. The first prototype had the snap-action solenoid threatening to beat the crap out of the delicate glass parts. Let's try to dampen that hammering.

Meanwhile, I spent a week in England, interviewing camera talent. When I was finished, we had eight camera-crew units, each with a lighting camera and an assistant camera. A single gaffer would find eight electricians.

Coincidentally, another stop-mo feature was in the works at the same time: Aardman Animations' *The Curse of the Were-Rabbit*. When both shows were crewed-up, every animation cameraperson in the realm was working.

A few weeks later, I was back, testing Hammer Cam Mark II. It was much less jarring, good enough to start making Corpse Cams.

Preparing for living and working in the United Kingdom for a year turned out to be the same as going there for good: fancy papers to be stamped, renting out our US house, piling personal stuff on a single pallet, cramming moco rigs in shipping containers, and divesting stuff that wasn't worth storing.

My beloved Chevy Geo Storm was in the latter category. Two days before takeoff, three Polish students were looking it over. The prospective buyer was taken by the red paint and the sports-car look. The girlfriend hadn't much to say. The business advisor, the one in the fake leather jacket, scrutinized inside and out, smelling a rat.

"Vaht ees zis?"

Oh, that was a small scratch on the 10-year-old car.

By now, the buyer had bonded with the car and was deaf to the nay-sayer. "I do not care! I am 100 percent going to *buy this car*!"

And he did.

When offered a free mattress to boot, as well as anything else left in the house, the biz advisor changed his tune.

"I *love* this country! Everyone are positeeve here!"

After we circled a third of the planet, we were in East London, home of 3 Mills Studios, where *Corpse Bride* would be made. Back in the 1700s, the site was built for producing gin. In September 2003, those red brick buildings were still standing and ready for us. They confirmed we weren't in California anymore.

My first step was meeting with David. He'd been on-site for a while now and knew this show would be a squeeze. He expected me on-site in two days, ready to start. No problem. I was expecting to spend my year mostly in another black-cloth shanty town, with few holidays off.

Our two days of freedom was just what the jet lag required. Our new town seemed familiar, but with surprises, like which way to look when

on a crosswalk. Also, we needed time to process the dialects and col-
loquial phrases. I figured my instant familiarity came from growing up
with English stories, films, and pop music. My favorite surprise was the
Tube, London's subway system. With nine million people in town, something smarter than freeways had to be used by most of the population.
Imagine: For less than three quid, you can step into the train (mind the
gap) and spend your commute with today's news in *The Sun*. So, next
morning I would step down from the Tube and get *on* with it!

Prep Time

A handful of people from the States were allowed work permits, mostly
heads of departments (HODs). The rest of the HODs and all the crew
would be Londoners.

Some work on sets and puppets was going on, but we were only
in our prep phase. I began with Mike and the story. The script was in
flux, taking on a "land of the dead" contrasting with the "land of the
living." Tim Burton had that in mind from the beginning. We needed
it, because the original fable couldn't support a feature film. The fable
offered that cool out-of-the-grave scene, then a lot of yapping about
"Should they wed or not?" and then, finally, Corpse Bride throwing in
the towel with grace. The inverse-worlds would complement each other
and create some variety. In Tim's universe, Victorians in their stuffy par-
lors would be the ironically dead-like living world, while real corpses
would cut loose in a perpetual Day of the Dead. Each craft would help
give life to Tim's notion, especially paint. The Victorians would get a
lot of grays and desaturated colors, while the reveling Dead would have
more color and contrast.

I wrote up some camera notes for enhancing Tim's concept. Basically,
the Victorians would get a conservative camera treatment in keeping with
their proper, measured lives: Keep the angles level, use medium focal-length
lenses, and make only prim and civilized camera moves. The Dead would get
to turn it all upside down, with arty angles, wide-angle lenses close on the
subject, and energetic moves. Have fun with it!

It would be the same with lighting: The Victorians need to know where
the light is coming from, and it should be purposeful and smooth. The

Dead don't care where the light is coming from as long as it's fun, colorful, and contrasty. Party on!

The next stop was Nelson Lowry, the art director, from Vinton's. *Corpse Bride* was his big break, and he was earning it. His concept art was inspiring and clear; this wouldn't be a prickly mock-*Nightmare*. His paintings looked like they were hundreds of years old, moody and romantic, with atmosphere. Translated to film, with more contrast and selective lighting, we'd be hangin' with Rembrandt and his homies.

Seriously, our Victorian subjects could benefit from adopting a few hallmarks from the Dutch Masters, especially that single-light contrast—*strong* contrast! Or consider the foreground characters, basking in nearby firelight, while the distant walls are charcoal gray. Such images are associated with the elegant, polished, and theatrical, at least in my view.

The puppet designs had geared up for a legitimate drama with serious themes; the key characters were smooth, lifelike, and capable of engaging the audience. I took my cue from the gorgeous Corpse Bride puppet. We, the camera department, were here to make a spooky but beautiful romance in a theatrical vein.

There were a few sets on animation tables that looked like large crates; all four walls were attached. A carpenter pulled one off, and there was a stuffy but beautiful parlor. The sets were considerably larger than usual in stop-mo. I wondered why. I knew this would make for a better finish on the film; the details on the props and puppets would be more lifelike. The depth of focus would expand, and the audience would feel the wider space, engaging with the story more readily.

Was that the intent? No. I found the reason on a visit to Mackinnon and Saunders, quality puppet makers. Mike wanted mechanical face movement on several key characters so the animators could adjust jaws, cheek muscles, and eyebrows from inside the head. They'd slip tiny Allen wrenches into hidden holes, twist a little, and the flexible skin would be pushed and pulled in any increment required. The puppets could be made to speak and emote with great subtlety. The mechanics inside had to be as compact as possible, because the size of the heads was governed by the gears and screws inside. The job of making the innards was literally in the hands of two small Asian women—nobody else had fingers small enough to do it. Head size, body, clothes, props, and sets all had to be scaled to those mechanical skulls.

I started out with a crew of Clive Scott, the gaffer, and Andy Bowman, the camera and moco engineer. Much of our prep was similar: rounding up "kit" for Clive and Andy's domains.

Clive had no problem laying cable with some of his crew and securing steady power. But when we fired up an Inkie with a 240-volt "bubble," we got a lot of heat, but not much usable light. Whatever the elusive culprit, the Inkies remained the lamp of *last* choice. The electricians renamed them "gimps."

We went to ARRI Lighting, one of the premier makers of lighting kits, and spent at least one crown jewel on brand-new ARRI lights in 300 watts, 650 watts, 1K, and 2K. Clive suggested another favorite in Britain: Strand's Micro Ellipse. If the puppets made their own show, they'd use them as spotlights; these were real ellipsoids in puppet scale.

Andy knew where the moco rigs were hiding in London, and we went on excursions to examine them. Most were home-brew contraptions, much like my spawn, and some looked more manufactured. By the time we stopped hunting, our menagerie boasted 10 species that could freely fly a camera and seven less evolved breeds that could move in a straight line, with pan and tilt.

As the sets and characters were delivered, I tested them for the screen. A typical task could be testing black crow puppets for optimum shine in backlight or roughing in a set, homing in on a suitable light treatment.

While lining up on an awkward angle, it occurred to me that the story guys could find a better composition if they were actually on set. We tried it with Mike and his story artist, shooting stills, options for individual cuts for this set. It worked well on a few scenes, and we all had fun, but the tightening schedule didn't allow for more.

It was time to bring on camera crews, one by one, to take ownership of their assigned sets and do a serious prelight. The animators were coming!

CHAPTER 44

The New World

When the first batch of Corpse Cams arrived, they landed directly in Andy's shop. A quick test showed that we could use them, but I wanted a bit more TLC from the solenoid. Andy was sure he could calm it down on-site. We didn't know that unforeseeable events would soon eliminate the need to bother with solenoids.

Like a bolt out of the blue came a change of the guard: The first line producer was gone, along with the producer. Allison Abbate was now line producer. She had worked under Kathleen on *Nightmare* and had risen to become a respected producer at Warner Bros., the studio paying for our show. Like Kathleen at Disney, Allison had backup from the Warner mothership.

One of her executive peeps, Chris DeFaria, senior vice president of physical production and visual effects, called Allison with a question for me.

"Why aren't we shooting on digital?"

Oh, the irony of it. If only his question had been put to others months earlier. I blew away the little black cloud of cynicism over my head; maybe this could be a second chance.

My explanation was an enthusiastic and agitated tale, hopeful, knowing that we were on the same image-sensor wavelength. And, in fact, we were. DeFaria and Allison were interested in giving the digital idea a shot. Manna from Warner would fall for a short time so we could prove it feasible. We also got Chris Watts, a VFX supe with imaging smarts. He could spearhead the testing and assemble a pipeline from camera to camera and to the editor's room.

Finally, if the tests were positive, we could go camera shopping. Better get crackin', because we were now poised to turn over several setups to the animators and start shooting in three weeks. The plan was to test several commercial off-the-shelf cameras only. We already knew there'd be no time to write code for an industrial camera, whereas digital SLRs would come with enough smarts to do what we'd need.

My list of must-haves included sensors roughly the same size of the 1.85:1 aspect ratio on 35 mm, the ability to use Nikon lenses, a pixel resolution at least or better than 2K, and the ability to display a RAW test frame in Photoshop. While waiting on developing a real color and density profile, I would need assurance that we were exposing correctly. It's too easy to adjust the image on the monitor instead of actually changing the lighting on set. With a RAW file adjusted to emulate the film test clips, we'd have a poor man's color profile, good enough to avoid such sins as underexposing.

The test was to compare images from a Mitchell film camera with images from the digital candidate. Each camera shot the same material: five setups lit and ready to go. Then all the images went to a color-grading facility, where I adjusted the digital images to better match the film.

Studying the film-outs in a screening room, I saw enough good images to allay concerns about minor glitches. I'd seen how stable the images were as JPEGs on a monitor. I showed the test to Tim and Mike. After I explained the glitches, the directors were pleased to continue going down the digital road.

Chris Watts and I had already agreed that the best candidate was the Canon EOS-1D Mark II N. Now was the time to write a check for 31 of them, close to the same number of sets we had to service. That was a big move in our jump to going digital, but we had more moves to make before we'd have an efficient system. Meanwhile, we began making shots.

Not everyone on my crew was elated by the last-minute change, and one bloke made a habit of bleating, "Digital may be new, but film *works.*" Aside from shock of the new, replacing a hefty Mitchell with a "GirlyCam" could be seen as a threat to one's manhood.

Without the niceties that came with working with a film lab, we needed a surrogate on-site. Chris worked out a system whereby Martin Pelham had a few "data wranglers" who would take the camera memory cards when they were full, then process and archive shots, run the digital projector, and develop any custom programs that would make the flow smoother. One gift from the wranglers was easy access to sequences from the intranet. Brilliant! We could easily match continuity with an adjacent shot.

Chris went on a hunt for graphic monitors of the CRT kind. They were getting scarce but were preferred for their accuracy, better than the newer, flat, LCD types. Each crew got one with a Power Mac G4 computer, both screwed to a trolley that had big, beautiful balloon tires to protect the hard drive. These "lighting stations" would be what we'd refer to while lighting. They were the only way to see an accurate image; the projector was especially inaccurate. Kudos to Mike for trusting my daily affirmation in the screening room: "It's not so plugged up. It looks great on the lighting station."

About that promised "real color and density profile," I was stuck on making the profile bend and tweak the RAW image to respond like it was shot on Eastman Kodak 5248, the film we used on *Nightmare*. Dmitry Lavrov of FilmLight Co. could do that. It took some doing, but it would be more accurate than eyeballing it. Instead, Dmitry analyzed color chip charts and gray scales shot on film and digital.

It permanently narrows interpretation of the raw camera data, like committing to a set of printer lights. It imposed a standardized monitor image in a situation where noodling with displays could lead to entirely different exposures and contrast ratios between crews.

Andy had his work cut out, too. In 2003, Canons had no way to run a live feed to the animators' frame grabbers. What they did have was a viewfinder we could modify enough to attach a small video camera in just the right spot. There's the feed, but we needed to look in the finder, too, for things like checking focus. Andy designed a swing-away joint that would click right back into video position.

He came up with several other must-have items: scaled-down matte boxes, mounts for moco focus drives, digital frame counters, remote shoot switches, moco interfaces, and a means of preventing animators from shooting with the work lights on. I kept finding new needs, and Andy was the go-to bloke. When he was overloaded, he'd see me coming and open with, "Yes, sir! Yes to *everything*." Maybe he felt that the Yanks were giving him a Colonial treatment.

Andy and I had an ongoing debate about which moco systems were the best, British or American. Later, our gentlemanly contest expanded to other channels in technology.

On their farewell day, the British Concorde supersonic jets buzzed East London, which was most impressive! Andy pointed out that the fleet had flown for many years, whereas the Apollo landings were only one-offs.

Harrumph, I had to stand up for NASA, if only by getting snarky:

"You're right, Andy. We just . . . went to the *moon!*"

Malcom Hadley, one of the lighting cameramen, had warned me about dust settling on the sensor. Every time we'd change lenses, microscopic dust motes could stow away and hide in the camera. The only way to see one on the sensor was to shoot a frame and look for one on the monitor. To get rid of it, you had to gently swab the delicate sensor. Shoot another frame. Did we get it, or was it still there? This could become a Sisyphean cycle, and it did.

What if we did all this in a high-tech cleanroom? Andy was game and made a desktop version, a see-through box that was fed filtered air, keeping the bad air out. Only one person was allowed to perform the operation. Want to change lenses? Bring your ailing camera to Andy.

Might as well upend another institution. I was puzzled by electricians waiting for their LC to meter the lights. Clive explained, "Sparks [electricians] don't carry light meters in the UK. Only LCs have them."

Was a light meter a badge of rank? Whether it was or not, I had a problem with it.

"This is a waste. The sparks are just faffing about when they could be advancing their shots."

After a congenial chat about cultural differences, Clive would tell his crew that we expected all sparks to carry meters. Nothing fancy, just be able to converse in foot-candles. After a couple of days, I noticed electricians wearing guilty grins, coddling their shiny, new light meters.

CHAPTER 45

Pretty Pictures

F irelight in a dark room brings its own drama and can guide the
viewer's eye. That goes for constrained window light, too. We tried
to use more shaping with shadows and highlights, as if working in
black and white. In the Land of the Living, subdued colors in paint and
clothing got us close—but not all the way—to B&W.

To make fireplaces useful for us, we needed to manipulate the light in
terms of both direction and reach. The light from a real fireplace doesn't
have much reach; it takes several lights behind the fireplace opening aimed
at who or what you want to see—for instance, two crossbeams and a middle beam, all scraping on the inside walls and spilling out to the room floor.
If you can't reach some character from inside, cheat a little; send forth a
special beam from somewhere convenient. Program them to flicker. We
insert the actual flames in post.

The scene that lured me into the job was all about moonlight, not a
flame to be seen. I called the scene "Bride Rising." It starts with Victor (the
unsuspecting groom) wandering in the forest, reciting his wedding vows,
mistakenly evoking the Bride and then fleeing from her, and, finally, the
Bride catching up to him in a whirlwind of crows on a stone bridge. Let's
make it spooky but beautiful!

The Bride's ascendance had to have some dynamic camera move; the
corpse just poking out of the ground wouldn't cut it. The best idea I could
come up with was switching places, with the Bride barely sticking out of
the grave and the camera at shoulder height. Then camera descends while

the Bride rises to her full height. The balance of power is reversed, with the Bride towering over Victor, seated on the ground. It was simpler than what I had in mind, but that's all we needed.

We had several sets for the scene, all covered with trees and snowdrifts lit by moonlight; those Micro Ellipse beams turned out to be the primary lighting. They gave us the control to home in on layers of trees and layers of scrim netting that created the background night mist.

The Bride had to look eerie but beautiful, and a Micro Ellipse beam behind her veil was just what we needed—a halo, glowing like you'd see in an old religious painting. With a little smoke in the air, we could have seen the moonbeams coming from behind her, but that would have stymied every other setup in the studio. Actually, there was a cheap and simple way to get the effect in post. All we needed was a green screen behind the Bride, and the rest was a straightforward digital process.

The glam recipe that had worked for Sally in *Nightmare* gave the Bride the same effect, a few clicks up in the diffusion filtering, purposely flattering lighting, and longer lenses. Acknowledging the Bride's star status, we even enhanced her bluish skin with Steel Blue gels.

When we got to making glam eye lights, the animator, Brian Demoskoff, had to land the puppet on the marks exactly where the eye light was. Lifting the puppet out of the ground was accomplished with a small elevator, so Brian could count on the Bride parking in the right spot. The Bride's lighting worked pretty well here, and we adopted that look throughout the film anytime she was being supernatural, angry, or self-sacrificing.

Anyone animating the Bride had the finicky job of animating her veil and wedding dress. That's right: They were animating cloth! Some cloth was veined with wire, and often, there would be an overhead veil rig consisting of armature joints attached to parts of her gown that couldn't stay up by themselves. These shots were considerably more time consuming to make, as you might expect.

Simon Jacobs and his AC, Christophe Leignel, shepherded the scene along while Stuart Galloway worked on the end of the scene, where Victor gets to a stone bridge and is cornered by the Bride. The storyboards had the camera spiraling in and around the odd couple. Stuart was the senior Kuper moco system cameraman, just the bloke to take on the challenge.

(In fact, Stuart had started on the show training most of the rest of the camera crew.)

For several reasons, it made sense that the bridge rotate, not the camera. For one, we didn't have the space to make a 360-degree green screen in the size needed. And even if we did, none of the rigs could reach that far. So, we rigged the bridge and the key light to rotate. All the camera crane had to do was move in on the characters.

Stuart still had to deal with multiple circles. To avoid twisting cables, he could only do one turn, then rewind to the same spot, then carry on the move as if no rewinding had been done. Every time he did another rewind, he was getting into deeper danger of ruining the animator's work. There were nerves of steel on that one.

For the background, Nelson Lowry made a 360-degree matte painting that included a photo of a small-scale church from the model crew.

This setup was so unkind that the animator had to skip the veil waving in the wind. Instead, this would be one of the few times we stepped up to an all-CG veil.

Once the whole four-minute "Bride Rising" scene was put together, it became one of my all-time favorites.

By this point in the story, we'd been in heavy drama for 20 to 30 minutes, and it was time to change to something lighter. We find our intermezzo in a colorful pub down in the Land of the Dead where a troupe of skeletons performs a jazzy retelling of the Bride's story. Call it "comic relief."

As fun as this scene is to watch, LC James Lewis and I had to work out quite a shadow conundrum. The challenge was lighting the skeletons with two different colored gel lights while creating only one shadow per skeleton on the stage wall; all those double-shadows would just be a messy jumble. After some epic failing at moving lights around, we gave in and decided to shoot individual elements that a digital-compositor could combine later.

The key element would be a single clean shadow—no skeletons, just shadows. That would let the compositor replace, stretch, and squeeze the single shadows as needed. Capturing such an element actually called for a second camera in our cramped quarters. We had to find a spot for the "clean-shadow camera" where the puppets weren't getting in the way so we could cast a sharp shadow with a tiny halogen bulb. Of course, James would have to switch lighting between cameras, each frame.

Our deus ex machina solution made it too easy. In the midst of shadow play, we flip to black limbo, behind dancing skeletons lit with saturated colors, while we keep changing to the music, in complementing pairs.

Happily, the Dead didn't spend their eternities in such hallucinatory lighting. Most of those twisted sets were bent in a theatrical vein, a good contrast with a "classical" lighting look. No worries; those underworld sets would never be mistaken for the Victorian world.

Besides making things pretty, our photography was expected to further the emotional tone. Most of the crew had a shot at an exercise in changing moods in the same setting. Three or more scenes take place inside a Gothic church. Here are the shooters and explanations of what they did:

Simon Paul's sequence took advantage of a stormy night to create a creepy atmosphere. Inside, we used a single candle as the primary source, uplighting a gaunt and scary pastor. Moonlight coming through the stained glass dimly defines columns and arches within, and flashes of lightning punctuate his dialogue.

Mark Stewart took the church in a spare and somber direction, setting the stage for a loveless arranged wedding. He used soft daylight to shape the architecture and enhanced it with a few unmotivated specials.

Several units, particularly Peter Sorg's and Simon Jacobs's, had a mega-scene that changes moods three times: a midnight wedding with a heartfelt exchange, a clashing sword fight, and a transcendent moment of self-sacrifice. Both crews created an uplifting feel, enhancing key areas of drama with brighter pools of moonlight. The Underworlders brought their spooky touch in the form of light scraping up the columns from holes in the floor.

As the duel worked as comic relief, I assumed we could get away with using red rim light on random surfaces to sharpen the air of danger. When the Corpse Bride brandishes a sword, she gets the "warrior babe" lighting: A strong underlight casts dark shadows and throws highlights on her sword. When the bad guy perishes, he takes on the Dead's blue glow, with a dark background.

For the uplifting finale, we'd saved our brightest moonlight of all, giving the Bride her most beatific and luminous treatment!

Katy on *Corpse Bride*.

CHAPTER 46

Visual Effects

To animation camera workers, shooting live-action elements is a guilty pleasure, like a baker licking frosting off the spoon. Bring on the smoke and fire, and let in the mist, ground fog, tear drops, and rain splashes! "Camera is at speed! Action! Cut!" Fun? Yes!

One day, while the crew was at lunch, AD Ezra Sumner and I grabbed all the smoke puffs, coughs, and twisting smoke we needed. Ezra did the puffing on his beloved cigarettes while I captured his stinky performance on my mini DV camera.

Andy Bowman and I shot the ground fog in "Bride Rising" by corralling dry-ice floes to fit the shots and shooting on 35 mm film. At the end of the roll, we caught rain splashes and tears sweeping in highspeed for more pathos.

Stuart Galloway was the master of our water tank setup. Originally, I was looking for a way to remove the burden of animating the Bride's veil. If we submerged a veil in a fish tank, the veil would drift elegantly with the currents. It looked great, but to follow the Bride's animation, we'd need some underwater moco move matching towing the veil.

We found a hefty aquarium that didn't break the bank, and Stuart did a serious test, right down to a composite. It worked, but the trick would never be as versatile as we'd need. That's when I looked into a CG solution.

The fish tank was still perfect for filming those "not of this earth" elements, like shimmering fairy dust and noxious vapors from a poisoned chalice (not to be mistaken for Ezra's twisting smoke). Stuart's magical splooge from a cracked egg was worth an "Ooo!" from the audience. That's where Bride and Victor *shwoosh* from the Land of the Dead to the Land of the Living. Thinned glitter paint deftly poured was the magic.

Banging our heads on a challenging moco puzzle could be fun, too—for instance, the bad guy's POV as he circles the Bride in a tight close-up. After wrangling with three or four axes to no satisfaction, James Lewis tricked the Kuper system into thinking the pan axis was 12 inches in front of the lens, inside the Bride's head. Now, when he commanded a single pan move, all the axes would work together, automatically sweeping the camera in a perfect circle. Clever was the lad.

The flight of the butterfly in the opening credits was a team effort that required pushing a single camera move through three sets, another puzzler. LC Graham Pettit started the move in Victor's bedroom set, flying out the window. Then James finished the move, drifting down to the street, another set. Then Stuart inherited both moves to fill in the middle part, flying around the town rooftops. To make it more of a challenge, Stuart's set is half scale. Take a bow, mates.

Now, who was putting together all these shots and elements? Much like the VFX work on *James and the Giant Peach*, we had a single effects company on *Corpse Bride*. The Moving Picture Co. (MPC) handled it all: compositing, painting out puppet supports, and CG animation.

Yes, there was more CG than the handful of veils. MPC created falling rain, flocks of butterflies and crows, smoke rings, and singing spiders (when we ran out of the puppet versions).

We also had a representative digital artist on-site. MPC set up four workstations that were supervised by Jessica Norman. We could set up a look, and Jessica would crunch a sample shot to send back to the mothership. Very useful.

I never thought of color timing as a VFX job, but times had changed. Some people were skipping the tradition of giving notes to the colorist as they watched the movie in a screening room. Instead, they were digitizing their negative and putting the entire movie in a system for image editing, a.k.a. "Put your movie in Photoshop!"

What a perfect match we would be, shooting and color-correcting in digital. I was fired up. We had scenes that needed some work, mostly in strengthening the mood and clarifying the subject. And MPC actually had the tech and a talented colorist. The only snag was that Allison said, "You aren't going to do it."

What?!

She explained that Tim was going to do the digital grade, and we wouldn't need to do it twice, as the dwindling budget could use a break.

Nolo contendere. It was Tim's movie!

Nonetheless, I just had to have a hand in it! I complained enough about the shooter being keeper of the image that a bone was thrown my way: two eight-hour timing sessions with Max Horton, the colorist, in his digital lab. Then I'd walk away, and Tim would have the lion's portion.

Better make the best of it; there would be no time for musing or dabbling. Max and I had to show up on the day knowing exactly what we wanted to accomplish and *why*. Before the digital intermediate day, I gave Max a copy of the movie.

"Take it home and watch it with your family."

I hoped that would help him assimilate those touchy-feely moods in "gradations."

Max appreciated that, and he responded by visiting the studio to see how we were lighting our setups. Max Horton: one of us!

In a more mechanical "make it look like this" mode, I armed him with 45 sample stills I'd tweaked in Photoshop, and copious notes on the look and dramatic tone.

On the day, we were in sync from the beginning. We'd nail several shots in a scene and then move on. We covered the whole movie that way until we ran out of time. Then we focused on special challenges. I left before deadline; Max would work on filling in the remaining shots.

I don't know how long he stayed, but on the next day, Tim saw a complete "DP's version," and he bought it. I heard that his only change was making the Bride's skin a deeper blue.

Digi-Corpse Cam Mortem

Corpse Bride may be the prettiest picture I ever worked on, but I'd remember this job more for our cobbled-together digital studio. It was a gamble that paid off as we'd hoped, but it didn't stop there. We got more limber every time we dreamed up another solution. Here are some dividends that focused on saving time:

Throw away your light tables and stop begging for film reference clips. Want to compare a shot against what we're lighting now? Just pull up the old shot on your lighting station, right on set. With that advantage in hand, we didn't need to shoot density wedges.

In fact, we could view a complete sequence while on set. The studio was wired up enough that camera, art, and production had that access—as long as the rats weren't gnawing on the cables.

Rigging a Canon was a breeze compared with lugging a 40-pound Mitchell. We could hang a Canon upside-down and squeeze it into tight quarters, like a snorkel lens. Or we could hand-hold it to find the next composition, snapping a few options to compare.

We didn't have to wait for overnight dailies. It was more like instant gratification. Anytime we shot film in alternating matte and beauty frames, we'd wait days before we could see beauty frames only. But skipping out the elements from a digital medium could be done in minutes, and Mike could approve the shot.

There was no need to scan film negatives or make telecine transfers. Scanning the whole movie would cost about $9 per frame.

I also liked being able to do a rough contrast grade on a single shot right in the projector. That was done by tweaking the projector's gamma controls just enough to verify that we had a healthy "negative" to work with.

On the caveat side, all that reviewing access came with a catch: It was seductive and easily abused in an endless shoot-view-tweak loop. CG animators can tell you all about the tweak cycle!

Take heed of the easy portability of digital devices. Someone once nicked the computer that fed the projector. Inside the missing tower PC were several hard drives containing our dailies—half of the movie to date. Was it merely misplaced? No, the security camera footage showed a hulking figure lugging a computer-shaped load away with utmost dispatch.

How bad was that? Well, it could've been worse. Without backups, the project would have been over, but we did have backups elsewhere. Still, we had the specter of a pirated half-movie floating around. Oh, well, they couldn't do much damage with that half. More likely, the slime bucket sold the computer to his fence for a few bob.

In the fullness of time, we finished, albeit considerably later than according to plan. It was time to go home. Katy and I took off on a brisk September morning in 2005, exactly two years after we'd arrived in London. The flight back was a chance to reflect on our adventures—and our future.

I felt lucky to have had such a great crew; everyone took on the extra task of learning a system still in development while using it to shoot a beautiful film. It was lucky that Katy could work on set as a volunteer painter and set dresser so we could experience the project together.

Henry Selick phoned me while we were packing for the flight. He'd seen *Corpse Bride* and said it looked pretty, and he had a new show brewing. We talked about me coming on if and when it was solid. He was curious about my recent digital experience. Were pixels really the way to go? Oh, yeah!

Henry had one more surprise: The project would be in Oregon.

I found Andy Bowman, last of my crew, on a quiet stage. He was dismantling my moco rigs for their sea voyage. We shook hands.

It was only after I was back in the States, with hands on the machines, that I found Andy's last tag. The alignment numbers on two mating parts were gone. Instead, to be sure of a good fit, one had to line up the words "Yankee" and "Doodle."

Pete refining a shot.

Jack Is Launched, and Sally Walks through Fog

The fog that almost kept Jack from taking off in his sleigh was dense and confining. We made it mostly with dry ice vapor and a strong photo fog filter on the lens. Also, we used a half-silvered mirror to add moving art clouds, Zero the dog, and his glowing nose.

After Jack is airborne, we find Sally, left in fog, yearning for Jack. This heartfelt moment needed a more sentimental fog. But what does sentimental fog look like? I didn't know exactly, but I knew what we could do. Jim Aupperle and Brian Van't Hul used layers of bridal veil. Some scrims had cutout wisps taped on as a moving gobo, projecting onto other veils. For a sentiment moment, Sally could move with the moving veils.

When Trey was animating, the veils had to be out of his way. To give him some work space, Brian rigged the veil frames on 3-foot motorized tracks. When he was ready to shoot, Trey would hit the button, and the veils slid back into place, the camera took a frame, and the veils moved out again. I look at that sequence and still appreciate what those guys pulled off 100 percent in-camera.

Certain animators could get in trouble in the close quarters between puppet and camera. Deep in the zone, they may feel nothing amiss while bumping the lens with their butt. We needed a way to give animators some breathing room. What if the camera just got out of the way?

Sally's "veil mover" script could be tweaked to make a "give me some space" script. Punch the shoot button and the camera slides in place on a moco floor track, shoots a frame, and slides back out.

Nightmare set.

CHAPTER 47

Birth of Laika

Back in the States, I had plenty of time to absorb the book Henry was adapting, *Coraline*, Neil Gaiman's shivery tale for kids. It would be several months before we were wanted in Portland, Oregon. Housing would be awkward, so we floated between friends and family. We hadn't noticed we'd adopted Brit accents, but some family members accused us of flaunting them: "Gimme a break! You're fakin' it!"

We seemed to appear a bit dodgy to strangers, too. While I was checking email in an internet café, a woman's voice from behind barked, "Step away from the computer!"

She couldn't mean me, could she?

"Take your hands off the keyboard and step away *now*, sir!"

Jesus! She had a gun strapped onto her leg.

"I'm Tammy of the FBI! Step away *now*!"

I could do that for the FBI. No problem.

It turns out she was on the tail of some loser who'd been trying to steal from a bank using the same computer I was using. It didn't help that I had no home address at the time. How about our last job address? "We've got one, but you won't like it." True that. Our claim that we were floating around, awaiting a puppet show that would hire us in Oregon, got the same disbelieving reaction.

While we were making pretty pictures in Britain, Will Vinton Studios had undergone a major transformation. Now it was Laika Entertainment, LLC, owned by Phil Knight, founder of Nike. Phil's son, Travis, had been an animator at Vinton for 10 years. Now he had double duty; he was animating in the studio and also handling the corporate side of the biz. Henry had signed on at Laika as a supervising director, and the rest of us would come from near and far.

Thanks to telephones and the internet, I could do a lot of prep while floating around. Until we had a script and some concept art to ponder, I'd concentrate on the camera-department essentials.

The most urgent matter was the cameras. Even if the fleet of Canons from *Corpse Bride* were available from Warner, they were probably thrashed. But more important, we'd never given the animators a clear image in their frame grabbers—nothing better than a tiny video cam looking in the Canon viewfinder. I went looking for industrial cameras that could fulfill the animator's dream of a sharp live feed on their grabbers.

A few candidates could do that, but most were lacking in other areas. Our *Coraline* cameras had to have these features:

- Affordable enough to use in quantity

- Still in production: no problem getting more

- Compact: much smaller than a Mitchell!

- Self-contained live feed

- Thermoelectric cooling (for long exposures)

- NIKKOR lens compatible

- Sensor size like 35 mm film and greater than 2k in resolution

- Film-like color response curves

- Software development support

Only one camera made it to the spec list: the Redlake MegaPlus EC11000. It wouldn't come ready to shoot like a "prosumer" camera would. There were no buttons, knobs, or viewfinder. It was more like a component in a custom system, always tethered to several other boxes. The Redlake was typically used in the industrial world in machine vision, searching for dead pixels on flat-panel TVs. Even a machine could get bored of *that* job!

A stop-mo capture system would be considerably different. The beauty of it was that we could tie everything together: camera, grabbers, moco, intranet, projector. It would be the exact fit for us, and there would be no need for workaround schemes to control willful consumer cameras.

The catch was that if we decided to go with Redlake, there would be more than a little programming necessary to customize the camera for our needs. We were lucky that Laika had some serious programming talent on hand. Before asking that a big check be written, I wanted to see one of these red anodized marvels demonstrated at Laika with the programmer who might eventually find it in his lap.

Meanwhile, there were other concerns: Henry and the producer, Mary Sandell, wanted to have some face time with me, and I wanted to see the standing camera-crew talent. So, on to Portland.

It was good to see Henry again, and we got right into the brief on *Coraline*. He said he liked *Corpse*, but he wanted to go a different way. This story was darker, more like *The Shining* for kids. This would be our first venture into full-on scary. We didn't want a romantic look; the story is contemporary, set during a gray Oregon autumn. Coraline, a plucky preteen, discovers a mysterious tunnel in her house that leads to a duplicate house and a duplicate pair of parents. Coraline quickly finds the fantastic Other World much better than the boring and bleak Real World.

Visually, we would uphold the Kansas and Oz motif, with Other World conceived as a distorted mirror image of Real World. Other Mother has some occult skills, and she seems to be the preferred mother, but she is vile to the core. For some bright relief, we'd have three over-the-top theatrical scenes designed to please a kid like Coraline.

Henry and I also shared a walkthrough of a dubious candidate for a studio, a vacant truck garage. The only positive it offered was that it was right across the street from the legacy Vinton/Laika studio, which was still making commercials. Detriment abounded, most notably the open oil-waste canals cut through the warped asphalt floor. Henry's take on it was "abatement." Besides, would he really *want* to be that close to the mother ship, hovering, second-guessing? Was there *anything* we didn't hate about it?

With Mary, it was meet and greet and a bit of amiable negotiation regarding my rate. It was about showing the producer that we're allies.

I met with cameraman John Ashlee Prat and stage/camera manager Toby Ethridge to compare notes on crew and camera gear. (John had been using consumer cameras for animation, which was a good sign.)

They gave me the number of a machinist who'd made a moco camera head they liked. This Chris Rosequist did nice work. Could he make several complete camera cranes at a reasonable price? The guys seemed convinced he could. Did it matter that he lived in Minnesota? No problem. Chris would start sending me drawings on the internet as soon as I gave him some specs.

It seemed premature, designing a camera rig before choosing a camera. But the other camera candidates were similar in form, and this downtime was too valuable to squander. I sent Chris a digital model of the Redlake to fit inside my specs. From that point on, he and I were in frequent contact, noodling details with an eye for cost.

Yes, for some time, I had been pondering moco cranes that were smaller and lighter, improvements made possible by featherlight digital cameras. Wouldn't the animators be happy to have simpler yoga positions to access their puppets?

CAD files were a natural for long-distance communication and quick turnaround, although I missed being there to make real-world checks on design details. Indeed, we ended up modifying several details later for just that reason. The design was as basic and economical as possible, intended to service many setups with motion control at the same time.

I ordered 11 rigs. Was that a lot? Not for the way Henry liked to use camera movement. Sure enough, those 11 rigs got swallowed up with our existing six cranes, and they were never idle.

CHAPTER 48

Roundup

Sometime in early 2006, Katy and I checked into a flat in Portland that was a short bike ride from Laika. We still hadn't found a studio for the film, but if Toby couldn't find one to rent, it would be entirely possible to build one from scratch. There was a hefty patch of ground available near Nike headquarters, and the cost of building a studio could be spread over the next three Laika features. The only snag I could imagine was time. How long would it take to build? Longer than I and any other camera crew could continue floating.

Meanwhile, I got to see a Redlake camera perform each built-in trick. My favorite was the ability to speed up a live feed; this trick was for the animators. They would be able to see their hands, while moving a puppet, as the camera sees it. The trick was done by changing to fewer bits per pixel and "binning"—that is, instead of processing every pixel, pick out only the second pixel, horizontal and vertical, or every third or fourth pixel. While using the 4 x 4 "bin," we could get a 15 fps live feed, albeit in black and white.

In fact, most Redlakes were *only* black and white, which is what their industry/lab customers wanted. For us, each Redlake would be modified to include the color mosaic layer you find in most digital cameras. That would be a commitment; there were no refunds for special modifications. Well, good. I felt confident about spending the bosses' money.

Laika's R&D team started on that "more than a little programming." We, the camera people, sent wish lists for this and that. The R&D team named their shiny new program "Flipbook"—like CG viewers, but with different duties. Starting with the basics, it had to see what the camera sees, take a frame, and add it to a shot. That was enough to start on.

"Can we see it scroll through the frames? Actually, it would be better if we could just . . ." R&D might never finish as long as somebody piped up with another idea. Or until a purse holder said, "You're done!"

After several discouraging walkthroughs, Toby found a property for lease, a very interesting factory. It wasn't a foundry, nor was it a dead-animal-rendering plant. It was a squeaky-clean shop dedicated to making computer cases. The shop floor was about a half acre, and upstairs was all the desk and art space we'd ever need. I campaigned for the building with zeal. We could get going right away.

Once we settled on the studio-to-be, many postponed activities kicked into gear. With Vinton's history in town, I thought finding local crew people would be a snap. Most were interested, but not everyone wanted to jump in. For some, the 20-minute drive from Vinton was too far. It was a lifestyle thing, I was told. Bohemian artist digs versus an Intel plant built in the sticks two or three decades ago.

I asked one of my must-have crew members to lunch in hopes I could bring him on board. Remember when Henry backed me into working on *Nightmare*? Maybe the ploy could work for me. When my prey was about to decline, I stood up just in time to shake his hand and congratulate him. "Good decision, man! You did the right thing! Welcome to the show!" I didn't stop until I'd backed out the door, leaving him laughing.

Bryan Garver came on as supervising gaffer happily. He'd worked in LA and knew all the local electricians, which made him quite valuable.

Not everyone I contacted in San Fran and LA wanted to pull up stakes, but I got some great cameramen and assistants in both cities. I also got two gifted camera-electronic-moco engineers, Steve Switaj and Chris Andrews. To top it off, Kirk Scott came on as stage manager.

After VFXing in New Zealand from *The Lord of the Rings* (2001) to *King Kong* (2005), Brian Van't Hul had just settled into a job at Disney. Would he be interested at all? A few days later, his email response read simply, "Yes."

I was given limited time to hire crew from other countries. I called Peter Sorg and Mark Stewart. Yes, they were happy to take the jobs they'd had on *Corpse Bride*.

Once we had a rough script, some concept art, and maybe some story-boards, I could slip over to right-brain mode. There was some interest in creating previsualization storyboards, maybe with animated camera moves. I sat with a CG operator and gave it a try. We had a real scene in the film to experiment with, and we built the terrain in Maya, found angles, and then created the camera move.

It was kinda fun, but the process didn't seem much of a time saver: The virtual sets took as long to line up as the real ones. I was glad to see the idea fizzle simply because we cinematographers love using creativity and intuition rather than making copies.

Plus, a meatier challenge was around the corner.

01:01:53

Jack Lands in the Statue's Arms

After being shot out of the sky, Jack lands in the arms of a statue and sings about his woes for roughly two minutes. Henry was rightfully concerned about boring the audience. How long could they watch Jack just singing there, maybe waving his arms? Not two minutes!

Henry wanted a special rig built to swing the camera around the statue, keeping Jack in frame. I thought it would be a neat way to keep things moving, and I offered Henry the Luxo Senior rig. We could save building a one-trick rig and add some variety, such as spiraling into a close-up. Sold!

Six months later, animator Anthony Scott had a great performance in the can, with fancy camerawork from the team of Jo Carson and Jim Matlosz. Everybody loved it.

I was haunting the studio one weekend and found Henry and Tim Burton reviewing a reel on the flatbed editor. When they got to poor Jack's song, Tim sped up the film. As the footage zipped along, Tim said, "Henry, you like this? I don't like it."

Henry seemed to bristle. "You have to run it at normal speed. It's a great scene, a lot of good work in it."

Tim disagreed. "I don't know. It's too slow. I never wanted it."

"Then why did you let me shoot it?"

"I just wanted to see how it would look. We should just cut it out. What do you think, Henry?"

Henry replied with an unearthly calm. "Right now, I'm seriously thinking about leaving the show."

That's when I decided three's a crowd and left. On Monday, we all marveled at a brand-new hole kicked in the wall.

Anthony Scott animating on *Nightmare*.

CHAPTER 49

The Third Dimension

A huge python was uncoiling from its tree, and its undulating path pointed toward me. Henry emitted a nervous chuckle while the snake slithered past him. I could reach out and touch its head while locked in eye contact with the magnificent animal. No, it wasn't a dream. It was the best 3D shot I'd ever seen. That serpent was so beautiful and believable I wanted her for a pet.

As we continued our prep, RealD founder Lenny Lipton had told Henry about his new 3D system. Here, in Lenny's LA screening room, we were getting up close and personal with his proof of concept. We were excited about the possibilities; stop-motion was made for 3D. I remembered being a little squirt and pressing my nose on a toy-store window. We could give the audience *that* perspective. They could *be there*!

Lenny's process overcame every technical snag that had made 3D infamous; he'd taken ingenious advantage of digital cinema to make the stereoscopic experience smooth and dependable. His enthusiasm about 3D as a new tool for the cinematographer was infectious.

How did he do it? Well, of course, digital magic could heal all the image flaws created by the imperfections in older 3D film systems, but that was just the beginning. In order to create an illusion as flawless as that snake, the magicians must know a lot more.

We wanted to make 3D shots like that snake—a whole movie's worth. It was within grasp. We still had prep time, and several 3D experts were eager to point us in the right direction.

Henry and the few camera people we had on-site sat with the advisors, taking in basic theory and noting experiments we should conduct. Some advisors were into camera-system design, and others were interested in how 3D could complement the story, define character and mood, and create special moments.

But *everyone* had a dog in one particular fight. Some called it "stereo gluttony"—when a 3D tenderfoot has a hankering to make everything "come out" enough to be grossly unpleasant. As our eyes struggle to take in too much 3D volume, there can be physical repercussions. Of course, it also tends to drive away audiences.

These advisors really loved 3D. Now, their greatest hopes and fears were clutched in our inexperienced hands. I promised them we wouldn't screw it up for everyone, already knowing I'd have to keep an eye on certain Y-chromosome-driven characters.

The next day, we were on our own, experimenting in baby steps. How is it that our brains can take flat images from our left and right eyes and crunch them into an image with 3D roundness we can discern, recognize, and understand? We didn't know how, but in our brains, a squad of 34,073,741,824 neurons certainly did. They worked every time.

We learned some new words: *interocular* and *convergence*. The distance between the left and right eyes is called the *interocular distance*, typically shortened to IO. The average adult IO measures 2.5 inches, or 64 mm, eye to eye. *Convergence* is the amount our eyes toe in to align each eye's image of an object. The more cross-eyed we get, the closer things look. If our eyes are pointed on parallel lines, things look like they are as far as a distant star. When those lines of sight go fully parallel, we say the star is "at infinity."

Because puppets hold still for multiple exposures, we could shift a single camera to the left and to the right to capture both 3D views. That was a big win; there would be no beam splitters between dual cameras, no searching for duplicate lenses with identical optical characteristics.

This was the beginning of our "3D sliders." My first idea was a two-axis rig sliding horizontally to achieve the desired IO and panning left or right to converge on objects. That panning axis could be a headache—too much mechanical slop. Lenny had a better idea. He advised leaving out the convergence axis and instead aligning in post by sliding one image over the other. We needed extra picture width for that maneuver, and a 3K crop of our 4K sensors allowed for it.

We had two designs for the sliders during the show. We were working in fractions of millimeters. The smaller new one was better at accurately sliding a camera into place.

The Flipbook took on 3D capabilities, including automated 3D capture and one of those red/blue 3D viewing glasses. Just put on the colored glasses, and you can see 3D on the monitor. It was useful for a quick check, but we needed Lenny's full system on-site; it was the only way to see what we were doing.

For our screening room, we installed a D-Cinema projector with a RealD polarizer, a box of polarized glasses, and a 30-foot silver screen.

We started with a question: Can we get away with building a smaller-scale set and placing it just behind the foreground set, or will viewing in 3D give away the trick to the audience? John Ashlee began experimenting with several forced-perspective sets built at different scales.

John's answer might have been, "It depends." A 1/2-scale background looked natural in normal stereo, and a1/4-scale background would work in weaker 3D. That was going to help on large exteriors, where a full-scale house was prominent in the background. (For stop-mo films, the term *full scale* refers to a puppet's world, not ours!)

In the same vein, it also seemed logical that a puppet world should be seen through a puppet's IO, a lot smaller than ours. We'd soon see. Paul Gentry's assignment was about establishing benchmarks for IO distances, shooting for the widest IO we could use before 3D gluttony kicked in. John found that no single distance would work for the myriad conditions we'd encounter, so Paul shot puppets in this matrix: close-up, medium, and full-body shots at different focal lengths and at different IOs.

We projected each frame in 3D and rated the puppet heads for round-ness—normal, extreme, and reduced. Not surprisingly, we found that the closer you get to the subject, the smaller the IO you need. Beyond "extreme" was a 3D no-man's land, which John named "Triple-Pinocchio" because it made noses stick out. No matter. Not even a chameleon could get cross-eyed enough to fuse both images into a single nose.

While I was putting together our IO cheat sheet, I noticed that, yes, when shooting in a puppet-scale world, we should use a puppet-sized IO. In fact, it took considerably less IO, less than I got from doing the math.

I also noticed that we'd been playing tiddlywinks so far, testing a single parameter, the IO, modified by distance and focal length. That got us into the game, and it was becoming fun, like a puzzle. The game had to expand to take on another parameter (alignment) and more complex conditions, more like real-world 3D shots. The situation I most wanted to tackle was deep sets.

We started with a close-up on a puppet with normal 3D roundness. Meanwhile, we had a distant house at infinity. Sometimes, something had to give, a compromise with IO and convergence.

By now, we knew enough to deliver basic 3D shots while staying out of trouble. As we gained experience, the game became more like chess; there would be greater challenges and more maneuvers with which to handle them. Soon, with a little more evolving, we were using 3D creatively.

In one instance, Henry wanted 3D depth to differentiate the Real World from the Other World specifically in sync with what Coraline is feeling. So, we kept the Real World at a reduced stereo depth, suggesting Coraline's flat outlook, and used full 3D in the Other World. At first, full 3D opens up a better world for Coraline, but when things go bad, we carefully exaggerate stereo depth to match her distress.

Advisor Brian Gardner introduced us to the "stereo arc," a graph drawn with curves in sync with what's happening in the script. He also pointed out that we could make a character seem powerful by thrusting him out into the theater or weak by keeping him "behind" the screen.

Similarly, a shot that recedes deeply behind the screen creates a sense of space and freedom. But switching directions, crowding images into theater space, makes us feel claustrophobic or otherwise uncomfortable.

Because IO was run on a motion-control channel, we could increase or decrease IO during a shot. We had the same freedom to animate alignment in post. The combination might have been that sublime snake shot: The python starts from infinity and stops right in our face! *Coraline* is full of memorable 3D tunnel shots, some genuine woo-hoo moments that were executed like the snake shot.

Gradually, we developed new skills. New info was shared crew-wide, often just before lunch. I was proud of my crew.

I was evaluating a lot of 3D shots that were in setup or ready to launch. Looking through the glasses was a straightforward way to get the feel of it, but I was looking for eyestrain makers. I'd turn on my laser to survey the depth; the laser dot showed where the screen surface was. From there, we could easily see what was close up and what was in the background. Then it was glasses off, and we could see both left and right images. Was it within bounds?

Even after the shot was in the can, we could finesse alignment by sliding right-eye frames against left. That allowed what I called a *stereo grade*, in which I'd review a cut sequence specifically to see how the shots cut together in 3D. The typical issues were cutting from a close-up to a distant subject; that left the audience struggling to snap from cross-eyed to wall-eyed! The fix? At the cut, the two shots had similar alignments; then we'd gradually slide into the deeper shot.

After constantly looking at 3D for a year and a half, we expected to develop immunity to extreme stereo and turn into 3D gluttons. We definitely pumped up our eye muscles, but we also learned to be more eloquent in the new language. We gained an eye for subtle differences in 3D, even a memory for depth. "The windows weren't as far away in the last shot."

CHAPTER 50

Shots, Clever
and Well Done

When everything comes together on a difficult and beautiful shot, it deserves a cheer. On *Coraline*, we had a lot of well-conceived and well-executed shots. Let's start with a big one.

Remember Henry's Kansas/Oz motif? He wanted an ongoing 3D illusion, specifically to increase the sense of confinement in Real World. First, build a set with a strong forced perspective, and then shoot in 3D to give conflicting cues on how deep the rooms really were. Later, we see establishing shots of the more appealing Other World shot from the same position, but built in normal perspective. The compositions line up on screen, but Kansas feels cramped, while Oz feels comfy.

These twin establishing shots depended on building the forced-perspective sets to an exact camera position. Because of that, the burden fell mostly on the carpenters, as new angles usually required a new build.

Our first establishing twin shot is in the Real Kitchen, wide on Coraline and her mother against the window. Cameraman Paul Gentry used directional soft boxes to throw backlight in through the window, with just enough front fill to keep it all looking rainy and bleak. He added a hidden surface-mount white LED to create a cold glow on Mom from her laptop.

The reason I assigned Paul to both kitchen interiors was the elaborate treatment the Other Kitchen would need. Paul was happy to get complex when necessary. I found some catalog photos of overlit kitchens, and Paul caught right on. He went for rose and yellow gels on focal spots to create pools and accents scraping down the wall, making the set bright and warm.

The twin shots of Coraline's bedroom worked better simply because one bedroom dissolved right into the other. However, the moving camera made it anything but simple. John Ashlee was dealing with two sets with radically different physical depths. It took numerous move tests and rebuilding architecture, even bedposts, to line up on a pivotal frame in the dissolve. This fancy ruse was beautiful by itself, but John's lighting carried on for maximum difference in mood; the Other Bedroom scenes had warm practicals and multiple spots shaping and picking out details designed to delight, but it was never overly bright, allowing the bright moonlight to play a part. In stark contrast, John rendered the Real Bedroom with chilly soft light from the overcast sky.

Another bait for Coraline is a magic, self-illuminated garden. Steve Switaj and the model shop provided a combination of fiber-optics, small incandescents, and LEDs embedded in fanciful animated flowers. As the shooter, Paul Gentry had another finicky job. The combo of the practicals, black-lit activated paint, and the moonlight came together as a beautiful scene. Some shots with growing flowers could be mistaken for CGI, but it's all real stuff. Sometimes, we shot Coraline separately so the flowers could be animated in reverse by trimming them frame by frame.

Frank Passingham, another cameraman from London, rendered a more dangerous version of the garden, tinting it with poisonous green moonlight and carefully diminishing the glowing plants while raising contrast.

In quite the opposite tone, Frank made the Other House exterior a beacon of light, overpowering the full moon with warm practicals in windows, outdoor lanterns, and architectural lighting. In effect, the house itself became the key light for a charming conversation between Coraline and a wise black cat.

Here's an all-time favorite of mine: Coraline discovers an opulent nineteenth-century theater in the Other Basement, where she enjoys a vintage burlesque show followed by a breathtaking trapeze act. Peter Sorg used many small MR16 architectural lights to streak up walls and low-voltage halogens for footlights. Adding other practicals, mini spotlights in motion, and a central China ball for fill, Peter surpassed the grandeur of our reference, which was London's Royal Opera House!

Taking full advantage of 3D in acrobatics, we're right up there with the daring performers, carving through auditorium space while quoting the Bard! Eric Leighton did the animating, while our growing 3D knowledge added the scope and excitement without nuking our eyeballs.

At one point, Coraline is thrust into a dark, dank, iron-plate cell where she meets three pale-green ghost children. Chris Peterson shot the ghosts separately on motion-controlled rods against green screen that covered the set walls. The same motion-control rigs repeated the movement during Coraline's animation, this time carrying light bulbs, creating interactive light that appeared to emanate from the ghosts. Chris activated glow-in-the-dark stars on Coraline's sweater with UV tubes and augmented them with blue-gelled movie lighting. This was another favorite; every aspect, from design to animation, helped to create one of the most chilling scenes in a stop-mo movie!

Later, when things go bad, the portal is dusty, dark, and full of cobwebs. Peter Williams hid sources wherever he could, relying on hidden cutouts and small hidden sources within the tunnel. This was one of many sets where white LEDs were put to good use. They worked well as Obie lights, too—mounted right on the lens.

For an even darker tunnel, Peter used a candle carried by Coraline as the only source. He mounted a tiny, high-current lamp at the tip of the candle and hid it from camera with an equally small piece of aluminum blackwrap. The lamp got so hot it had to be turned off between exposures; this was automated by the moco. With a candle flame added by the visual-effects team, the source looks genuine, with natural falloff.

Peter W's experience with tunnels made him the guy to deliver several point-of-view shots in those squeezy spaces. The camera was rigged on a pole so it could just get through. Note the shot had hands; it looked silly, but it worked.

Chris Peterson created that ultra-3D point of view as the magic portal stretches toward infinity. The camera was inside a very large sock as we pulled up and away, stretching several feet high.

The last shot in the movie was actually shot last. Mark Stewart set up on five stages to shoot elements that would be combined into one long, meandering camera move. It would go through a garden party, then rise up over the house, landing in the same composition as the film's opening shot. Soft, yellow key light and enveloping bounce fill rendered a more appealing color and contrast ratio than the standard cold, rainy look.

With five completely different moco rigs in play, Brian Van't Hul and Nic Marrison took the precaution of motion tracking each rig as it played back its version of the move. They compensated for variances that turned up, making all the elements track each other accurately.

As a camera crew, we were very fortunate to get a chance to experiment with practical 3D on a long-running production. Circumstances gave us opportunities to test other theories on the job. I like to think we came out of *Coraline*'s 83-week shoot a little smarter.

For example, we had been warned that digital paint-out of puppet supports would not work in 3D because the digital paint would reveal itself, floating in the same space as the removed support. That's true if one is working on a 3D computer model, but we were going to treat each 2D frame like a separate shot. It was not the disaster predicted, but the compositors had to be very consistent on both "eyes."

Brian Van't Hul shot a lot of live-action effects elements with a Red One digital camera. He shot them all in 2D amid concern that they would be revealed as flat, but time and money limited us to this approach. The best example of his success is a sequence featuring thick ground fog that was added in post. By layering several 2D fog elements in proper 3D alignment, he created a believable illusion of full depth.

One theory our work upheld was that scenic flats would reveal themselves in 3D. That proved to be true. We had to move painted backgrounds significantly farther from the set, even when they were seen out a window. Fortunately, we were in a big building.

Katy and Tim Taylor on *Coraline*.

Katy on *Coraline* set.

Father's study. *Coraline* set.

CHAPTER 51

At Technicolor

At Technicolor Digital Intermediates (TDI), colorist Tim Peeler lent his practiced eye to our successive grades for 2K D-Cinema, 3D, film emulation, and home video.

All through production, we had worked in sRGB color space, so it would be a comfort to work from that familiar territory (converted to Rec709) instead of a standard conversion to film space. TDI accommodated, responsibly warning us that Rec709 had a mismatch with the film's gamut, and the DLP projector wouldn't display certain colors when we got to the film-print emulation, even though they would appear in a film-out. It was a little disconcerting, and I asked for a film-out of one scene that dropped out its green key light. As predicted, it came back on film with colors very close to those I had been used to seeing.

Since then, Joseph Goldstone and Josh Pines at TDI have developed a means of working within the DLP limits, so we can see a DLP-friendly replacement color interactively during the grade. Josh has described their method as "limiting the underlying gamut of the film-out to match the color gamut of the DLP."

Yes, this amounts to a slight dumbing down of the range of colors we can put on film, but it also makes it possible to see the result interactively in the DI session. You pay your money and make your choice. It's nice to know the option is there, but anyone considering this path should consult an expert at the lab.

With deep respect, I salute the *Coraline* crew for successfully shooting the most ambitious and technically challenging film in the stop-motion genre. Working responsibly and with professionalism, everyone produced consistently beautiful work.

A Twist in the Studio

"Wrap" was in the air, but the building wasn't going to be emptied. There were already several new gleams in Laika's eye. Throughout *Coraline*, we knew Laika intended to overlap films in production. To most of us migrant film workers, it held the potential for steady paychecks—a rarity and a dream.

That made the stakes higher for the aspiring staffers, skewing the dynamics and leading to competition, tension, and, on occasion, drama. This was my first job that had a human resources department, two nice ladies who were charged with many tasks, including mediating complaints such as hurt feelings and stolen staplers, corporate style.

There had been a changing of the guard during production, and Laika had a new producer from Aardman Animations. I knew she had a tough job ahead and offered to share my viewpoint. Not interested.

Flash forward to early 2009, after the show was finished and only a skeleton crew inhabited the studio. The estimate was that it would be a year before the next picture would start. Laika would lose talent. Maybe we could fill the wage gap with that kiddie film I'd dropped several years ago. I called the author, and he was excited about the idea. The new producer was less so.

It wasn't a surprise or a letdown. The lack of work left me free to chase a childhood dream: I wanted to build an airplane! Granddad had done it, making him a hero in my eyes. His one-seater was powered by a Ford Model T engine. Nowadays, you can buy plans for one. I found a 1920s design that suited me (open cockpit and two seats, so Katy and I could enjoy the breeze).

Another guy, William Wynne, had instructions to modify a Chevy Corvair engine for swinging a propeller. It wasn't as crazy as it sounds. The 'Vair engine was designed by borrowing light-plane engine features, like a VW, but bigger. I found that the most interesting, so that's where I began.

The first move was to find a usable Corvair corpse to revive. Scrounging around, I got a decent motor for $50. Score! The FAA requires that you keep a builder's log on your plane, so I decided to make my log in the form of a home movie. I shot video of the disassembly, repairing, machining installing, welding, and assembling.

Several months of fun in the garage went by, and then a Laika rep called. The studio people wanted to buy my moco equipment, and I agreed to a bargain sale. Handing over all that stuff, I felt weightless; the equipment takes a chunk of space.

I took this to be a hint that my services were not required at Laika. It was not a huge surprise, considering the chilly relationship I had with the new producer. She'd already hinted at another shooter, someone from Aardman. It had to be the bloke I'd heard about who yelped "Foul!" when this bloody Yank purloined the job on *Corpse Bride*. That's showbiz, and it was his turn now, brother.

After some time passed, Henry and I met for lunch. It was good to see him again now. We'd built up some tension (*Coraline* had been a tough show for everyone), but that had dissolved. He was busy on another picture, this time with Disney/Pixar. Apparently, Henry and we misfits from his posse would not be called back to Laika.

On the upside, Henry's show sounded like a DP's dream. Shadows were to be a big part of the central theme. In fact, the story included a living shadow girl. Doubtless, this show would be spooky. I imagined there'd be a lot of shadow play and tricky in-camera shots of the shadow characters—all in my comfort zone.

I'd be getting my hands dirty on this one, a camera unit with assistant and electrician. This show would be smaller than the last picture, so I'd have more time away from DP tasks. I had the summer of 2010 to pull up stakes and move south to the Bay Area.

The airplane engine was nearly finished, and I had to see it run before the new movie became my world. I tweaked it to perfection and set it up at a nearby airport. On the big day, some gearhead buddies and Katy were on hand. When the propeller first spun, they all cheered, and I felt like a kid seeing his first stop-mo dinosaur take a step: "It's alive!"

For 45 minutes, I let it chop the air and tug at the test stand as we grooved to the sweet, thrumming engine music. It was just the right note for a new adventure.

Lovers on the Snow-Covered Hill

Our romantic ending had to look softer and less like German Expressionism. The smoothed-over spiral hill was made especially for the scene. Just sitting in work light, it evoked an old Christmas card covered with glitter. Ray Gilberti got into the mood, softening the moonlight and then giving the scene a subtle glow with just the right diffusion filters.

Animator Tim Hittle, thoroughly smitten by his new girlfriend, had his own inspiration. You might remember the proud gait in Sally's march up the hill. Tim planned it, saying, "I'm gonna make her walk like a bride!"

CHAPTER 52

In the Shadows

The Shadow King, Henry's new show, had the potential to be the best job I'd had since *Nightmare*. We set up shop back in the same neighborhood. This time, we moved into a vacant chocolate factory, which seemed like a good omen.

Besides the shadow girl, we'd have a kid named Hap, who could make his own shadow magic with his fingers, and a giant shadow monster. It would be challenging, but with some creativity, we'd be practicing shadow sorcery!

The initial storyboards showed many shadow effects, and we favored in-camera effects as the way to achieve them. If a shadow was ranked as a character, the shadow should be right there on set.

I brainstormed practical ways to shoot those images. I thought, for instance, that there had to be a better way to create hand shadows than directly animating a puppet's tiny fingers against the light. We'd lose time, shadow sharpness, and possibly even finesse in the performance.

I wondered about making a series of puppet hands to create the final hand pose incrementally. It could be easily done with a 3D printer. Eric Leighton, our animation director, had a similar idea; he proposed creating partially animate-able hands that could be preformed to throw a specific shadow. These ideas would work in certain conditions, but when we needed larger shadows or when access to the animate-able hands was difficult, we'd need something more robust.

I got excited about what we could do with a high-definition video projector, thinking the projector lamp could serve as the source while playing a shadow animation. Hang the projector above the puppet or place it under the floor or even behind a translucent set wall; there would always be a way to get the angle we'd need. But if our lighting design just couldn't accommodate, the projector could work to produce a separate shadow-only element by projecting negative shadow onto a darkened set.

What about "emergo," shadow characters floating away from the wall? My non-CG solution was a jointed puppet made of soft aluminum, shot as an element. It all sounded good, but so far, it was just guesswork.

Eric and I started making several tests using one of those newfangled projectors. One interesting shot had the shadow girl cavorting on a tall building. Another featured a jolly-looking character who doesn't see his shadow growing into a giant monster.

Confident that we had some reliable new tricks in hand, I turned to my always-evolving cluster of prep tasks. Henry had said he expected thorough tests on everything: "We aren't going to wing it this time."

We didn't have the extra time; the city of San Francisco would come through with a generous chunk of cash if we started before a certain date, and our budget was counting on it. Better get smart with our priorities!

I'd always started early on gearing up: lighting, grip camera, and moco. Some stuff we could get with a phone call, but 14 moco cranes built to spec? That takes a while!

I went to Joe Lewis of General Lift, LLC, a longtime go-to guy in LA. In his shop, Joe showed me this and that, and we traded sketches and specs. When his work was done, we had a proud fleet of the most evolved camera robots for that mission—and our price.

Canon had recently added a Live Preview option to its digital SLR cameras. (How recently? Mid-2007, when *Coraline* was already in production!) We could now run a wire to a monitor and see exactly what the professional-grade Canon EOS 60D sees without any R&D of our own.

Finally, we needed a program like Laika's Flipbook that could add each frame to a shot and provide the other animator tools. Fortunately, Jamie and Dyami Caliri had been developing such a program. It's called Dragonframe, and if you're interested in shooting your own stop-mo, look it up; it's the way to go.

Another top priority was signing up a crew. That was easy with veterans from Skellington and ILM in town. I'd call my guys in, one at a time, when needed. In addition to our stage manager, Kirk Scott, Steve Switaj came in early to create lamps that threw supersharp shadows, operate moco, and handle any other tech jobs required.

As start day approached, we had set and puppet on stage, ready to begin our first scene: Hap makes shadow tricks in a dark closet. There were about 17 cuts in the scene, great for working out lighting design.

I liked the notion of having only two light sources: Hap's flashlight and a scary water heater. In another era, they'd call it "noir style"—strong contrast, sharp shadows, and stark simplicity. From *Citizen Kane* to *The Night of the Hunter*, a lot of us know that look.

Pity I didn't use the phrase "film noir" while discussing the scene with Henry. We might've gotten off to a less bumpy start. After I'd told my first unit to prep a setup with stark contrast, I arrived on set and found them putting up a soft overhead silk. That was a surprise.

"What's with all that overhead fill?"

"Henry wanted it."

Surely, this couldn't be what Henry wanted. All that fill light would make the scene look like an old TV sitcom. We'd fix that. I decided to get rid of the eyesore and see how much the boss liked it. Carl Miller and his crew looked pained, caught in the dilemma of serving two masters. The boss didn't see it my way after all.

The bumps continued. Besides differences in lighting, we had a rift over priorities as I put my tasks in prep order. For a few weeks, I concentrated on creating a look book, imagery that showed what I had in mind for the film. I shot a variety of lighting setups and combined them with written descriptions and stills from noir-style movies. I might have done that sooner, but I was still reading from the old "wing it" script. Regrettably, my 30-page document didn't give Henry what he wanted.

Laurels upon us for civility while carrying out the exit interview, while in producer Mark Miller's office. Gentlemen, all.

But after I was given the boot, it wasn't a wrap. They still had an agenda. Would I be interested in returning to working as one of my unit cameramen? Sure, that was better than expected, and it was an offer to get my hands gloriously dirty again.

Mark also asked if I could suggest a DP to replace me. Finding a candidate should've been easy, but the only interested party seemed to be Peter Sorg, back in the UK.

Then, Henry got up to leave, and he offered me his hand, in honor of our two-by-two careers; that made us stronger.

It was a Friday, and it was getting late. Mark and I were still cleaning up some details. He asked, "When do you want to tell your crew? Do you want me there or not? Take some time to think about it."

That was trusting, leaving it to me. Nobody ushered me out the door.

Driving home, I wondered how the guys would take it.

The following Monday, Kirk Scott was quietly poring over the camera budget when I told him: "You probably should know that I got bounced last week."

He remained quiet, besides dropping his forehead on his desk. It was just a single skull-to-wood "clunk." He remained in the awkward pose for about five minutes, without making a peep.

Once out of his reverie, Kirk rounded up the crew. Soon, Kirk had an office full of cameramen and noise—to the tune of "WTF?" I told the crew what to expect; the show was still looking for a new DP, and I'd come back after a couple months, looking forward to joining them as part of the crew.

Suddenly, I had the time to make a flight simulator, to get more out of those Saturday flying lessons.

Forced Landing

After two months, I returned to the set. Peter Sorg greeted me with a friendly smile. We punched each other's shoulders—guy code for "This arrangement will work out just fine." Pat Sweeney and his assistants were setting up another scene. I was glad to see all of them.

There were two scenes for me. They were interiors with moving traffic lights and a moving camera as the character Hap and his brother go to sleep. My new/old job was starting out fun. Tim Taylor assisted, and Mike Catalano was the electrician.

With our first batch of happy animators in play, we moved on to setting up a long tunnel set. It was an interesting challenge to light, and we had to give the animator the ability to puppet three characters well into the tunnel. Using tricks from *Coraline*, we got our animator shooting.

Before he finished, there came a mysterious call: Everyone was to report immediately for a meeting with Henry and Mark Miller. All 150 of us convened in a large room. Mark introduced a Disney producer, Jim Morris. Jim had been a straight shooter in the past, and he hadn't changed. He cut straight to the chase: Disney couldn't find a way to make a profit on *The Shadow King* and had decided to shut it down.

Closing down a show mid-production isn't unheard of, but it was still a jolt. The more invested you are in a project, the more you want to see it finished. You want to keep up with your peeps, and the steady paychecks don't hurt, either! I didn't worry about starving, but I knew those flying lessons would have to go.

I looked over some of the other faces in the room. Some were pale, while others looked flushed. One lady burst into tears, and a few wore slightly deranged grins. The general mood was fairly mellow. The ultimate in mellowness was Paul Gentry, who'd just driven up from LA to report for duty.

Henry closed the meeting by thanking everyone. It was August 14, 2012.

You Can't Afford It!

Two years later, I was walking downtown and stopped to ogle a 1964 Ford Mustang that had been beautifully restored—"cherried-out," as they say.

There was a voice behind me . . . "You can't afford it!"

It was Kim Marks, a fellow cameraman, home from shooting a season of *Mad Men*.

We talked about the usual, what we'd been doing and what might be coming up. I had recently shot two short animation pieces for a new guy, Jon Peters. One was a teaser for a possible feature. Kim was hopeful about another season of *Mad Men*.

We chuckled about the fickle business.

"Your only way to know that you're retired is when they stop calling you."

The Lost Words

Katy, bless her heart, suggested that I shed some light on another story. It began in 2009, running in parallel with this book. For reasons of plain macho pride, *never* would I write the adjacent story. She said that the story could help people. It's just a few points of interest I found to be useful for some with a certain condition.

Back in 2009, I was getting puzzled about the narration on my home movie. I would stumble over a script that I had just written. Over months, I found difficulty in making the right sounds to blurt out a simple sentence. After a dozen takes, I had a decent performance in the can. Then, whatever the glitch was, it disappeared.

Over several years, my stupid-tongue tricks appeared more often, like fumbling the airplane's ID while broadcasting on landing status. Sometimes, I couldn't understand people in meetings. It was difficult to understand Katy too. I just passed it off as the noisy room.

Several people told me to have my hearing checked. When I aced the test, I decided to find a neurologist. This was my formal introduction to "primary progressive aphasia." The brain doctor's description of aphasia sounded very familiar. I took it as throwing a wrench into my language skills, all of them. Over years, you lose such abilities as speech, decrypting *other's* speech, reading, writing, and finding words.

The only "feature" I had *not* encountered was writing. Could the pen become my best way of slinging words back and forth? Yes, at least for now, but someday, my writing ability would decline, and its number would come up too.

Suddenly, I felt it was time to quit kicking that biography down the road and get moving, before the option would be taken away. Knowing nothing about writing, I expected to cruise through several months, scribbling away, and come up with a best seller. In reality, it took me *four years* to finish this comical chronicle.

It's not because of the speed I plinked on the keys; it was much more like the prep to do before I could start making letters appear on the laptop. I had seen enough synopses, scripts, and storyboards to know the need for a plan. Start with a timeline, studded with bare-bones chapters. That would be a blueprint, the big picture. From that, I'd begin on a very rough draft, something solid enough to polish.

The patchy draft was easy; my long-term memory was always excellent, but my vocabulary had been slipping. Words faded away, slowly, then faster, as the weeks, months, and years moved on. But for the grace of an online thesaurus, this book would have read like a *Dick and Jane* primer.

Why four years? Include all the normal life activities that burn time; that's the time eater.

Let's shift to those few points of interest that I mentioned. I hope you find them to be useful, comrades.

To begin, my speech was working unsuitably, failing me, but there was another medium for communication. The pen helped me to level the field of interaction. With text, I can take my time, cobbling together a sentence, and nobody is waiting for me to dig up that vanished word. Also with text, I can take my time, reading someone's sentence over and over until I get it. That is exactly how I meandered through writing my book.

Besides having alternate ways to communicate, would there be some further value? At least, I can tell you that all that time has become a boot camp for this language-challenged writer. For instance, when I gear up to write a word, I sound the word in my head, just like when I prepare to blurt out the word in speech. A *sound* equals a *letter*. So, within the process, I get a mini workout in spelling.

Besides all the mental stretching and exercising, I noted something else as significant; while I was polishing the chapters, *more* story details were bubbling up. Interesting: I certainly hadn't been trolling for them. Maybe there was a tangle of memory neurons, fishing for those added details.

Nonetheless, my big picture had expanded, in a better way. While tickling the ivories, I was in the best situation to relive selected scenes from my life. Pictures have been known to be the worth of a thousand words, but a lot of material plays better in writing. I'm happy to have some writing to round out my photo album. But, it was much better than that; I could communicate in a substantial way.

Perhaps, you'd like to have something like this, but you don't have to burn so much time. A journal seems more reasonable.

More than having the bird in hand, I enjoyed the process, just *doing* it. Sure, it was a challenge, but when I won over the obstacles, finishing a line or a paragraph, it felt good. And it's even sweeter knowing that I thwarted my brain-eating antagonist for another day! Good luck in your challenges; we are in silent kinship. Just knowing that, I find helpful.

—PETE KOZACHIK
April 2018

ACKNOWLEDGMENTS

T o everyone who appears in this manuscript, I thank you for the humanity you bring to this book. A cameraman does not live by widget alone. There are about 280 of you, more than I can name, so I'm singling out a few for more acclaim.

Good old Mom: With a whisper, she started my career, and she's been my preeminent follower for six decades.

Tim Burton: He dreamed up *Nightmare*, launching many futures, including mine.

Henry Selick: He chose me on *Nightmare*, became a long-term friend, and partnered our complementary careers.

Teachers and mentors: I've been lucky, having Irene Tejada, Flip Ferington, Phil Kellison, Bill Tondreau, Alex Funke, Dennis Muren, and Phil Tippett.

Camera crews: You guys make me proud! You've been the talented, can-do boots on the studio floor, with the dedication to deliver.

Thanks to Eric Swenson for the photos of us at work on Henry's films.

Katy Moore-Kozachik: the brightest star in my universe! This sweet and smart lady is the one who suggested writing this book.

My editor: I knew the book was in good hands with Rachael K. Bosley, who took a first pass at editing my book and who has been editing my *American Cinematographer* magazine articles through the years. She's as good as it gets!

I also want to acknowledge Steve Pizello and David E. Williams from *ASC Magazine* who have been incredibly supportive throughout the process.

I also want to thank my many friends and colleagues who have reached out to me and have supplied information and photos for the book. In no particular order they are—Anthony Scott, Eric Swenson, Gretchen Schafenberg, Henry Selick, Jim Matlosz, Justin Kohn, Ray Gilberti, Timothy E. Taylor, and Tom Proost.

And thanks to Jon Peters for his friendship and care.

To all of you on this page, you should take a bow!

About the Author

PETE KOZACHIK lives in Northern California with his wife Katy and their three cats.